Dayton

THE GEM CITY

By Bruce W. Ronald and Virginia Ronald • Photography by Karen Copher

Dayton: The Gem City

a pictorial and entertaining commentary on the growth and development of Dayton, Ohio

by Bruce W. Ronald and Virginia Ronald

To our parents and parents-in-law,
who made it possible for us to work together

Publishers:
Larry P. Silvey
Douglas S. Drown

Managing Editor:
Kitty G. Silvey

Editor:
Ellen Sue Blakey

Art Director:
Rusty Johnson

Assistant Art Director:
James Michael Martin

Historical Photo Editor:
Judith Wehn

Current Photographer:
Karen Keith Copher

Manager of Production:
Mark Radcliffe

Project Director:
Ches Cochran

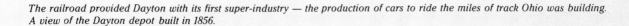

The railroad provided Dayton with its first super-industry — the production of cars to ride the miles of track Ohio was building. A view of the Dayton depot built in 1856.

Copyright 1981 by Continental Heritage Press, Inc., P.O. Box 1620, Tulsa, Oklahoma 74101. All rights reserved.

Library of Congress Catalogue Card Number: 81-65678

ISBN: 0-932986-20-X

Dayton: The Gem City is one of the American Portrait Series published by Continental Heritage Press. Others include:

Akron: City at the Summit
Charlotte: Spirit of the New South
Cleveland: Prodigy of the Western Reserve
Columbus: America's Crossroads
Denver: Rocky Mountain Gold
Des Moines: Capital City
Detroit: American Urban Renaissance
Fort Worth: The Civilized West

Houston: A History of a Giant
Indianapolis: Hoosiers' Circle City
Los Angeles Two Hundred
Miami: The Magic City
Milwaukee: At the Gathering of the Waters
Oakland: Hub of the West
The Saint Louis Portrait
The San Antonio Story
San Diego: California's Cornerstone
San Jose: California's First City
Tulsa Spirit

Sponsors and benefactors

The following Dayton area firms, organizations and individuals have invested toward the quality production of this historic book and have thereby expressed their commitment to the future of this great city and to the support of the book's principal sponsor, The Montgomery County Historical Society.

ABC American of Dayton Inc.
Advanced Machinery Concepts, Inc.
The American Lubricants Company
Amolé
Annthony Engineering Company
Arco Industries, Inc.
Atkinson Transfer, Inc.
Auto-Valve, Inc.
Aztec Graphics, Inc.
Baldwin & Whitney Ins. Agency

B.D.I./Flack
The Beerman Realty Co.
*Bendix Automation & Measurement Division
*Benham's
*L.M. Berry and Company
*Blue Bird Baking Company
Bon Builders, Inc.
Brown & Hughes, M.D.s, Inc.
*Carillon Park
*Central Printing Company
The Central Trust Company
Citizens Federal Savings & Loan Association
Citizens of the city of Kettering, Ohio
City of Dayton
Clark Consolidated Industries, Inc.
Click Camera Shops
Coletti Design
Mr. & Mrs. Harold F. Collins
Mr. & Mrs. Richard F. Collins
Continental Consultants, Inc.
Coopers & Lybrand
Crown Lift Trucks
Danis Industries Corp.

*Dayton Area Chamber of Commerce
Dayton Legal Blank Co.
*Dayton Malleable Inc.
The Dayton Performing Arts Fund
Dayton Plumbing Supply, Inc.
*The Dayton Power and Light Co.
Dayton Progress Corp.
Dayton Sure-Grip & Shore Co.
Dayton Typographic Service, Inc.
*Dayton-Walther Corporation
Dayton Women's Civic Clubs
*The Daytonian
C.H. Dean & Associates, Inc.
Delco Moraine Div. GMC
Domicone Printing Services
Dowler Opticians, Inc.
Duellman Electric Co.
Economy Linen and Towel Service Inc.
*The Elder-Beerman Stores Corp.
Engraving Arts Inc.
Ernst & Whinney
E. George (Babe) Ferguson
Frigidaire Divisions, W.C.I.
*Gem Savings Association
General Motors Acceptance Corp.
The Genuine Parts Co.

*Good Samaritan Hospital and Health Center
Gray America Corp.
Great Trails Broadcasting Corporation
Greater Dayton Heating & Cooling, Inc.
Group 2 Communications Inc.
GZK, Inc.
H & H Industries, Inc.
Harris Corporation, Business Forms Systems Division
Hartman & Dean Equipment Corp.
*Heidelberg Distributing Company
Helmig Lienesch Doench & Associates
Mrs. Glendora G. Hipple
Home Environment Center
*The Huffy Corporation
IBM Corporation
Kaltenbach & Associates, Inc.
Kastle Electric Company
Kelly Services Inc.
Kettering Medical Center
Jerry L. Kirby
Kircher, Hilton & Collett, Inc.
Knerr Insurance Agency, Inc.

Kniess Saw Co., Inc.
Kohler Food Service Inc.
Mr. & Mrs. Floyd G. Koller
J.R. Kuntz Company
Kurz-Kasch, Inc.
LaForsch Orthopedic
  Laboratories, Inc.
Lamar Outdoor Advertising
*Ledex Inc.
Maurice J. Leen Jr.
Lincoln Storage & Moving
Lorenz & Williams Incorporated
The F.W. Lotz Paper & Fixture
  Company
M & M Precision Systems, Inc.
*The E.F. MacDonald Company
Manpower, Inc.
Marconi Avionics, Inc.
*The Martin Electric Company
McCauley Accessory Division of
  Cessna
*Mead Corporation
Metropolitan Life Insurance Co.
Miami Products & Chemical Co.
*Miami Valley Hospital
Miami Valley Parking Corp./First
  Street Garage

Robert E. Miller
Monsanto Research Corporation
*Montgomery County Historical Society
*NCR Corporation
Robert C. Neff
NEWCO-FREBCO Inc. Electrical &
  Mechanical Contractors
Northrup Corporation
Northwestern Mutual Life
Oakwood Rotary Club
The Olt Insurance Co.
Oregon Historic District Society
James C. Oren & Associates, Inc.
The H.J. Osterfled Co.
Parking Management, Inc.
Patterson-Trane Service Agency
*Philips Industries Inc.
Don Phillips, Quality Food & Vending
Pioneer Standard Electronics Inc.
Poeppelmeier Co.
Polar, Inc.
*Ponderosa System, Inc.
*Price Brothers Company, Inc.
Professional Marketing
  Communications, Inc. (PMCI)
Jane T. Reece
Refrigeration Equipment Co.

Donald Renner Company
*Reynolds + Reynolds
Ralph Rhoden Painting &
  Decorating Inc.
Robbins & Myers, Inc.
Ken & Fern Routson
Royston/Ward Fine Jewelers
J. Gordon Rudd, Attorney at Law
Ryan Homes Inc.
Edward M. Rybicki
*St. Elizabeth Medical Center
Schriber Sheet Metal & Roofers,
  Inc.
Mr. & Mrs. Roger R. Schultz
*Shopsmith, Inc.
Smith & Schnacke
Donald E. Sortman Co.
Specialty Machines, Inc.
*The Specialty Papers Company
SRA Dayton-Beavercreek,
  R.A. Martin III
The Standard Register Company
State Fidelity Federal Savings &
  Loan Association
Stengers Ford Inc.
Techneering Sales, Inc.
Third National Bank

Tires Unlimited, Inc.
Touche Ross & Co.
Tradin' Post
The Trane Company
TRW/Globe Motor Division
United Color Press
United Systems Corp.
The University of Dayton
Valdhere, Inc.
Van Dyne Crotty Inc.
*Vulcan Tool Company
Irl C. Wallace
WAVI/WDAO Broadcasting
  Corporation
*WDTN TV2
Western Ohio Neuroscience
  Group, Inc.
WHIO TV
*White-Allen Chevrolet/Honda
*Winters National Bank and Trust
  Co.
Wisco Products, Inc.
Zenith Pattern Products, Inc.

*Denotes Corporate Sponsors. The
histories of these organizations and
individuals appear in a special section
beginning on page 175.

It's the people.

There is nothing special about Dayton's history— and there is a lot that is special.
That is not a contradiction.
The city was shaped by Indian wars, hardy pioneers, greedy men and philanthropic men (often the same),
natural disasters, transportation systems, wars and national events.
But most other cities were shaped the same way.

To many Daytonians, this general truth has created a sense of unimportance, a sense that has been reinforced
by one television network which chose a suburban Daytonian as "the average voter" in 1976.
The average epithet is only partially true.
Dayton does personify prototypical America, especially mid-Western America.
It is a good test market for the nation at large because it is typical.
But it grew to be a major American city because its people were atypical.

John Patterson may not have invented the cash register,
but he did invent welfare and modern selling techniques.

The Wright Brothers did invent the airplane, and in the short space of three years, they also perfected
the lightweight internal combustion engine, the propeller and the glider.
Kettering did invent ethyl gas, but he also invented
the portable electric generator, the "buzz bomb," electric ignition
and the electric self-starter which made automobile driving an amateur—and asexual—sport.
Lib Hedges, on the other hand, built a real estate empire from a definitely sexual business.

Dayton: The Gem City is the first major history of the city in almost 50 years.
And it is the first history to see Daytonians not as saints but as human beings—
often flawed but still capable of greatness.
It is a popular history more than a scholarly work (a 1917 history covered far less time
and was at least three times as long), but every effort has been made to eliminate errors.
Still errors will appear, and stories often encompass more than one truth.
It is our hope that we have corrected more mistakes than we have committed.

—Bruce and Virginia Ronald

7

A winter evening tête-à-tête on Courthouse Square.

LNA   "T

How bad was
and horrendous
the dubious dist

Contestants in
test were to subm
novels. Originato
19th-century aut

Dazed by the
entrants from 50
"The camel died
sulkily and, buffi
the journey began
minor inconvenie

For her victor
picturing Snoopy
"It was a dark an

more than a million Americans, the American Cancer Society stated, "A preliminary study of dietary factors showed no higher rates of coronary heart disease and stroke in people who ate a high-fat diet than in those who did not."

Actually, only 36 percent of the fat in the U.S. food supply comes from beef, pork, poultry and fish, while 42 percent comes from vegetable sources, such as oils, shortening and margarine. There is reason to believe that by substituting vegetable fats and oils for beef fat in our diets, we could be doing ourselves more harm than good. Recent research on animals suggests that

about nine g
48 percent of the

Fact: Red m
source of iron;
serving of beef s
of the recomme
ance for an adul
"heme iron," a t
five times more
the body. Hem
booster effect on
eaten with the i
iron in spinach,
available unless
tion with anoth

Fact: Three
beef contain 16
amount of lea

CHAPTER ONE

THE FIRST DAYTONIANS

Celoron de Blainville buried a lead plate at the mouth of the Miami River to notify future travelers of France's claim to the area.

"…all the woods over the land is of great plenty…"

"We found the clover to be as high as the middle of a man's leg. In general all the woods over the land is of great plenty and of all kind that grows in this colony except pine."[1]

When John Peter Salley wrote his description of the Miami Valley in his journal in 1742, he did not know he was writing about a land already inhabited for at least 14,000 years.

Built on a buried valley 400 feet deep, Dayton sits over the Teays Stage Hamilton River, a massive underground river at the bottom of the valley. The Illinois and Wisconsin glaciers filled in the depression with sand and gravel deposits. Here and there are outcrops of shale, shaly limestone and limestone which was used for burial slabs by some prehistoric men.

Overlying the gravel and Niagara limestone is the rich silty loam which produced the deciduous and coniferous forests that scientists call post-Pleistocene. The weather then was both colder and wetter. The receding Wisconsin glacier provided a home for moose, elk, deer, mastodon, giant beaver and caribou. (A mastodon tooth was found in Dayton in 1829 near the mouth of Stillwater River. Given to the Cincinnati Museum as a curiosity, it is tangible evidence of the existence of exotic prehistoric animals. Remains of a giant ground sloth can be seen at the Dayton Museum of Natural History.)

In the Dayton area, there are few artifacts of the Paleo-Indians (*paleo,* old) who tracked these mega fauna (large beasts). Paleo-Indians were hunters and nomads. Since they followed migrating animals, they needed no permanent settlements. They used flint tools—spear points, knives and scrapers. The fluted spear points were made by hitting a piece of flint with a hammerstone. After a rough lance-like shape was formed, final shaping was completed by pressure chipping —pushing off tiny flakes with a bone or antler tool. The center of the point was channelled to make space for the split end of the wooden shaft. Probably the shaft and point were bound together with animal sinew. Knives and scrapers were made in a similar fashion. Hides of animals could then be scraped before being used for clothing or shelter. Other than the flint, no remains of the Paleo-Indians have been unearthed.

Sometime around 6000 B.C., a new prehistoric Indian appeared in the Miami Valley. About that time, the climate in the area changed. It was both warmer and drier. This encouraged the growth of hardwoods—oak, hickory and beech. Animal life adapted. The Paleo-Indians may have moved northward after the big game, or they may have remained, adapted and intermixed with the new peoples, generally known as Archaic Indians (*archaic,* also old). Archaic culture lasted 5,000 years, to about 1000 B.C.

Archaic man was not only a hunter but a fisherman who supplemented the protein in his diet with grains, fruits and nuts. Less nomadic than the Paleo-Indians, Archaic peoples still moved frequently. Probably they followed a regular cycle in their wanderings, returning to an area when the local plants ripened. They had stone pestles for grinding seeds and nuts and stone axes for chopping trees.

Remains of mats and baskets, bone, slate and shell jewelry, as well as bone and shell tools and simple pipes for smoking, reflect their developments. Such items were included as grave goods—items buried with the dead. The grave goods may have had a religious significance. Burials did tend to follow patterns. Often the bones were sprinkled with red ocher. The graves were usually elliptical, three or four feet in diameter, and the dead were often buried in a bent position, knees to the head. The unearthed bones give some clues to the physical

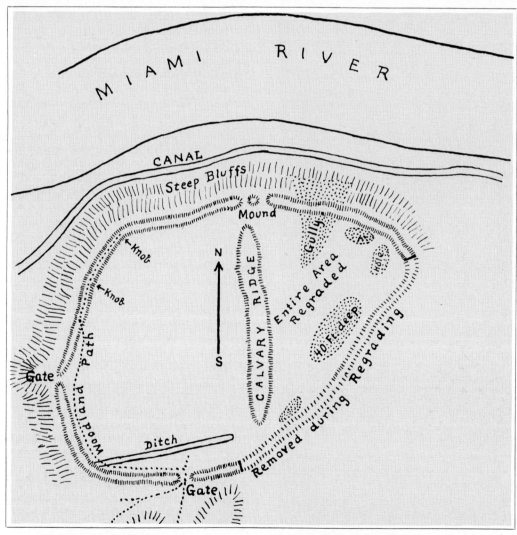

DAYTON'S EARLIEST SETTLERS: The Miamisburg Mound (above) is the largest single Adena mound in Ohio; a drawing (below) depicts the arrangement of prehistoric Indian earthworks; archaeologists delve into the trash pits (facing page, left) at the 60-acre Incinerator Site used by Indians around A.D.1180-1210 ; three of the houses on the site outlined with posts (right) measured about eighteen feet square and were of wattle and daub construction. A cedar post at village center may have been used to fix corn planting time by the stars.

characteristics of the Archaic Indians. The men were about five feet to five feet four inches tall, the women were three to four inches smaller. They had a high incidence of arthritis, rickets and abscessed teeth, and the infant mortality rate was high.

In the Dayton area, a slightly different group of Archaic Indians also existed. Called Glacial Kame for their habit of burying their dead in kames (hill-like gravel mounds) left over from the glacier, these Indians are also noteworthy for their grave goods which included exotic shell ornaments from the Gulf Coast and copper beads from eastern Wisconsin, indicating a large trade network. The Glacial Kame period probably began about 2500 B.C. and lasted over much of the northwest Ohio Valley until 1000 B.C.

Stonehenge-on-the-Miami

In southern Ohio, the Woodland Indians spanned the time period from 1000 B.C. to A.D. 1000 in three main phases. The early Woodland Indians were the Adena ("mound builders"). The Adena mounds were cone-shaped and used for multiple burials, sometimes over a period of many generations. The Adena Miamisburg Mound, 68 feet high and 850 feet in circumference, is the largest single mound in Ohio.

The Adena built elaborate mounds because they did not move often. In their primitive slash-and-burn agriculture, they used digging sticks for minimal cultivation. A cultivated plot would last three to four years, then a new one would be cleared and the old left alone for several years. Although Adena Indians cultivated pumpkin, squash, sunflower, amaranth and perhaps corn, they remained hunters, fishers and gatherers as well.

Trade networks were more extensive than in the Archaic period. Some jewelry was elaborately carved. Copper, slate and shell jewelry was popular.

One of the Adena's more unusual practices was head deformation. Babies were strapped to cradle boards, causing their heads to be artificially flattened at the back. Physically much larger than Archaic Indians, the Adena were in turn dwarfed by the next group of Woodland Indians, the Hopewell. Taller, more slender, much less rugged than the Adena, the Hopewell were much more sophisticated.

The famous mounds in Ohio are almost all Hopewell or Adena in origin, including the Fort Ancient earthworks south of Dayton. These groups were responsible for the mysterious earthwork of circles and squares covering more than 31 acres located at the bend of the Great Miami River (present-day West Carrollton).

One important aspect of Hopewell life was the extremely elaborate trade network. Exotic materials collected from South Carolina (mica and quartz), Lake Superior (copper), Wyoming (obsidian), Gulf of Mexico (shells) and other places were often made into ceremonial jewelry and artifacts. Effigy pipes and Hopewell pottery have been found as far away as Georgia and Mississippi.

About A.D. 500, the Hopewell culture began to disappear. The reasons are unclear. Perhaps drought or floods. Perhaps the trade networks disintegrated. Warlike marauders may have forced them from the Miami's banks. Whatever the cause, the Hopewell Indians were influenced locally by the Mississippians who settled near the Hopewell mounds at Fort Ancient. Although they did not create Fort Ancient, these Indians did create the first culture known in Dayton.

The Indians picked a good place to settle. Of 496 sites listed in the Ohio Archaeological Survey for Montgomery County, 100 or more are in Dayton. Some were visible when the city was settled in 1796; a few are visible yet today. A park bench sits atop an old Indian mound in Triangle Park. Dayton has one excellent Fort Ancient Indian site, called the Incinerator Site. On these 60 acres, in addition to the Fort Ancient remains, artifacts were found from the Hopewell and Adena periods and even some points from the Archaic and Paleo-Indian periods. The Dayton Museum of Natural History has been excavating the Incinerator Site since 1969. The Incinerator Site has been dated at about A.D. 1200. The group of Fort Ancient Indians lived on the bank of the Great Miami for about 25 to 30 years. By then, probably because the ground was exhausted and the firewood depleted, they moved on.

In the eleven years of excavation, a clear picture of a farming and hunting community has developed. The Fort Ancient Indians settled on the Great Miami floodplain and built a stockaded village of about 25 houses. A circular stockade was made of wooden posts thrust into the ground. Immediately within was the ring of village houses, all facing a tall red cedar post in the center of the village. Each house was similar, almost eighteen feet square, and made of wooden posts. Branches were woven between the posts, then mud was daubed on to fill in the spaces. This wattle-and-daub construction was topped with a thatched roof with a smoke hole over the central fire pit.

Pottery remains suggest a matrilinear culture with family designs remaining in defined areas, since daughters did not move but sons did.

eaten as were bear, raccoon, squirrel, beaver and turtle. Turkeys may have been raised for food;[3] they did comprise about six percent of the diet.

Pottery remains suggest a matrilinear culture. If a style of pottery is confined to one group of houses and not in general use in all areas, archaeologists infer that a mother taught her daughters the family design. If her daughters later moved to their husbands' homes, the family design would have shown up in other households.

Following in the footsteps

The Mosopelea Indians may have been the link between Fort Ancient and modern Indians. All we know of the Mosopelea is the name and stories that they left the Miami Valley sometime before 1673.[4]

Since that time, Dayton has been home territory to at least two different Indian groups. The Indians who first met and traded with white men were Miamis. The Miamis apparently moved into the Montgomery County area about 1700. They are part of the Algonquian language group. In 1750, Christopher Gist, trading with the Miamis, wrote,

Sunday, 17 February
This place…is fine, rich level Land, well timbered with large Walnut, Ash, Sugar Trees, Cherry Trees, it is well watered with a great Number of little Streams or Rivulets, and full of beautiful natural Meadows, covered with wild Rye, blue Grass and Clover, and abounds with Turkeys, Deer, Elks, and most Sorts of Game particularly Buffaloes, thirty or forty of which are frequently seen feeding on fine Meadow: In short it wants Nothing but Cultivation to make it a most delightfull [sic] Country.[5]

Sometime about 1780, the majority of the Miamis were driven out by the more warlike Shawnees. More and more white men began to move into the area. This set up the classic Indian-pioneer confrontation. Both groups believed the land was theirs, and thus the stage was set for Dayton to be a minor part of what the early settlers would call the "Miami Slaughterhouse."

The large red cedar center pole may have been used for astronomical sightings, according to J. Heilman, curator of anthropology at the Dayton Museum of Natural History and Roger R. Hoefer, formerly of the museum. The alignments obtained using this post indicate April 24 as the time to plant corn and August 20 as the time to harvest the green corn.[2] The amount of burnt corn found "ceremonially" (not in the trash pits) tends to back up this assumption.

The stockade was surrounded by corn, squash and bean fields. Meat was killed, caught or fished out of the forest and streams. It included more deer (75 percent) than any other source, plus elk (nine percent). Shellfish and fish were also

"On the Banks of the Miami — 1776" by Don Caron.

The Indians and white men began as friends, but within 40 years, the two groups were bitter enemies. Part of the reason was a difference in the white men who confronted the Indians during that time. In the early days, the white men were traders whom the Indians welcomed. By the 1780s, however, the white men were settlers, a group who tried to restrict the Indians' movements and take over much of their land. It was no wonder the Indians looked upon them in a different light.

The first commercial traders to reach the Miami Valley came by land and not by river. British fur traders, operating in what is now western Pennsylvania, blazed a "Trader's Trail" from Logtown on the Ohio River to Pickawillany, just north of current day Piqua. They followed Indian trails which were probably old buffalo paths. It was a successful venture, and soon pack trains of ten or more horses were crossing what would become Ohio, to trade for beaver, deer, fox, bear and raccoon skins. In return, the Indians received fabric, shirts, coats, gartering, rings, wire, knives, red dye, the always-popular beads, powder and lead for bullets.

A large, two-story blockhouse was erected at Pickawillany, and one report claims more than 50 English traders were known to have traded there. A group of Miamis even moved to Pickawillany to trade, abandoning relations with the French *coureurs de bois* (traders) to the north.

The English trade route apparently did not exist before 1747 or 1748, but it did not take the French long to respond to the competition. On June 15, 1749, an expedition of 180 Canadians, ten Indians, twenty soldiers, six cadets and eight officers left La Chine (near Montreal) to solidify France's claim to all the lands along the Ohio River. It was led by Captain Celoron de Blainville and accompanied by Father Bonnecamps.

Celoron left lead plates at the mouths of the rivers as he passed, restating France's claim of territory. After leaving the final plate at the mouth of the Great Miami (which the French called *Riviere a la Roche*), Celoron and his men headed north toward Pickawillany on September 1, 1749, arriving at the blockhouse thirteen days later.

Neither Celoron's nor Bonnecamps' journals describe Dayton's site, but the water was so low that half the expedition had to leave their canoes and march. "This was thought," Bonnecamps says, "to have [occasioned] the loss of Monsieur de Joannes, how having undertaken to follow a savage who was going to hunt, lost himself in the woods." Three days later, he appeared "at a bend in the river, conducted by two Miamis."[6]

France laid claim to the Ohio country in 1749 with buried lead plates.

The chief was La Demoiselle (young lady, spinster or dragonfly; the English called him Old Britain). At Pickawillany, Celoron told him, "By these belts of wampum, I set a boundry [sic] to all passages which lead to the Beautiful River [Ohio], so that you go there no more, and that the English who are the ring-leaders of this very evil work may no longer approach this land that belongs to me. . . . I break off all trade with the English, whom I have notified to retire from off my territories; and if they come back here again they will have reason to be sorry for it."[7]

A mystery...

■ *Celoron has many spellings. Canadian records suggest Celoron de Blainville. Most early histories call him Celeron de Bienville. It is not known whether Pierre-Joseph or his brother Jean Baptiste made the expedition in 1749.*

La Demoiselle was polite enough—"We do not speak from the end of our lips but from the bottom of the heart,"—but said he would not leave as "the season is too far advanced."[8] Celoron gave up, burned his canoes and returned home. But Celoron's threat was not from the end of his lips, either.

Early in the morning of June 21, 1752, an army of 240 French and Indians attacked the blockhouse at Pickawillany, demanding that the English traders be surrendered. They were—except for two the Indians hid. One wounded trader was killed, scalped and his heart eaten raw. Old Britain (La Demoiselle) suffered an even worse fate. He was shoved in a tub, boiled alive and eaten. The Miami Valley was free of the English for more than a quarter of a century.

War with the Indians

After the French and Indian War ended in 1763, American settlers considered the West open for exploration. The settlers of western Virginia and Pennsylvania moved westwards, seeking a frontier they could call their own. They found it in Kentucky.

It took tough men and tougher women to survive in the wilderness. Few ever reached 40 years of age. It was survival which motivated and shaped these early Kentuckians, and, if they had any other time, their thoughts turned to owning vast stretches of the choicest land. These first settlers believed that "tomahawk rights" would make them rich. In essence, if a man found land he liked, he would blaze a distinctive mark on each of the four corners of the land and the land would be his. The concept drove the early Kentuckians to explore and press farther and farther into the wilderness.

But it was not an uninhabited wilderness. The Shawnee Indians—having been forced from their lands in Florida, Georgia and later the Carolinas—were in no mood to be moved again. The Kentuckians, however, were relentless foes. When a white man was found scalped, the Kentuckians would scalp two Shawnees. Bitter, unforgiving warfare threatened the lives of everyone on either side of the Ohio River.

Even before America proclaimed her independence, the British had enlisted the Indians on their behalf. Since Americans were pushing the Indians out of their homes and hunting grounds, the Indians quickly sided with the British. Besides, the British had money, and the Americans did not.

In 1780, Captain Henry Bird led a raiding party of 150 English and Canadians plus hundreds of Indians from Detroit into the wilderness. The expedition came south on the Maumee from Lake Erie, portaged to Loramie's Creek, down the creek to where Pickawillany had stood and south along the Miami. The British army of perhaps a thousand fighting men passed the site of Dayton and reached the mouth of the Great Miami on June 13.

The plan was to attack the fort on the site of Louisville. But the Indians—fearing that the famous Indian fighter, Colonel

The War of Independence pitted colonists against Redcoats and the Red Man. In 1780, Col. George Rogers Clark (above) fought one of the war's longest battles against 600 Indians who sided with the British.

George Rogers Clark, was there—refused. Instead, they proceeded east to the Licking River and south along it to Ruddle's Station, which they captured, and a day later, they captured Martin's Station. About 300 prisoners taken from the two settlements were forced to march back to Detroit. "I procured a guide through the woods," wrote Bird. "I marched the poor women and children 20 miles one day over high mountains, frightening them with frequent alarms to push them forward."[9] Those who could not keep up with the march were killed. Some of those who made it to Detroit were sold as slaves.

Kentucky was humiliated. The frontiersmen demanded revenge, and George Rogers Clark—one of the most competent of all American revolutionary war leaders—was ready to lead them into battle.

Raising an army of about a thousand men, Clark crossed the Ohio August 1 and marched up the Little Miami to "Chelecanthy" (Clark's own spelling for the Indian town north of current-day Xenia). No Indians were present. The army burned the corn and buildings and moved on to "Pickawey," about six miles downstream on Mad River from the site of Springfield (where the George Rogers Clark Memorial Park is now).

Shortly after two in the afternoon, a pitched battle took place. The cannon (or cannons—reports vary) which Clark's men struggled so hard to bring won the day for the Americans. The three-hour engagement involving 1,000 Americans and over 600 Indians produced few casualties on either side, but it was one of the largest and longest battles of the Revolutionary War.

Two years later—1782—a cleverly led British raid south of the Ohio River succeeded in leading a force of Kentuckians into a bloody ambush at Blue Licks. More than 60 Americans were killed. (So many were killed out of so few inhabitants that courts could not be held for months in certain Kentucky counties for lack of men to serve on a jury.) Clark again raised a thousand-man force and retraced his path northward, but the Indians had abandoned both Chelecanthy and Pickawey. Following an Indian trail to the Miami River, Clark attacked a number of Indian towns near current Piqua, but most of the Indians had fled.

Rum in the rain

Skirmishes continued. A small band of Shawnees would cross the Ohio and steal a horse. A somewhat larger band of Kentuckians would cross the Ohio and steal a dozen Indian horses. Although the British (expecting the peace talks which would end the Revolution in 1783) had ordered no more major raids, it was still easy to die on either side of "The Beautiful River."

In the summer of 1786, an Indian raid resulted in the death of Patrick Henry's brother-in-law. As governor of Virginia,[10] Henry authorized a raid against the Wabash Indians near present-day Fort Wayne, Indiana. George Rogers Clark offered to lead the troops. After some delay, more than enough troops arrived, and Clark authorized Colonel Benjamin Logan of Kentucky to march with a separate force against the Shawnees at the Mad River's headwaters (Plalely Lake, now called Indian Lake, north of Urbana). Logan had 700 men which he formed into two regiments; one was led by his brother John Logan, the other by Robert Patterson of Fayette County.

Patterson was born in Pennsylvania in 1753 and moved to Kentucky in 1775. He helped found the town of Lexington. He was a fighter, and in 1778, he served with George Rogers Clark

A misplaced tale or two

■ *All Dayton histories written after 1880 say Robert Patterson camped at the site of Dayton after the 1782 expedition, adding that "a lively little skirmish took place here." There is no record of such a stop or battle in more than a dozen existing memoirs, including Patterson's. It is possible (but unlikely) that Clark's army did return via the Great Miami and therefore Dayton. A similar story has Patterson camping on the site for a few days on his return from another expedition in 1786. Since Patterson was badly wounded on this later excursion and no army would linger long in enemy territory, the story makes little sense. But where the stories came from remains a mystery.*

in Illinois. He was with Bowman at Chillicothe (Old Town) in 1779 and with Clark again in 1780 and 1782, having risen in rank with every mission.[11] On the march to the mouth of the Licking, Patterson was delayed by rain and impressed a barrel of rum for his troops. As Colonel Logan was to report later, "in consequence of its effect, the army was somewhat delayed in crossing."[12]

On the afternoon of October 6, 1786, the Army split up and attacked seven Indian villages. In a skirmish, an Indian struck Patterson in his right hand with the muzzle of his rifle. (The wound apparently remained open until Patterson's death in 1827.)[13] Patterson was court-martialed for the rum incident. It was "in some measure irregular," and he was sentenced to be reprimanded.[14]

Despite the Indian and settler difficulties, some Ohio lands had already been sold for settlement by land speculators. Other lands were reserved for Revolutionary War veterans. The only trouble was that the Indians—not the Americans—still ruled Ohio.

Late in 1790, Congress authorized General Arthur St. Clair to send General Josiah Harmar on a punitive mission against the Indians living near the site of current day Fort Wayne, Indiana. Not having enough regulars, St. Clair asked for Kentucky militia to march with Harmar. Harmar would have been better off alone. Kentucky—which had previously sent men of the caliber of Daniel Boone, Simon Kenton, George Rogers Clark, Benjamin Logan and Robert Patterson—now sent the very young, the very old and the very drunk.

"Attacked about one hundred Indians, fifteen miles west of the Miami village, and from the dastardly conduct of the militia, the troops were obliged to retreat," wrote one of the regular officers, Captain John Armstrong, describing the action of October 19, near present-day Fort Wayne. "I lost one sergeant and twenty-one out of thirty men of my command . . . many of the militia threw away their arms without firing a shot."[15]

The Indian leader was Little Turtle, and this excellent tactician struck again with equal success a few days later. Again the militia panicked; again the regulars paid the price. Harmar burned some villages and some crops at a cost of 183 officers and men killed. And Little Turtle was far from through.

Arthur St. Clair took personal command of a new army a year later. St. Clair had a few more regulars than Harmar but

still relied on the completely undependable Kentucky militia. St. Clair's strategy was to build a number of safe forts as he marched northward. He built Fort Hamilton on the Great Miami (naming a future town in the process). Then he proceeded west and north on a route that approximates today's U.S. 127. Fort Jefferson was next. St. Clair proceeded due north to the site of today's Greenville—and disaster.

"On the fourth [of November, 1791] at day break," wrote an 18-year-old pack horseman whose father had been killed and scalped by the Indians in Cincinnati less than six months earlier,

> I began to prepare for returning and had got about half my luggage on my horse when the firing commenced. We were encamped just within the lines on the right. The attack was made on the Kentucky militia. Almost instantaneously the small remnant of them that escaped broke through the line near us and this line gave way, followed with a tremendous fire from the enemy and passed me. . . . Not more than five minutes had yet elapsed when a soldier near me had his arm swinging with a wound. I requested his arms and accoutrements as he was unable to use them, promising to return them to him and commenced firing. The smoke was settled about three feet from the ground but I generally put one knee to the ground and with a rest from behind a tree, waited the appearance of an Indian's head from behind a tree or when one ran to change his position. . . . Hearing the fire at one time unusually brisk near the rear of our left wing, I crossed the encampment. Two Levy officers were just ordering a charge. I had fired away my ammunition and some of the bands of my musket had flown off. I picked up another and a cartouch box, nearly filled, and ran ahead nearly to a large tree where I changed my piece and fixed my bayonet. . . . I think there was about thirty of us. I was soon in front. The Indians ran to the right where there was a small valley filled with logs. I bent my course after them and found I was with only seven or eight men. The others had kept straight forward and had halted about thirty yards off. We halted also and being near to where the savages lay concealed, the second fire from them left me standing alone. My cover was a small sugar tree or beech, scarcely large enough to hide me, and most of the Indians in the hollow from fifty to seventy yards distant directed their fire at me. The balls struck the tree and many plowed along the ground at it's [sic] root. One moved my hat but did not cut it. . . . I then retreated, running my best, and was soon in. By this time our artillery had been taken. I know not whether the first or second time our troops had just retaken it and were charging the Indians over the creek in front and some person pointed me to an Indian running with one of our kegs of powder, but I did not see him. There were about thirty of our men and officers lying scalped around the pieces of artillery. It appeared the Indians had not been in a

FRONTIER FOES: The rights to Ohio were fought for by folk hero Daniel Boone (left), and by Arthur St. Clair and Simon Kenton (above left and center) against Indian leaders such as Little Turtle (above right).

THE TREATY OF GREENVILLE: "Mad" Anthony Wayne commanded the battles and signed the treaty which eventually opened southern Ohio to American settlement.

hurry for their hair was all skinned off....The ground was literally covered with dead and dying men and the Commander gave orders to take the way....In a short distance we were so suddenly among the Indians, who were not apprised of our object, that they opened to us and ran to the right and left without firing. I think about two hundred of our men passed through them before they fired, except a chance shot....I fell in with Lieutenant Shaumburgh....Corporal Mott and a woman who was called Red Headed Nance. The latter two were both crying. Mott was lamenting the loss of his wife and Nance of an infant child. Shaumburgh was nearly exhausted and hung on Mott's arm. I carried his fusee and accoutrements and led Nance. In this way we came together and arrived at Jefferson a little after sunset.[16]

The author of the memoirs was Benjamin Van Cleve, who would become one of the founders of Dayton.

Embarrassing defeat and final victory

St. Clair had 623 killed and 258 wounded of his army of 1,290. Civilian losses were not recorded, but the total dead —including a number of women—probably exceeded 800. (Custer was to lose only 267 men in 1876.) The loss of more than 40 percent of the total U.S. Army in the West embarrassed the fledgling country and infuriated President Washington.

After a few futile peace attempts, President Washington and Secretary of War Henry Knox finally selected "Mad" Anthony Wayne to lead the Army. Wayne was a stern commander, even rigid, but he seems to have been fair to his troops. Wayne would have preferred his troops to enter battle without bullets. He had fought the Creeks in Georgia and knew that they dreaded the bayonet. To the Indians, the white man's army was the "long knives," and Wayne became known as "the chief who never sleeps" because he drilled, drilled, drilled his rabble into an effective, disciplined army. Although he distrusted muskets, he made his infantrymen fire them often. He held competitions and included his riflemen as well. If an infantry company won, they received an extra ration of whiskey. If the riflemen won, they got nothing—they were supposed to win.

In the fall of 1793, the site of Dayton was again bypassed as

Wayne moved his army up the Miami to his winter quarters in a huge fort he called Greene Ville in honor of the American Revolutionary hero, Nathaniel Greene, who had been Wayne's friend and neighbor in Georgia.

Sensing that the Americans were close to success in their plan to drive the Indians westward, and much preferring the Indians to Americans as neighbors, the British in Canada decided to bolster Indian support by building a new fort near what is now Toledo, Ohio. It was a clear violation of The Treaty of Paris which ended the Revolution, but the British felt the gamble was worth it.

In June of 1794, an attack—almost certainly led by British officers—was made upon a foraging party from Fort Recovery, a fort that Wayne had constructed north of Greene Ville on the site of St. Clair's defeat. The Americans were badly mauled at first but rallied to fight their way back into the comparative safety of the fort. For two days, the Indians tried to capture Fort Recovery. For two days, the Americans held them off, inflicting many casualties. For the first time in the Northwest Territories, the United States had successfully held a position. Some historians believe this battle was the real turning point of the Indian wars.

This time, Kentuckians cared enough to send their very best. About 1,600 militia joined Wayne, and he marched his men north from Greene Ville in July 1794. A surprisingly humble Wayne wrote Henry Knox, "The fortuitous events of War are very uncertain. But this I can promise that no conduct of mine will ever require the kind paliative [sic] of a friend—or cause that great and good man Our Virtuous President to regreat [sic] the trust and confidence that he was pleased to repose in me."[17]

Wayne's next letter, following the Battle of Fallen Timbers, was—justifiably—less restrained. "It's with infinite pleasure that I now announce to you the brilliant success of the Federal army under my Command in a General action with the combined force of the Hostile Indians & a considerable number of the Volunteers & Militia of Detroit on the 20th Instant, on the banks of the Miamis, in the vicinity of the British post & Garrison at the foot of the rapids."[18]

After the anticlimactic Battle of Fallen Timbers (both Wayne's legions and the militia fought well, if briefly), the war was over. On August 3, 1795, almost a year after Fallen Timbers, Wayne signed a treaty with the Indians at Greene Ville. The treaty opened all of the southern half of Ohio to American settlement.

CHAPTER TWO

STRUGGLE FOR SURVIVAL

A plat of Dayton as it appeared in 1802.

Long before Wayne's legions had cleared the Indians from the Ohio lands, the land prospectors had their eyes on the land at the mouth of the Mad River. Judge John Cleve Symmes of New Jersey contracted with the U.S. Congress in 1787 to buy all the land between the Great and Little Miami up to the Mad River for 66.66 cents per acre.

The convoluted details of the land transaction are contradictory and sketchy. The resulting confusion nearly destroyed an embryonic Dayton. The government offered Symmes the southern twenty miles of his proposed purchase, but he felt he should have been awarded all of it. Without a firm contract, Symmes set out from New Jersey in late July 1788 for the territory he believed was his. He arrived at the site of Cincinnati and started out to explore his land. Colonel Robert Patterson, Israel Ludlow and John Filson went with him. Filson, who had just completed an exceptional map of Kentucky, literally disappeared on the expedition. Patterson, Matthias Denman and Filson had planned to create a town. After Filson's disappearance, Ludlow became the third partner. They wished to call the town Losantiville (*L* for Licking, *os* for mouth, *anti* for opposite —the city opposite the mouth of the Licking River). Governor St. Clair spared the world Losantiville by naming the town Cincinnati for the Society of Cincinnatus, a group of Revolutionary War officers.

In spite of the Indians, a preliminary survey of the Miami lands was made by Benjamin Stites. He was so impressed by the site of Dayton that he entered into a contract to buy the entire seventh range of townships to build a town called Venice at the mouth of Mad River which he wanted to call the Tiber. (The Italian Tiber flows through Rome and is nowhere near Venice.)

In a letter dated May 1789, Symmes described the Mad River country: "But what I call the beauty of the country is the many prairies which lie in the neighborhood of Mad River."[1] Judge John Cleve Symmes was a good judge, probably honest but certainly stubborn and vain. While Congress finally did award him all the lands he asked for, Symmes could not make the payments. There were severe irregularities in his land dealings and his record keeping.

Seventeen days after the Treaty of Greene Ville, Judge Symmes sold the seventh and eighth ranges between the Great Miami and Mad rivers on one side and the Little Miami on the other—about 60,000 acres—to Governor Arthur St. Clair, Israel Ludlow (who already owned the site of Hamilton, Ohio), Brigadier General James Wilkinson and Jonathan Dayton, senator from New Jersey. (The latter two, although acquitted in the courts, are condemned by history for their involvement in the Aaron Burr conspiracy, allegedly to form a private army and to seize Spanish territory in Louisiana and Mexico.) These proprietors thought Dayton the most pleasing name of the four owners. The others—St. Clair, Ludlow and Wilkinson—had major streets named for them. Since these three were Federalists, they named one street Jefferson to appease the Democrats.

Making a mark on the land

Benjamin Van Cleve was one of the area surveyors. He worked for Daniel C. Cooper. The team of which Van Cleve was a member went up the Little Miami while Cooper headed north along the Great Miami to build a rough road. When both teams converged at the mouth of the Mad,

FOUNDING FATHERS: Dayton became a town on April Fool's Day 1796. Founders included surveyors Benjamin Van Cleve (upper left) Daniel Cooper (lower left) and Colonel George Newcom (lower right). Jonathan Dayton (upper right), a New Jersey senator, was one of the original owners of the land. Dayton's name was chosen by the purchasers as "the most pleasing" to grace the township.

they found six Wyandot Indians there. "They behaved very friendly," Van Cleve wrote; "they gave us some of venison jerk [*sic*] and we in turn gave them a little flour, salt and tobacco."[2]

Van Cleve must have liked what he saw because he and 45 other men agreed to become settlers. In March 1796, three separate parties with a total of 55 or 60 men, women and children set out from Cincinnati to create a new life in the wilderness.

Thompson's party, including Van Cleve, set out by boat and arrived first. Samuel Thompson had married Benjamin Van Cleve's mother, Catherine. They had their two young children with them, one only 3 months old. Their pirogue (boat) was decked (roofed) to provide some protection from the late March weather.

George Newcom also left Cincinnati overland on March 21, 1796, with the largest party—five bachelors and seven men with wives and families. Ten more had left a few days earlier in a party led by William Hamer.

On April Fool's Day, 1796, Thompson's pirogue landed at the head of St. Clair Street. Early Dayton historians were fascinated with the question of whether Catherine Thompson or 9-year-old Mary Van Cleve stepped out first. Whoever it was, the town of Dayton had begun.

The first step for survival was to erect a shelter. The pirogue was broken up for lumber, trees were felled to clear land for planting, and the logs turned into cabins. Some of the locations are still known. Newcom's Tavern was located at the southwest corner of Main Street and Water Street (now Monument Avenue). Samuel Thompson's cabin was on Water Street between St. Clair and Mill streets (now approximately Patterson Boulevard). Mrs. McClure's cabin was on the

Dayton's first settlers arrived by land and river. Samuel Thompson's party came by decked boat and included a 3-month-old child among its passengers.

southwest corner of Water and Mill streets.

In the summer, three more families came to settle—Jerome Holt, Robert Edgar and Daniel Cooper. Holt was a brother-in-law of Van Cleve; Cooper was a surveyor; Edgar was his chain-holder. Cooper would become the struggling town's most prominent citizen.

Life for the pioneer settlers was almost unbelievably difficult. Most were attracted to Dayton because they had no money. The free land offered was their chance for survival, self-esteem, perhaps wealth. Each pioneer received an in-lot of 99 x 199 feet for a home and vegetable garden, and a ten-acre out-lot (away from the town's center) for a farm. There are three slightly different early town plans all drawn by Cooper (in 1802, 1805 and 1809), but basically the in-lots covered an area running between the Great Miami on the north to Sixth Street on the south and from Wilkinson on the west to Mill Street on the east. Earlier plans went farther west. The 56 original out-lots were mostly to the east of Mill Street. (George Newcom must not have been superstitious; he chose for himself lot 13 of the 381 in-lots.) Benjamin Van Cleve—the basic source for early Dayton history — was apparently not cut out to be a farmer. "I raised a very good crop of corn this year," he wrote of his first year's effort, "and in August took the ague severely [probably malaria] and did not get able to labor until spring. I received my pay for my possessions in Cincinnati. . . . I sank the price of my lots, my corn was mostly destroyed and I was about forty dollars in debt. I gave eighty dollars for a yoke of oxen, one of them was shot, twenty dollars for a cow and she died, flour cost me nine dollars a barrel, corn meal one dollar a bushel at Cincinnati, other articles in proportion, and the transportation to Dayton was two dollars

and a half per hundred weight."[3]

The next year, Van Cleve moved to Little Beaver Creek, seven miles distant and raised a crop worth 1 pound, 17 shillings. Van Cleve computed his loss at 16 pounds, 17 shillings and sixpence. He returned to surveying with Israel Ludlow in order to survive.

In the winter of 1796–97, Dayton Township was formed. It was a vast area containing parts of current Montgomery,

Rubicon Creek provided the power for a sawmill and "corn cracker" beginning about 1816.

Greene, Miami, Clark, Champaign, Logan and Shelby counties. The tax returns for 1798 are still extant. Daniel Cooper was tax assessor, George Newcom was collector. The 138 taxpayers paid a total of $186.665, and Cooper charged $7.21 for the assessment, which more than covered his $6.25 tax—the highest in the township. Robert Edgar, who had just helped George Newcom build his fine two-story tavern, paid $1.33. Newcom paid $2.69.[4] By the fall of 1800, George McDougal opened a store on the second floor of Newcom's Tavern. Dayton was too small to need a store, so McDougal traded mostly with the Indians, obtaining honey, pelts and jerked meat.

William Hamer, the Methodist minister who led one of the three groups to Dayton, apparently built the first mill (where Monument and Patterson streets now meet). But in 1799, Cooper built the mill that put Dayton on the map. He also built a distillery on his farm two miles south of Dayton on Rubicon Creek. A sawmill and a "corn cracker" similar to Hamer's mill followed. Soon Cooper was getting business from all around the area, and Dayton had its first industrial fatality. John Davis was chopping ice from the waterwheel at Cooper's mill when the wheel started under him. He was dragged under and crushed.

The Indians were making warlike noises again, so the young community of nine cabins built a blockhouse at the site of Monument and Main. It never had to be used for war. Instead, it became the first schoolhouse. Benjamin Van Cleve taught there from September 1 to October 31, 1797, until he had to harvest his corn crop. Later that year (or early in 1800), he returned to teach for another three months.

Even though the Indians remained basically peaceful, they caused the settlers some trouble. Early histories record that the Indians had the nasty habit of calling all the settlers (men and women alike) by their first names. The Indians were often drunk and unruly, and many were left to sleep it off in the corn crib behind George Newcom's tavern. Jailed whites were kept underground in his dry well.

By 1800, Dayton had erected a church building. A Presbyterian church stood at the northeast corner of suburban Third and Main streets. The windowless log cabin, seven logs high, was erected two feet off the ground and was unchinked, letting in plenty of light and air. The community's first graveyard was also there. The general site would become the crossroads of Dayton.

But Dayton was dying. Symmes had not made good on his

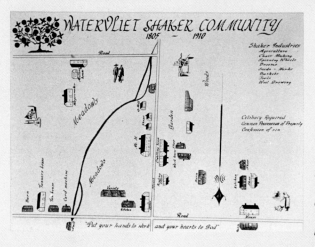

Shake, rattle and bark

■ *About the time Dayton's devout Presbyterian ancestors landed, a revivalistic fever began to sweep across the western United States. The conversion of hundreds to the schismatic or New-Light church was often accompanied by "a species of exercises of an involuntary kind, which seemed to have been substituted by the Great Spirit, in the room of the falling, &c. which had been among the New-Lights. The principal of these, were the rolling exercise, the jerks and the barks."[16]*

Dayton had a New-Light congregation as early as 1801, although it worshipped in homes not a church. The New-Lights were themselves split by revivalism and by Shaker missionaries from Mount Lebanon, New York. By April 26, 1805 (or 1806, dates vary), Dayton's New-Light, or Beulah, congregation had become the Beulah Shaker congregation. The early converts included Eunice Patterson, James and John Patterson (brothers of Robert) and Katy Stewart, a Patterson sister. Records in 1803 show fourteen Shaker families living on Beaver Creek, where they farmed in common. The 800 acres the colony owned at the height of its development were located in Van Buren Township. There a grist mill, a Believers' Fulling Mill and a carding mill were all established.

Shakers were peace-loving, celibate and industrious. The Beaver Creek community made woodenware, wagons and brooms, and all Shaker villages were renowned for their high-quality seeds. In May 1811, after the Dayton newspapers had frequently ordered them to move on, the community was mobbed. Still they refused *to leave. Other Shaker settlements were more seriously threatened. In nearby Lebanon, Union Village was burned, and some Shakers were shot. But the Dayton community had fewer problems than most. Some believed the peacefulness of the Dayton colony was directly related to the "blessing of Dayton." A Shaker at Union Village had a vision requiring him to put a curse on Lebanon. Francis Bedle and Richard McNemar proceeded to do so by riding through the streets, waving their hats and shouting curses at the village. After cursing Lebanon, they rode north to Dayton where the town was blessed in exactly the same manner. As a result, many settlers moved from Lebanon to Dayton—and the Watervliet community thrived.*

The name Watervliet was officially given to the village in 1813 to honor the Watervliet Shaker community in New York state. By 1832, a printing press had been established, and Watervliet was the western hub of Shaker printing.

Since celibate communities could only grow by conversion of new members and celibacy proved difficult to sell in Dayton, the Watervliet community slowly died out. In 1906, the state of Ohio bought the farm and the brick buildings which were all that remained of the thriving village founded by the "other" Pattersons. Part of two buildings (much remodeled) and the interior of the Dayton State Hospital farm barn are all that is left. The few remaining pieces of furniture and memorabilia are now located at Kettering-Moraine Historical Society Museum.

contract, and the U.S. government was demanding payment from the settlers. The demands were modest—only $2 an acre—but few could pay the price. Some left in disgust; new settlers were afraid to settle in the area because their land titles might be contested.

In 1802, only five families were living in Dayton—Newcom, Thompson, John Welsh, Paul Butler and George Westfall. Once again, it was Cooper who saved the day. He purchased preemption rights to the entire area and worked out arrangements with both the settlers and the government. A year later, Ohio became a state and Dayton, tiny Dayton, the county seat of huge Montgomery County.

Montgomery County included all of today's Preble, Miami, Darke, Shelby, Mercer, Van Wert, Paulding and Defiance counties and parts of four others. Dayton Township was one of four subdivisions and included about 6,300 square miles. Total white male population over 21 at the time was 526. (The entire state had only 15,413.)[5]

Things began to happen to the early, empty town. Courts were held. A jail was built on West Third Street at the cost of $299. A post office—with County Clerk Benjamin Van Cleve doubling as postmaster—was built at First and St. Clair. Henry Brown built the first store building on Main. Colonel Robert Patterson arrived in 1804 and purchased from Cooper a huge tract of land south of Dayton.

In 1805, the town of Dayton was incorporated. It now boasted a new graveyard between Fifth and Sixth streets near Ludlow as well as the first library in the state. There were two true marks of success—a brick tavern and a brick house.

And in March 1805, Dayton had a flood.

BRICKS AND BANKING: By the early 1800s, Dayton needed a school. The result: Dayton Academy, a two-story structure at Third and St. Clair (right). Bearded John Harshman evolved from farmer to bank president during his 45 years in Dayton (below, seated).

Tiny Dayton became the seat of Montgomery County and boasted a brick courthouse in which to conduct area legal business.

Nature and the Red Napoleon

After the flood—a severe one—some settlers wished to move the town to higher ground. But unwiser heads prevailed, and a levee was built instead.

As new settlers arrived, the center of the town slowly shifted to the south along Main Street. The early histories record most new arrivals, complete with family biographies.

"In the summer of 1805, Jonathan Harshman, one of the earliest settlers of Montgomery County, arrived in Dayton from Frederick County, Maryland, and purchased a farm five miles from town," began one entry regarding the arrival of a prominent Dayton family. "He was for many years profitably engaged in farming, milling and distilling and made a large fortune. He also had a store in Dayton. [In] partnership with John Rench they traded for country produce, which they sent down the river to Cincinnati and New Orleans. In 1825 he was elected a member of the Ohio Legislature. In 1845 he was elected

Famous Indian leader Tecumseh (left) had plans to expel the white man, but was foiled at the Battle of Tippecanoe by William Henry Harrison (right).

president of the Dayton bank and served till his death, March 31, 1850."[6]

The town needed a school, so the Dayton Academy was opened in 1808, although its handsome two-story brick building at the northwest corner of Third and St. Clair streets was not completed until late in 1810. Cooper donated the lots the building would occupy, plus two choice lots at Third and Main which were sold to fund the project. The academy's first teacher was William M. Smith, who taught in his home until the school was built. In 1820, the Dayton Academy adopted the Lancasterian teaching method. It included student monitors, tickets of merit (playing ball on Sunday cost a scholar 25 tickets) and no exams.

In late 1808, *The Dayton Repertory,* a four-page weekly newspaper, was founded. There may have been an earlier paper of a few issues published in 1806, but there are no surviving copies and Douglas McMurtrie, author of *Early Printing in Dayton, Ohio,* suspected this ghost paper was merely legend.[7]

Early newspapers were very poor sources of local history, except for birth and death notices. All local news, even election results, was common knowledge, not worth committing to print. Instead, early papers usually published news from Europe or the East Coast, copied from Eastern papers which finally made their way to Cincinnati, then to Dayton, via the weekly mail.

But the advertisements in those papers remain interesting. In 1808, Daytonians could shop at John Compton's, H. G. Phillip's or Steele and Peirce's store. John Dodson was a carpenter, John Hanna ran a weaving establishment. John and Archibald Bunns had a "factory" which made sickles, and D. C. Cooper offered to card wool for nearby sheep farmers.

Reid's Inn became the place to meet in early Dayton. David Reid was opposed to paying the $10 license fee for running a tavern, so he called his place an "Inn or House of Entertainment." It was between First and Second streets on the west side of Main.

By 1810, Dayton was a growing town with keelboats heading north and south on the Great Miami. It boasted a brick courthouse, the Dayton Academy, five brick houses, 26 frame houses, nineteen hewn log houses and seventeen cabins. Commerce included a printing office, six taverns, five stores, two nail factories, a tannery and a brewery; three each of saddler's shops, hatter's shops and cabinetmaker's shops; a gunsmith, a jeweler, a watchmaker, a sickle maker and a wagonmaker, in addition to smiths, carpenters, masons, weavers and dyers. The population was 383. (Only 131 were men 16 or older.) They paid $865.785 in taxes.

Dayton even had suburbs. South of Third was Cabintown. A ravine west of Wilkinson was Rattlesnake. An area east of town was called the Commons.

In 1811, Dayton did not have a flood—it had an earthquake instead. The first shock was on December 16, 1811, between two and three o'clock in the morning. Afterquakes occurred the following day, later in the month, late in January and on February 13. "Although no material damage was done by these earthquakes, the people, and animals and fowls as well, were very much alarmed. Persons who experienced it in youth, spoke of it in old age with a shudder of horror."[8]

The legends that grew up about the famous Indian leader Tecumseh were fabulous, often fantastic. But one thing was certain—he was a born leader, and he nearly succeeded in rallying many of the Indian tribes to expel the white man. He might have—had it not been for his brother and William Henry Harrison.

Tecumseh's brother (possibly a twin or triplet) was called

Riverbound Dayton was linked with the rest of the world when two bridges, one free and one toll, were built in 1817 and 1819. Toll charges: two cents if by foot, three cents if crossing by horse. Sketch by Thomas Wharton, 1832.

The Prophet. He was certainly a fanatic, perhaps insane. While Tecumseh was away gathering support, The Prophet told his braves that he had made a spell so the white man's bullets would pass through the warriors without injury. William Henry Harrison, governor of Indiana Territory, commanded about 800 men whose bullets refused to be bewitched, and The Prophet was defeated at the Battle of Tippecanoe. The defeat destroyed Tecumseh's original plan and forced him to ally himself with the British who were anxious to revenge their earlier defeat.

America was eager for war. Britain and France were fighting and threatened U.S. ships on the Atlantic. American sailors were impressed at sea and forced to serve the English. Swords rattled. In 1812, before America declared war, President James Madison called on Ohio to supply 1,200 militia for one year's service. Dayton was chosen as the gathering site. General William Hull, governor of Michigan Territory, was chosen to lead them. It was a terrible decision.

Dayton, with its population of almost 500, was suddenly quadrupled as it hosted 1,500 to 1,600 soldiers. Two regiments were on the Commons to the east of town, a third regiment was camped to the south. Ohioans were asked to sell at least one blanket per household to the militia to keep the men warm and dry, and less than 200 Dayton women sewed 1,800 shirts for the troops in a three-week period— well before sewing machines. General Hull marched the men to a training camp three miles away on the west side of Mad River on May 26, 1812. Meanwhile, the volunteer rifle company of William Van Cleve (Benjamin's younger brother) marched forth to guard supply trains from marauding Indians.

On June 1, some dozen days before the war would be officially declared, Hull marched the Army north toward Detroit. He was an excellent marcher; even though a road had to be constructed from Urbana northward, the Army managed an incredible nine and a half miles per day and reached Detroit on July 5.

Hull decided to enter Canada, and 188 Ohio militiamen promptly said they could not be expected to fight on foreign soil and would not cross the border.[9]

A small detachment of Ohioans fell into an ambush at the hands of Tecumseh and his men. When a larger detachment met the same fate, Hull returned to the comparative safety of Detroit. A bold expedition of about 1,300 British regulars, Canadian militia and Indians marched on the American position. Although the British had no real hope of capturing Detroit, Hull—apparently terrified—surrendered. The British claimed to have captured 2,500 Americans, but 2,000 is perhaps more honest. It was not an auspicious beginning for a war. Hull had one regiment of regulars with him. These were taken to Canada as prisoners. The militia was disarmed and sent home. Few of the Daytonians, if any, had fired a shot.

Hull was court-martialed, found guilty of neglect of duty and bad conduct and sentenced to be shot. He was not executed, but his reputation was destroyed. Dayton land speculator James Wilkinson also had his military reputation ruined in the War of 1812.

William Henry Harrison was not having an easy time as governor of the Indiana Territory, so he dropped a few hints that he would not object to doing his duty in war. He was made a brigadier general and proved an exceptionally able commander whose troops adulated him. He refused hot meals and warm beds because his men could not share the same comforts.

For some reason, Harrison wanted Kentuckians, not Ohioans, in his army. The Ohio militia came forward to Harrison and were told—very politely, of course—that they were not needed. After Commodore Perry's brilliant naval victory on Lake Erie, the Army caught up to the British and their Indian allies at the River Thames near Detroit. Harrison ordered Colonel Richard M. Johnson's mounted Kentucky riflemen to charge a weakly-defended line; the plan worked perfectly, and the battle was quickly over. Tecumseh was killed and probably mutilated. His old enemy, Simon Kenton, was there as an invited guest of the army. When Kenton saw the mutilated Indians, he walked away saying, "There have been cowards here."[10]

In the West, the war was essentially over in 1813.

In 1814, Dayton had a flood.

Of Bibles, banknotes and bridges

Samuel Forrer visited Dayton in 1814. "At the early day there was a house and a well in an oak clearing on Main Street, near Fifth, surrounded by a hazel thicket," he wrote in his reminiscences, published in *The Journal* in 1863. "It was a noted halting place for strangers traveling northward and eastward, in order to procure a drink of water and inquire the distance to Dayton! [Forrer meant the thickets were so overgrown you could not see the city for the trees.] The embryonic city was confined to the bank of the Miami River, between Ludlow and Mill Streets, and the business—storekeeping, blacksmithing, milling, distilling, etc.—was concentrated about the head of Main Street."[11]

Reid's Inn had supplanted Newcom's Tavern as the focal point of the town. Reid was now Major Reid, thanks to his service in the War of 1812 (although Reid may not have done anything other than march north and walk home). After Perry's victory on Lake Erie, the patriotic innkeeper had a sign erected bearing Commodore Perry's words, "Don't give up the ship."

A bank with the unlikely name of the Dayton Manufacturing Company was begun in 1813. Only two years later, counterfeit Dayton Manufacturing Company notes appeared.[12]

On April 12, 1815, the Dayton Female Charitable and Bible Society was formed. It cost $1 to join, and dues were 25 cents per quarter. The names reflect the power of the growing merchant and landowner society of Dayton—Patterson, Cotton, Welsh, Crane, Peirce, King, Reid, Hanna, Steele and Spinning.

A market house was opened in 1815. One hundred pounds of beef cost $3 to $3.50. Somewhat later, whiskey cost 12.5 cents per gallon.

So far, Dayton had been completely bound by Mad River on the north and Great Miami River on the west. It was only in 1817 that the first bridge was completed across the Mad at Taylor Street. In January 1819, the Miami was crossed by a toll bridge owned by Patterson, Peirce, Reid, Phillips, Steele, Houston, George and King. A person on foot could cross for two cents; if he rode a horse, it cost three cents.

Stage coaches began carrying people and freight. The Cincinnati and Dayton mail stage, owned by John Piatt of Cincinnati and D. C. Cooper of Dayton, began a line over the route in June 1818.

Sometime during this period, Daniel Cooper had sold his home on Rubicon Creek to Robert Patterson and had moved into town. In 1818, he started to build a large brick home on the southeast corner of First and Wilkinson. Apparently Cooper, who was then 44, purchased a bell for the Presbyterian church and carried the bell by wheelbarrow to the site, injuring himself. He suffered for six weeks before dying at about midnight August 13, 1818. Perhaps there were more vivid characters in the course of Dayton's history, but few, if any, did more for the city. Cooper's combination of business acumen and philanthropy served as a model for other Dayton leaders to follow. (There is a park named in his honor; the Montgomery County Public Library stands there today.)

Before the big time

From 1820 to 1827, a nationwide economic depression slowed the growth of the young frontier city. In 1820, the population of 1,139 was welcomed to see an elephant named Columbus at Reid's Inn for 37.5 cents—half price for children. (A year earlier, Reid had displayed the first African lion to be seen locally.)[13]

A squirrel hunt in April 1822, netted 1,000 squirrels.

Butter was five cents a pound in July 1822.

In 1824, the "Haytien government" paid for 24 Dayton "people of color" to emigrate to "Hayti." Most returned later, according to early historians.

The first execution in Dayton occurred March 28, 1825. John McAfee murdered his wife and was hanged on a gallows (where Sinclair College is now) just east of the river. Nearly everyone in the county "was assembled at the gallows."[14]

Dayton's first fire engine arrived in 1826. It cost $226 and probably was not worth it.

In 1828, Dayton had a flood.

The *Dayton Journal and Advertiser*, January 6, 1829, described the city on the eve of the canal era:

"During the year 1825, thirty-six brick buildings and thirty-four of wood have been put up. The whole number of brick buildings in Dayton on the first of January 1829, is one hundred and twenty-five: of stone, six—of wooden buildings, two hundred and thirty-nine. . . .The public buildings are a courthouse, jail, public offices, and Presbyterian, Methodist, Baptist and New-Light meeting houses. The jail is of stone, the rest of brick. In sight of the town are a gristmill, a fulling mill [a process of shrinking and thickening wool fabric], a carding house, a cotton factory, a double sawmill, a simple sawmill, a shingle and lath factory, a cornmill and an iron foundry. There are in Dayton five taverns, sixteen dry goods stores, four drug stores, thirty groceries, twelve carpenters, eight masons, three millwrights, three tan yards, two breweries, two sickle factories, four hat factories, five saddler shops, nine shoemaker shops, five cabinetmakers, four chairmakers, three painters, three coopers, four wagonmakers, one coachmaker, five blacksmith shops, four watchmakers, one tinner, one coppersmith, ten tailor shops, one ropewalk [a rope factory], two tobacco factories, two stone cutters, one gunsmith, seven doctors, thirteen lawyers, two printing offices, with many other items too tedious to mention."[15]

By 1829, the population was approaching 3,000, but many of the original settlers were no longer among them. Daniel Cooper was dead, Benjamin Van Cleve had died in 1822 and Robert Patterson in late 1827. However, they had done their work well. All Dayton needed to succeed was a ditch about twenty feet wide and 250 miles long.

McAfee's Confession

■ *The trial of John McAfee aroused much interest in the small frontier community. It lasted two days, and McAfee was sentenced to be hanged March 28, 1825. On that morning, crowds began to come in from the country. At 10 a.m., he was taken from the jail, seated in a carriage and attended by the Reverend Father Hill, a Catholic priest from Cincinnati. Guarded by the militia, he was conveyed to the gallows erected west of Dayton near the Miami River. As was common practice of the time, McAfee made a public confession of his crime and was then hanged at 3 p.m.*

The story became a song with numerous variations and was popular throughout the Midwest.

CHAPTER THREE

POLITICS, PLAGUE AND THE IRON HORSE

The Miami and Erie Canal moved Dayton crops to market. The boat above floated around 1850.

The Miami Canal linking Dayton to Cincinnati took four years to build (1825-29) and was an immediate success. The Beckel House (left) was one of Dayton's most important early hotels.

After the great success of the Erie Canal in 1819, every state wanted a canal of its own. Canals certainly were needed in Ohio. Almost all the major settlements were either north on Lake Erie or south on the Ohio River. The interior towns such as Dayton grew marvelous crops. But they had difficulty getting the crops to market as the Miami River was often closed to traffic by fish traps and low water. The major Ohio canal was to be the meandering Ohio and Erie Canal from Cleveland—via Akron, Coshocton and near Columbus—to Portsmouth on the Ohio River. But, to keep western Ohioans happy, a Dayton-to-Cincinnati canal was to be built, with a promised extension to Toledo. Ground was broken for the Miami Canal at Middletown on July 21, 1825.

On January 25, 1829, the first boats—the *Governor Brown,* the *Forrer,* the *General Marion* and the *General Pike*—reached Dayton from Cincinnati. The canal was an immediate success. Cincinnati was nicknamed "Porkopolis" because of the hog traffic along the ditch. In March and April of 1831 alone, the canal carried 58,000 barrels of flour, 7,000 barrels of whiskey, 12,000 barrels of pork, 18,000 kegs of lard, 750 hogsheads of ham and—incredibly—1.8 million pounds of bacon.

The year 1829 was a year of major growth for Dayton. Timothy Squier opened the National Hotel next to the already thriving Beckel House on Third Street. A new market house was planned between Third and Fourth. (It eventually extended all the way from Main to Jefferson.) This caused quite a furor. The more established Daytonians who lived north of Third called all the land to the south "Cabintown" and wanted the market built north. But the people of Cabintown had more votes, and the market was built south of Third.

The canal was a significant factor in Dayton's growth. By 1830, Dayton's population was 2,954, an incredible increase of more than 40 percent in two years. The canal was making Dayton an important interior town.

In 1832, Dayton had a flood. Cincinnati, however, had a more disastrous flood, and Mayor John Van Cleve (Benjamin's son, an imposing man of over 250 pounds) helped raise $202 which Dayton sent to help Cincinnati's flood victims.

Dayton philanthropy was counterbalanced by Dayton tom-foolery. On the eve of presidential balloting in 1832, Democrats erected a tall hickory pole near the courthouse, complete with an American flag, to remind voters to elect "Old Hickory" Jackson. The Whigs were not amused, and two angry crowds gathered. Finally, Van Cleve, Dr. John Steele and a few other city leaders marched to the offending pole and announced that the Dayton Council had ordered the pole's removal. It was chopped down, reportedly saving a "bloody riot." After the election, a canal boat arrived in Dayton from Miamis-burg bearing an even larger hickory pole to celebrate Jackson's victory.

Cholera, color and counterfeit carpets

Until the mid-1820s, the early settlers were mostly the English and Scotch-Irish who had settled much of Colo-nial America. But the canals were slowly changing that. On December 17, 1832, a canal boat arrived in the town with 25 German immigrants. All were sick with cholera, and one

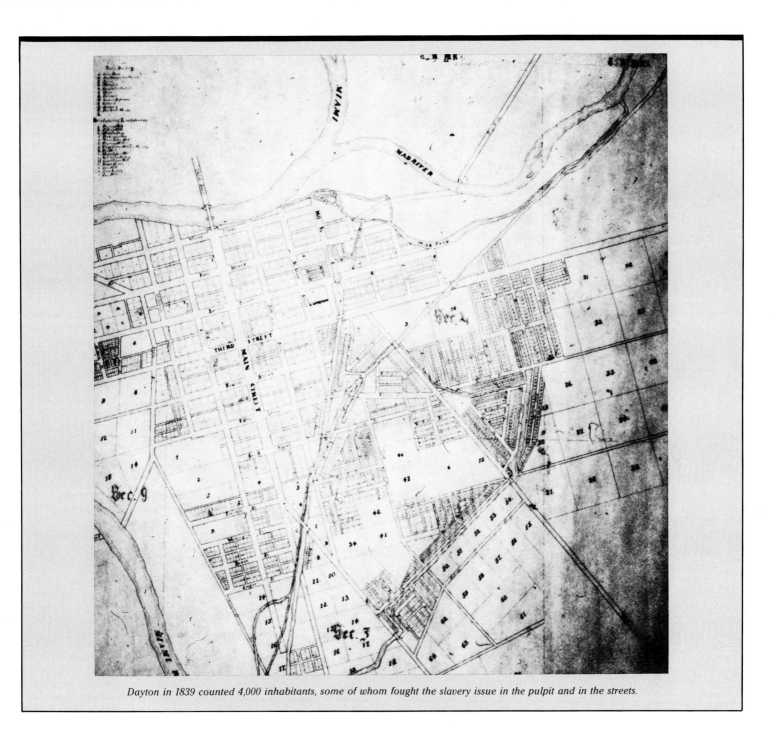

Dayton in 1839 counted 4,000 inhabitants, some of whom fought the slavery issue in the pulpit and in the streets.

had died on the trip north. All were shoved into a tiny room, and seven later died as did two men whom the town had hired to nurse them. A year later, cholera struck again, killing 33 Daytonians—a tragically high number for a town of only 4,000 inhabitants.

In 1838, Dayton had a park, a number of handsome new churches and the stirrings of racial hate. Even as a territory, Ohio did not allow slavery. While some Kentuckians brought black men and women with them when they settled—Robert Patterson brought 24—they were theoretically servants not slaves. But lawsuits brought as early as 1805 proved Patterson actually had slaves.[1] Some, including Edward Page, were freed and allowed to vote in Ohio.

Dr. Hibbard Jewett was Dayton's best known abolitionist. When an out-of-town lecturer delivered an abolitionist speech at Union Church on Main Street, February 13, 1839, the man was egged, forced from the pulpit, beaten by the mob and forced to recover at Jewett's house. During the same night,

the mob destroyed the homes of blacks and looted Union Church. *The Journal* newspaper usually breathed fire in its editorials. But this time, it chastised the mob with a surprisingly even-handed admonition. After pointing out that the paper did not support abolition in any way, it asked, "But we put it to every reflecting man in the community to say whether he can do otherwise than condemn these acts of violence.... Shall the mob or the law be supreme? That is the question."[2]

As more families and diverse groups moved in to take jobs, more conflicts arose. "In 1841, a young girl, so light in color many people thought her white, came to make her home with her people, in the vicinity of Wayne, Fifth and Eagle streets. A mob formed among the lower classes, and in February, when the thermometer was below zero, they drove the black families from their cabins, pulling down and burning many of the houses. The owner of one of the cabins stabbed the leader of the mob, Nat McCleary, and killed him.... Many died and others left town."[3]

Man-made channels provided manufacturers such as Stilwell and Bierce with hydraulic power.

Before the canal and the availability of cheap labor and cheap power, farming and a few small family businesses comprised the town's commerce. But the conditions were ripe for manufacturing.

To create industry required power. At first, the rivers provided it, but this limited industry to the riverbanks, and the river often proved to be a sporadic supplier. So hydraulics, or hydraulic races, were built. These man-made channels "fell" (dropped in elevation) at an even rate to provide constant, steady power.

In 1829, James Steele dammed the Miami north of town and created what later was called the Dayton View Hydraulic. The Cooper Hydraulic, built in 1838, was 50 feet wide and 700 feet long and ran between Third and Fifth streets. A third hydraulic, running off Mad River, was completed in 1845 and ran almost three miles. The drops were surprisingly small—twelve feet for Cooper's, fourteen feet for the other two. The three combined provided 170 "run of stone." (One run was approxi-

CHOLERA CURED FOR 50 CENTS
Howe's infallible
diarrhea preventative
and cholera cure

■ *Handbills tacked to covered bridges, fenceposts and other conspicuous places announced that the cholera epidemic was again in Dayton.*[14]

On May 22, 1849, 19-year-old William Munday died of cholera after having been confined to his bed about twelve hours. He had returned the day before by canal boat from Cincinnati. Twenty days later at the Kline House, "a working class Boarding house,"[15] *Mr. Kline supervised a workman digging a ditch to drain the stable yard. Both Kline and the digger died. Six boarders also contracted the disease and died. The Kline House was closed, and liberal amounts of lime were applied for fumigation.*

The first stage of cholera is diarrhea, restlessness, nausea and chills. It is followed by severe diarrhea, painful vomiting, cramps, thirst and circulatory failure. Death may occur within as little as three hours. The bacteria causing cholera are transmitted through stools of infected patients. The poor sanitary conditions of 1849—no garbage removal, no sewer system—were ideal for the disease.

By June 13, Dayton historian Maskell Curwen reported the disease was epidemic. "During that period, business was almost entirely suspended: the markets were deserted,

except by a few wagons and the streets whitened by the quantity of lime, scattered in the gutters. The number of deaths, as near as could be ascertained, was two hundred and twenty-five. During its continuance, a board of health, headed by George B. Holt, and a cholera hospital, under the management of Dr. Edmund Smith, were established, and every attention shown to the sick and dead that humanity demanded."[16]

The first Friday in August, Mayor John Howard proclaimed as "a day of fasting, humiliation and prayer."[17] *Businesses were told to close, and the people were to meet in "their several places of public worship at 10:30 o'clock a.m. to ask God's mercy."*[18]

"The Orphan Asylum. . .a neat brick building, on the brow of the hill, about a mile south of the Court House, was used in 1849 for the cholera hospital."[19] *(The asylum later became the Widows' Home and, later still, the site of the Protestant Deaconess Hospital which became Miami Valley Hospital.)*

Dr. John Wise remembered seeing 60 patients a day. Public funerals were eliminated, bodies carted to the burial ground, sometimes an entire family on one wagon.[20]

How to avoid cholera

■ *Of the exciting causes [of cholera], one [is] the premature laying aside of flannel and other warm clothing. In addition to this getting wet in a shower—remaining long in damp places—sitting in a strong current of air at night—and sleeping with but little bed covering—should all be carefully avoided. . . .A second class of exciting causes is connected with diet. Loading the stomach with any kind of food, especially at night, may bring on the disease. . . . In fact a nourishing diet is best; but should be plain and digestible. Meat or boiled eggs, should be eaten every day. Boiled ham, corned beef and poultry, corned mutton, and well-seasoned, beef steak are the best. . . .Veal, fresh pork*

and fresh fish should be avoided. Of salt fish, mackerel and salmon are too hard; but codfish with potatoes is proper. Old cheese is safe, and macaroni prepared with cheese may be eaten. Hot bread should be avoided—stale bread or crackers only, should be used. Of culinary vegetable mealy potatoes, well boiled hominy and rice, are not only the best but all others had better be omitted. . . .Those who drink malt liquors at their meals should limit themselves to freshly brewed beer, well hopped. As to brandy and whiskey, they cannot prevent cholera.
Daniel Drake, M.D.
Cincinnati, May 11, 1849[21]

mately the same as eight horsepower.) The canal—which was really two canals in Dayton—provided still more power.

Samuel Forrer, an engineer and canal expert, made his home in Dayton in 1817 or 1818. In 1839, he was appointed superintendent of the turnpikes around the town. Dayton had the canal, but it did not have the National Road.

In 1806, the young United States had begun plans for a road to connect the East with the new West. At first, National Road construction was brisk, but then things slowed to a crawl. It was probably 1838 (reports vary from 1836 to 1840) when the road reached neighboring Springfield. Daytonians tried everything they could to bring the National Road to Dayton. The government was not impressed, but since the road ended temporarily in Springfield, it was fair game for Dayton's entrepreneurs.

Dayton built a turnpike (presumably with the services of Forrer) from Springfield to Dayton, complete with counterfeit mile-marker signs which made the Dayton Turnpike look exactly like the National Road. Apparently it fooled some travelers who complained of being "hijacked" by the Daytonians' turnpike.

The first Montgomery County Fair was held on October 17 and 18, 1839, at Swaynie's Hotel (less than five months old at the time) located at the head of the canal basin. The carpets in the hotel were made by the Dayton Carpet Company, manufacturers of the first flowered ingrain carpet west of the Allegheny Mountains. Dayton historian Robert Steele reported with pride that "the Dayton carpets were sold in the stores of Cincinnati and other western towns as imported carpets, and purchasers did not discover the deception."[4]

Other than carpets, the fair was devoted to a get-rich scheme which appeared at least twice during the 1830s. Silkworms were (supposedly) the way to quick and easy riches. All anyone needed was the ever-lovely *Morus multicaules* (mulberry) tree, a few thousand cocoons—and plenty of time to feed the voracious little critters.

Judging from the fair's involvement with the committee on silk, Dayton was just as gullible as the rest of the country, including the carpet buyers in Cincinnati. The Dayton Silk Company was incorporated in 1839 with a proposed capitalization of $100,000. Vast sums of money were lost. Since the population of Dayton in 1840 was but 6,067, such wild speculation must have severely hurt the delicate economy of the young town.[5]

Dayton's second favorite pastime

Although the working days were long, there were few amusements to fill the evenings and Sundays in the Miami Valley. Without television, movies, radio or baseball, and with few magazines, newspapers or women of easy

---

Poor Tom is free

■ *A short time ago a negro man, who has lived in this place two or three years under the name of Thomas Mitchell, was arrested by some men from Kentucky and taken before a justice under a charge of being a slave who had escaped from his master. The magistrate, on hearing the evidence, discharged the black man, not being satisfied with the proof brought by the claimants of their rights to him. A few weeks afterwards some men armed, employed by the master, seized the negro in our main street, and were hurrying towards the outskirts of the town, where they had a sleigh in waiting to carry him off. The negro's cries brought a number of citizens into the street, who interfered and prevented the men from taking him away without having legally proved their right to do so. The claimants of the negro went before the justice again, and after a long examination of the case on some new evidence being produced, he was decided to be the slave of the person claiming him as such. In the meantime a good deal of excitement had been produced among the people of the place and their sympathies for the poor black fellow were so much awakened that a proposition was made to buy his freedom. The agent of the master agreed to sell him under the supposition that the master would sell him his liberty, and a considerable sum was subscribed, to which, out of his own savings, the negro contributed upwards of fifty dollars himself. The master, however, when his agent returned to Kentucky, refused to agree to the arrangement, and came himself. . .to take the negro away. Their first meeting was in the upper story of a house, and Tom, on seeing those who were about to take him, rushed to a window and endeavored, but without success, to dash himself through it, although, had he succeeded, he would have fallen on a stone pavement from a height not less than fifteen feet. He was prevented, however, and the mas-*ter took him away with him and got him as far as Cincinnati. The following letter received by a gentlemen in this place gives the concluding account of the matter:*

Cincinnati, January 24, 1832

Dear Sir: In compliance with a request of Mr. J. Deinkard, of Kentucky, I take my pen to inform you of the death of his black man Ben, whom he took in your place a few days ago. The circumstances are as follows: On the evening of the 22d inst., Mr. D. and company, with Ben, arrived in this city on their way to Kentucky, and put up at the Main Street Hotel, where a room on the uppermost story (fourth) of the building was provided for Ben and his guard. All being safe, as they thought, about one o'clock, when they were in a sound sleep, poor Ben stimulated with even the faint prospect of escape, or perhaps predetermined on liberty or death, threw himself from the window which is upwards of fifty feet from the pavement. He was, as you may well suppose, severly injured, and the poor fellow died this morning about 4 o'clock. Mr. D. left this morning with the dead body of his slave, to which he told me he would give decent burial in his own graveyard. Please tell Ben's wife of these circumstances. Your unknown correspondent,

Respectfully,
R. P. Simmons

Tom, or as he is called in the letter, Ben, was an industrious, steady, saving fellow and had laid up a small sum of money; all of which he gave to his wife and child when his master took him away. A poor and humble being, of an unfortunate and degraded race, the same feeling which animated the signers of the Declaration of Independence to pledge life, fortune and honor for liberty, determined him to be free or die.

—from The Journal
date unknown,
describing an event January, 1832

An 1843 artist provided one view of Dayton from the city's Steele's Hill where the Dayton Art Institute stands today.

virtue, the thoughts of men in the Miami Valley turned to politics. And in 1840, the time was ripe for Dayton to play its first important role in national politics.

The Democrats under Andrew Jackson had led the country for eight years. When Jackson did not run for a third term in 1836, Martin Van Buren soundly defeated William Henry Harrison and others. In 1840, Harrison ran again, but Van Buren—who gave the impression of being a fancy-living snob, totally lacking the common touch—was no longer popular.

Harrison was a strong popular candidate, especially in the West. Although he had been born in Virginia, Harrison had arrived in Ohio late in 1791, married John Cleve Symmes' daughter and made his home next door to Cincinnati in North Bend, Ohio. He was the hero of the Battle of Tippecanoe—he had successfully led troops in the War of 1812 and defeated Tecumseh and the British at the Battle of the Thames.

A slur (apparently from a member of his own party) claimed Harrison would be content to sit around his log cabin and drink hard cider forever if he were given a pension of $2,000 a year. That log cabin/hard cider reference was all the Whigs needed.

Dayton's first intellectual, John Van Cleve, was ready. His *Log Cabin* newspaper achieved national attention and well deserved it. Van Cleve did all the illustrations, wrote the songs and verse and probably many of the articles. It was a vigorously written paper, bombastic but brainy and sinfully sarcastic to Van Buren—"that used-up man."

On September 10, 1840, the 27th anniversary of Perry's victory on Lake Erie, Dayton was ready to welcome Harrison, the hero. On September 8, 1840, Dayton's population was 6,167 —and on September 10, it was more than 80,000! The Whigs had begun to arrive on the ninth—military units and a dozen canal boats loaded with men. Local Whigs displayed banners of free food and lodging for the asking. One arriving procession was five miles long. Speeches were made, and the *Log Cabin* reported favorably on them all. Harrison was apparently not the spellbinder, but Daytonian Robert C. Schenck proved a powerful Whig orator—and a major force in local politics for many years. Dayton basked in the political excitement and fervor. Politics, often violent and divisive, had become Dayton's second favorite pastime.

Harrison won the election. Tippecanoe (and Tyler, too) received 2,469 votes in Montgomery County to 1,339 for Van Buren and vice presidential candidate Richard Johnson who (under the command of Harrison at the Battle of the Thames) had led the decisive cavalry charge. Harrison was 68 when he took office. He died a month following his inauguration, perhaps of pneumonia but more probably of the medical treat-

LOG CABIN

NO. 7   PRICE--25 CENTS IN ADVANCE.   DAYTON: O.

LOG CABIN.

Saturday, June 27, 1840.

LOG CABIN CANDIDATES.

FOR PRESIDENT.
WM. HENRY HARRISON.

FOR VICE PRESIDENT.
JOHN TYLER,
THE INDEPENDENT VIRGINIAN.

FOR GOVERNOR OF OHIO.
THOMAS CORWIN,
THE WAGON BOY.

NEW SERIES.

This is the first No. of the New Series. There is no great variety in it, but the quality of its contents will make up for that. There is an admirable song written by Jno. W. Van Cleve and the music accompanying it engraved by him, will. Gen. Harrison's official account of the Battle of Tippecanoe, with an exact sketch of the Battle Ground handsomely engraved. And a most animated description of the Great Convention at Fort Meigs. No one will feel the want of variety after reading these articles.

Those who wish to subscribe for the New Series, should send in their orders as soon as possible so that we may know how many will be needed.

The price it will be recollected is but 25 cts for the 7 numbers. We hope our friends will calculate the proposals to their respective neighborhoods.

BATTLE OF TIPPECANOE.

The plate of this celebrated battle ground, and Gen. Harrison's official despatch to the War Department, detailing the particulars of the fight, occupy a large portion of the space to day. We copy the despatch, with the Message of President Madison, transmitting it to Congress from Niles Register (vol 1, page 307, Dec 28, 1811.) The conduct of Gen. Harrison, at the Battle of Tippecanoe has been made the subject of innumerable slanders on the part of the Locofoco leaders. It would be tedious to enumerate them, as in the present state of the canvass, there is no necessity for republishing the powerful refutations which have already deprived the calumnies of their power to injure, and will ultimately prostrate the party which has set them out among the people as facts worthy belief. The account here given, forms a part of Western History, with which all should be familiar. And which, while it abounds with matter of deep interest to the whole American people, forms a chapter of events in Log Cabin Times, scarce equalled by any things in important influence over the lives and prospects of the early settlers.

The plate gives a fine representation of the Battle Ground, and may be relied upon as correct. All who visit the spot speak of its great advantages for the purpose for which it was selected; and they do not fail to remark, too, that no where in the vicinity is any ground to be seen, which could be occupied by an army in the territory of an enemy, with any regard to the safety of those who composed it. The Battle Ground lies west of the Wabash river about one mile, and about four miles south of the river Tippecanoe. It is in Tippecanoe county Ind six miles from Lafayette, the county seat. The ground occupied by the encampment is the southern point of a beautiful dry and timbered ridge, which terminates at the Tippecanoe. The west side is steep and not of easy ascent—that towards the Wabash does not rise so abruptly. The camping ground is now under fence and belongs to the State of Indiana. Gen. Tipton, entered the land occupied by it and presented it to the State.

The Harrisonian will celebrate the Fourth of July, at Richmond Ind. and they invite their friends from Ohio to visit it on that day. The number present on the occasion, is expected to be very large.

SATURDAY--JUNE 27.

SUCCESS TO YOU, TOM CORWIN.

BY JOHN W. VAN CLEVE.

TUNE.—HERE'S A HEALTH TO THEE, TOM BREEZE

Success to you, Tom Corwin!
Tom Corwin, our true hearts love you!
Ohio has no nobler son,
In worth there's none above you.
And we will soon bestow
On you her highest honor,
And then our State will proudly show,
Without a stain upon her.
Chorus,—Success to you, Tom Corwin.
Tom Corwin, our true hearts love you!
Ohio has no nobler son
In worth there's none above you.

Success to you, Tom Corwin!
We've seen, with warm emotion,
Your faithfulness to freedom's cause,
Your boldness, your devotion.
And we will ne'er forget
That you our rights have guarded;
Our grateful hearts shall pay the debt,
And worth shall be rewarded.
Chorus,—Success to you, Tom Corwin, &c.

Success to you Tom Corwin!
We've call'd you from your station,
To have a while in other hands
The guidance of the nation;
For now our Buckeye land,
The land of our affection,
Requires your aid against the band,
That hold her in subjection.
Chorus—Success to you, Tom Corwin, &c.

Success to you, Tom Corwin!
Our hearts are all united,
To free our country from misrule,
And see her honor righted.
With Harrison and you,
We'll gain a triumph glorious;
Our cause is just, our hearts are true,
Our cause shall be victorious.
Chorus—Success to you Tom Corwin, &c.

Presidential Election in Ohio.

In almost all the newspapers that have published a table of dates of the coming elections, the Presidential Election in Ohio is put down as taking place in November. This is an error. The 30th of October is the day. The second section of the law of Ohio "to provide for the election of electors of President and Vice President of the United States," fixes the election on "the first Friday, preceding the first Wednesday in December." In the present year, "the first Wednesday in December" is on the 2nd day of the month—The first Friday preceding that day, is therefore on the 27th of November. The second Friday is on the 20th of November, the third is on the 13th the fourth is on the 6th, and the "FIFTH" is on the 30th day of October.

The Miami Valley in Convention

Amidst the State, district and County Conventions, which have been going on in Ohio, a big meeting in the Miami Valley has been called for from various quarters—and Dayton has been mentioned as a central and desirable place at which the multitude which the Valley would send forth, might congregate. The 10th of September the anniversary of Perry's victory upon Lake Erie, has been suggested as a proper time. All these things we say have been talked about of late among the people in this and the adjoining counties. And arrangements to carry into effect, what the people desire, will doubtless be made by a public meeting in Dayton.

THE SPRINGFIELD RAISING.

The Republic details the proceedings of a meeting of 6,000 or 8,000 of the yeomanry who met there by appointment on Thursday last in a spirited and attractive manner. At Springfield the sorrowful intelligence reached Gen. Harrison of the death of a son whom he had left at home in health. The blow was as severe as it was unexpected. He remained in Springfield but a short time, after he received the letter. The thousands there assembled sincerely sympathised with him.

THOMAS CORWIN

The Lebanon Star of Friday says, that Mr. Corwin's health is so far restored as to promise a speedy renewal of the intercourse with the people of this State which he was engaged in when attacked by the disease from which he is now recovering. This will be good news all over Ohio. The anxiety of the people to hear Mr. Corwin is constantly expressed.

DIED,

Very suddenly, on Tuesday evening last, at the residence of his father, at North Bend, Dr BENJAMIN HARRISON. He was in the 34th year of his age. This intelligence will be a very great shock to the General, as the Doctor was in good health, when he started for Fort Meigs
Cincinnati Daily News, June 19

A Straw in the Wind.

A vote, in regard to the Presidency, was lately taken on board the steamboat Queen of the West on the passage from New Orleans to Cincinnati. The whole number of passengers on board, including deck and cabin, was 213; and the aggregate vote was as follows: For Harrison, 135; for Van Buren, 78—being very nearly two to one in favor of the people's candidate.

Unmitigated Cruelty!

Ritchie, the Editor of the Richmond Enquirer, says he has marked the name of "Wm C. Rives from his subscription books!" Mean, man, how can you, standing as you do, on the verge of the grave, exercise such unheard of cruelty toward a poor, weak fellow-mortal like Mr. Rives? It is doubted whether the victim will survive the blow!

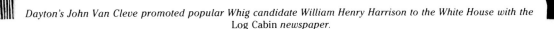

Dayton's John Van Cleve promoted popular Whig candidate William Henry Harrison to the White House with the Log Cabin *newspaper.*

William Henry Harrison (left) had plenty of Dayton help in his election bid, including orator Robert C. Schenck, listed on the Louisiana broadside above.

ment given him for pneumonia.

Politics continued to obsess Daytonians who were always eager to listen to promises and enjoy a good meal. In late September 1842, Henry Clay came to a Dayton Whig barbecue. Although the excitement and novelty of Harrison's 1840 visit was not equalled, the crowd reportedly was even bigger. Dayton welcomed an estimated 120,000 strangers. Speeches were made at the Jefferson Street end of the market house (between Third and Fourth), and dinner was served on two great tables, each 800 feet long. Local Whigs put out the red carpet. David Stout entertained "108 guests overnight and many more at dinner."[6]

Passing of Peasley's Pleasure Garden

■ *In 1832, Morris Seely (Dayton mayor for two months in 1841) had a plan to bring a canal to the rapidly-growing eastern portion of Dayton. He bought land for a very circuitous route from Third Street to Wayne Avenue to Richard Street, past "Africa," then southwest on a zig-zag course to join the main canal slightly north of the fairground site. The idea was that the properties along Seely's Basin would gain in value from being on the canal.*

Seely apparently saw his canal as a service to industry, not pleasure—with one exception.

Peasley's Pleasure Garden, on the west side of Warren Street, was designed in 1833 as a place for "pleasure and refreshments."[12] It was not a success. Few parties "were taken to the garden in boats down the canal to the basin, where the horse forded the canal, and towed the boat up the basin to the garden."[13]

Seely's Basin had a short life. Soon prime properties along the route were sold at ridiculously low prices—lots at Fifth and Wayne sold from $5 to $30. In 1836, a loan the city council floated had one-tenth of the money earmarked for filling in the unhealthy Seely's Folly. But as late as 1866, it was still there. When severe flooding occurred in the southern part of the Oregon district, residents blamed Seely's Ditch. Some say an angry mob took the law into their own hands and dammed the ditch by torchlight.

Most of the route is now obscured by U.S. 35.

Earlier in 1842, ex-President Martin Van Buren visited Dayton. He drew about 60 people for a dollar-a-plate dinner.

Immigrants set the pace

Although public schools were held in rented rooms as early as 1831, the public school system in Dayton really began in 1838 with the construction of two schools. One was on Perry Street, the other on East Second. In 1842, two more schools were opened in rented rooms. But as money was tight, the school board only ran school for one quarter, one month and one week, until the money was exhausted. German school was authorized in 1841 but not initiated until 1844. In the German schools, one-half the time was given to instruction in English.[7]

By 1850, about twenty percent of Dayton was foreign-born, with the German people accounting for almost three-quarters of that total. Almost 40 percent of the 1,008 people in Ward Six (to the southeast of central Dayton) had been born in Germany.

From the beginning, the German immigrants were the most patriotic Americans in town. They were among the first to volunteer for the Mexican War.

The Mexican War created great excitement in Dayton. Huge crowds gathered to send off the hastily-raised troops who left for battle on the canal boats.

The first Dayton company was sent home since more troops gathered than were required. Later groups were not so lucky. Dayton provided the First Ohio Infantry with 77 riflemen in Company B and another 77 in the mostly German Company C. The men marched to Cincinnati where they received rousing patriotic speeches in both English and German before taking steamboats to war. The men of Company B suffered badly, losing 33 men, sixteen at Monterrey.[8] Only 86 men of both companies returned to a candlelight celebration which included fireworks and the firing of "Mad Anthony," the cannon left behind by Wayne's legions long before. Another company of 100 men—the Dayton German Grenadiers—fought at Contreras, Churubusco, Chapultepec and Mexico City. Only 36 of them returned to a picnic celebration in July 1848.

Riding the railroads

Railroads were built long before the steam engine. England had a crude early version of a railroad in the sixteenth century. Horses or mules could move more tonnage hauling freight on rails than they could over the rough early roads. The first steam railway was opened for business in England in 1825, and five years later, a miniature steam locomotive was in Dayton at the Methodist church.[9] The track was laid around the interior of the church and carried people for a small fee.

Before 1839, Dayton had a horse railroad. Built by Joseph Cribmore, it ran from Beavertown (probably near the Dayton State Hospital on Wayne Avenue) to where the canal intersected Third Street. Since the wagons (loaded with choice limestone) went downhill all the way, a single horse could handle the heavy weight. The limestone was used to construct a new courthouse around 1850, and Dayton marble, much in demand, went both north and south on the canal.

Steam railroads came to Dayton relatively late.

In 1832, the Mad River and Lake Erie Railroad tried to sell stock in Dayton with little luck. Dayton was just not interested. It had the canal which was being extended—it reached Piqua in 1837 and Lake Erie in 1845. That gave Dayton access to New York City via the Erie Canal. Businessmen apparently believed the railroads would benefit Cincinnati and injure Dayton. The *Dayton Journal and Advertiser* concluded Dayton needed the tariff of distance from Cincinnati's "concentrated capital" to protect itself.

It was not until 1845 that the city government was con-

vinced that the iron horse would be an asset. It authorized a subsidy of $25,000 for the Mad River and Lake Erie Railroad and a similar amount for the Dayton and Western four years later. By 1851, the Mad River and Lake Erie connected Dayton to Springfield and the north via Sandusky. It also went to Cincinnati and later became part of the Big Four system (Cleveland, Columbus, Cincinnati and Indianapolis Railroad). The Cincinnati, Hamilton and Dayton was also completed in 1851.

In 1852, the Greenville and Dayton was opened. It used the tracks of the unfinished Dayton and Western to enter Dayton proper. The Dayton and Western, finally completed in 1853, went from Dayton to the state line near Richmond, Indiana, where it connected with another railroad to the west. The Dayton and Michigan Railway began service to Troy, Ohio, in 1853. It eventually reached Toledo in 1859 (but it never did reach Michigan). Thus in a span of about two years, Dayton went from a town without railroads to a center of railroads with connections north, south, east and west.

But two years before Dayton had welcomed a single iron horse, a canny school teacher had correctly anticipated America's—and Ohio's—great railway boom. In 1849, Eliam Eliakim Barney—and his friend Ebenezer Thresher—founded what would become Dayton's first giant industry.

E. E. Barney had been born in New York, taught school in Schenectady and Granville College (later Denison University) before moving to Dayton as the principal of the Dayton Academy. In 1841, he went into the sawmill business but returned to teaching in 1845 as the principal of Cooper Female Seminary.

Ebenezer Thresher, to whom Barney had sold his sawmill, approached Barney, and the two men agreed upon a manufacturing venture. At first, the two had no idea exactly what to make, but Thresher conceived the idea of constructing railroad cars. They bought some land on the upper hydraulic at lock 21 of the canal, built a plant and, late in 1849, proceeded to begin building cars which they shipped by canal boat.

Dayton's temporary geographic disadvantage turned out to be a blessing, as Ohio built more miles of railroads between 1850 and 1860 than any other state in the union. Ohio needed lots of railroad cars, and the Barney and Thresher Company was ready. By 1853, about 150 workmen were forming 15,000 tons of pig iron and 2.5 million feet of lumber into six freight cars and one passenger car a week.

Thresher left the company in 1854, and the Panic of 1857 reduced the work force to 50 or 60 men. But the company recovered quickly, and by 1859, employment was back to at least 160. The annual product value was almost a quarter of a million dollars, and annual wages equalled $78,000. While

FREIGHT CAR KINGS: Railroading came late to canal-run Dayton. The first tracks opened in 1851 and it took two former millers, E.E. Barney (left) and Ebenezer Thresher (right), to show Dayton the railroad's potential.

DEPOTS AND DEPOSITS: A view of Dayton's depot (above) was probably a familiar sight to one of the city's leading bankers, Valentine Winters (right), who logged the growing payrolls.

these figures may not seem overwhelming today, the Barney and Thresher Company (soon known by the more familiar name of the Barney and Smith Company) was Dayton's first super-industry. It bought massive amounts of local lumber and supported local foundries. The payroll created service industries, purchased land and built homes. One hundred of the factory workers were home owners—quite a feat at that time.

Barney was an interesting man. "Dour and taciturn, he constantly made rounds of the plant, looking for and resolving production problems in every department," wrote Dr. Carl Becker, professor of history at Wright State University. "He tolerated no waste, incompetency, or 'dissipation', releasing men on more than one occasion for these heinous sins. . . . Ever an innovator, he adopted new inventions in production and design whenever possible and personally developed at least seven improvements on cars for which he received patents. The community . . . regarded him as a brilliant man; and in the public mind he and the car works were one and the same entity. Giving the city its initial prominence in industry, he became . . . its first legitimate hero. In a sense, though, he prefigured the next great industrial personality of the community."[10]

Roman and Greek for America

In 1844, the corpulent John Van Cleve, Samuel Forrer and Horace Pease were chosen commissioners to secure plans for a new courthouse. Pease had an international sophistication rare for midwestern America. He conceived the idea of

Dayton created a national landmark in 1850 with its Greek Revival courthouse, key to an urban renewal plan more than a century later.

designing the courthouse along the lines of Athen's Temple of Theseus. Cincinnati architect Howard Daniels drew up the plans for a heavy Roman-style courthouse inside an almost pure classial Greek exterior. His unusual treatment of the rear of the building made Dayton's courthouse a national landmark, one of the finest examples of a large building in Greek Revival style. Completed in 1850, it would prove to be the key to an urban renewal plan more than a century later.

Despite the courthouse pretentions, Dayton was still a small town, and its steps toward growth slow. From early in 1843 to the middle of 1845, Dayton had no bank. The Dayton Manufacturing Company had become the Dayton Bank, but its charter had expired and the operation was closed out. In June 1845, a bank was formed with Jonathan Harshman as president and Valentine Winters as cashier. The Dayton State Bank followed a month later. In April 1852, the Exchange Bank was opened with Valentine Winters as president.

The telegraph came to Dayton on September 17, 1847, even before the railroads—an unusual sequence of events in mid-American history.

In 1847, Dayton had a flood.

On February 5, 1849, Dayton was first illuminated by "Crutchett's Solar Gas."

In 1851, Ohio declared that cities had to follow certain general rules. Since Dayton had only 10,976 people in 1850, it became a "second-class city." (It took 20,000 to be first class.)

Two of the leading lawyers in town were Robert C. Schenck and Clement Vallandigham. Both brilliant, both sarcastic, both supported to the death by rival newspapers (in one instance, literally), the two men were bitter political enemies. Their conflict, perhaps more than the Civil War, would determine Dayton's history for the next five years.

Woodland Cemetery was financed by trees removed for burial plots.

City of the dead

■ *Dayton was perhaps the first city in the West to create a suburban cemetery.*

Just as Third and Main gave way to Fifth and Ludlow as a burial ground, Fifth and Ludlow gave way to one of the most beautiful cemeteries in America. Woodland Cemetery was the creation of John Van Cleve. A mile south of the city, on one of the finest hills near town, Van Cleve took 40 acres of heavily wooded area and engaged Samuel Forrer to create a city landmark. Woodland was well named; the cemetery society sold off trees from the site to reduce the costs of operation. The first burial was Allen Cullum in July 1843.[11]

*Believed to be
John Van Cleve.*

The Raging Canawl

In 1847, John Van Cleve and his friends left Dayton for Chicago to attend a river and harbor convention. (At that time, the population of Dayton was approximately 10,000 —and so was the population of Chicago.)

They went by canal boat and lake steamer, then returned by lake steamer, railroad and stagecoach. Among the party were Senator Thomas Corwin, Ohio Governor William Bebb, Robert Schenck, local businessmen Horatio Gates Phillips and John Lowe, their wives, children and nursemaids.

Van Cleve proceeded to write a poem about the journey which he published in The Dayton Journal and Advertiser. The poem continues for more than 300 lines, describing the journey up and back.

A Traveler's Journey

Twas on the twenty-eighth of June, a company left Dayton,
Upon a boat that started with a very pleasant freight on.
All going to Chicago to attend a great convention,
With various other things in view it's not worth while to mention.

• • • •

We traveled quite safely, though not very fast,
And the locks, and the bridges, and aqueducts passed;
And if there was danger, we passed through them all
Without any harm on the raging Canawl.

• • • •

In eating and drinking we fared very well,
But of comfort in sleeping, there's not much to tell;
Where the company's large, and the boat is but small,
There's a poor chance to sleep on the raging Canawl.

• • • •

We passed by Defiance, and while they locked down,
The most of the company walked into town;
And then we went on about four miles, where all
Of the River Maumee is a raging Canawl.
At the guardlock, as some one had uttered the wish,
To have the next morning a breakfast of fish,
The steward provided enough for us all,
And we had them next day on the raging Canawl.
Just after he purchased them, Robert Schenck took
One out of his basket, and fixed on his hook,
Then close by the side of the boat let it fall,
And again jerked it out of the raging Canawl.
On this an old Yankee, who foolishly thought
That the fish had just then by Schenck fairly been caught,
Took the rod, in the hope that he too might make a haul,
And fished until night in the raging Canawl

• • • •

*While Dayton's Main Street looked busy in 1850, it was still only a second-class city by official Ohio standards.
A first-class rating required 20,000 people, and Dayton was only halfway there.*

CHAPTER FOUR
CIVIL WAR AND RECOVERY

The Miami River levee offered strollers a pleasant afternoon in 1872.

On Third Street, businesses wide and varied served Dayton, including the Pricer & Smith blacksmith shop (above) circa 1882, and the Phillips House (right), about 1859.

lthough its life as a carrier of cargo was ending, the canal had done its job. Dayton was now the third largest city in Ohio. The population edged past 20,000 in 1861, and slightly less than one-quarter of the citizens were of foreign birth, most of them German.

The Miami and Mad rivers bounded the city on the north and west. Dayton extended east to where Linden and Springfield streets currently intersect. The southern boundary ran along Jasper, Main, Union and Wayne (just north of where the National Cash Register Company would later build).

Although there was no water department, the thriving city had a city infirmary, an orphan asylum, a board of health (no doctor was on the board), a police department consisting of a marshal and six men, and seven volunteer fire companies overseen by the chief of police.

Strange bedfellows

aytonians believed that politics were worth fighting for, and they often did. The election of 1860 was the most exciting political contest since Harrison's campaign of 1840—and far more complex.

The Democrats had split over the issue of slavery and state's rights. The Northern Democrats nominated Stephen A. Douglas; the Southern faction chose John Breckinridge. The popular John Bell of Tennessee ran for the Constitutional Union Party, while the Republicans decided on Douglas' former debate opponent, Abraham Lincoln. That was confusing enough for a nation, but it was worse in Dayton.

Clement L. Vallandigham, a successful Dayton lawyer,

was elected to the U.S. Congress in 1856. Active in national politics, he became one of the leaders of the Copperhead movement (Northern Democrats who supported state's rights, also later known as Peace Democrats). Dayton, a town with a large German and Southern population, was ideal for the brilliant lawyer. The Germans violently opposed the introduction of cheap black labor. The Southerners (called Butternuts) had carried their distrust of blacks with them as they moved north.

Vallandigham's major local political enemy lived within shouting distance on East First Street. He was Robert C. Schenck, another lawyer-politician and another brilliant public speaker. Schenck had served as a member of the Ohio Legislature and was a member of Congress from 1843 until 1850. On the same day that Lincoln spoke from the courthouse steps in September 1859, Schenck addressed the crowd later, suggesting that Lincoln would make an honest, sensible president. Lincoln reportedly said that it was the first suggestion of his name for president.[1]

Valiant Val

Clement Vallandigham

■ Clement Vallandigham was a man whose time never came. He arrived in Dayton in August 1847 and purchased The Western Empire *and a print shop for only $150. Although he never finished college, Vallandigham had taught school and studied law. A friendly man, he prospered but was less than successful in his early attempts at politics.*

In 1856, he and Lewis D. Campbell were both sent to the 35th U.S. Congress because the winner was in dispute. Two weeks before the close of Congress, the results were official—Vallandigham had won by a narrow margin. Vallandigham was a Western Democrat and his political base was a combination of Southern farmer, German and Irish. Vallandigham raised and commanded a militia company of both Germans and Irish. At that time, Dayton had far more in common with the South than the East; most commerce was with the South. The buyers of Montgomery County farm produce and ice (a major export) were in New Orleans, not New York City.

Vallandigham was reelected in 1858 and 1860. He quickly became a leader of the Peace Democrats. Even after war was declared, Vallandigham was for peace. "I am for peace," he said, "a speedy, honorable peace with all its blessings."

With the country at war, "Valiant Val" was an embarrassment to Lincoln, the Republicans and "War Democrats" alike. Still he spoke for a significant number of Americans, especially Western Americans.

In the lame-duck session of the 37th Congress, Vallandigham strongly opposed the almost dictatorial anti-war acts. He argued against the Conscription Bill which allowed the rich to avoid the draft by buying their way out. Vallandigham was accused of being a traitor, a secessionist and a blackguard.

On April 13, 1863, General Burnside (the term, sideburns, comes from his name) issued General Order 38 which forbade "declaring sympathy for the enemy." In a two-hour speech on May 1, 1863, Vallandigham declared that General Order 38 was superceded by "General Order, Number One, the Constitution of the United States." He asked the crowd to hurl "King Lincoln" from his throne.

At 2 a.m. on May 5, 1863, 60 Union soldiers arrived in Dayton from Cincinnati. They marched to Vallandigham's home on East First Street and arrested him. By dawn, Valiant Val was in Cincinnati. "VALLANDIGHAM KIDNAPPED. A DASTARDLY OUT-RAGE! WILL FREE MEN SUBMIT?" Those were the headlines of The Western Empire *the following day. Editor William Logan clearly was furious. He called for "terrible retribution" and got it. That very night, a mob marched on* The Journal *office between Third and Fourth on the west side of Main Street and burned it.* The Journal *never missed an issue.* The Western Empire *did. Editor Logan was arrested, and the newspaper suspended publication until August 1863.*

Vallandigham was court-martialed although he was a civilian. Found guilty on twelve of thirteen specifications, he was sentenced to be imprisoned. Lincoln, unaware of the proceedings, read about the Copperhead's arrest in the newspapers. The embarrassed Union sent Val to the South, the Union Army abandoning him near Confederate lines.

A few months later, Vallandigham was in Canada—and running for governor of Ohio. He was soundly defeated on October 13, 1864, although only losing Montgomery County by 40 votes. Lincoln was reported to have telegraphed about his defeat, "Glory to God in the highest; Ohio has saved the Union."

After the war, a discredited Vallandigham turned to the practice of law quite successfully. In 1871, while defending Thomas McGeham who had shot a man in a Hamilton barroom brawl, Vallandigham picked up a gun he thought was empty and shot himself in a room of the Golden Lamb Inn in Lebanon, Ohio. His burial at Woodland Cemetery was, according to Dayton's famous Lincoln scholar, Lloyd Ostendorf, "the largest and longest funeral procession known to Dayton's history."

Vallandigham had the backing of *The Western Empire*. Schenck and the Republicans had *The Journal*. During the elections of 1860 and 1862, no stone was left unthrown. The bitterness of the editorials inspired riots, fires and probably the murder of *The Western Empire* editor, J. F. Bollmeyer.

Vallandigham won the congressional election in 1860 and quickly became a thorn in the side of the Lincoln administration. After war was declared on April 12, 1861, Robert Schenck volunteered to fight, and Lincoln, perhaps remembering Schenck's political aid, appointed the lawyer (who had no combat experience) a brigadier general of volunteers.

Three-month soldiers

L incoln called for 75,000 volunteers on April 15. Dayton's Lafayette Guard (or Yager, because of its predominantly German makeup), the Montgomery Guard, the Dayton Light Guard and the Washington Gun Squad were essentially marching units with attractive uniforms and plumed hats, much in demand for parades and parties. But they quickly responded to Lincoln's call. When they left for war, via the train to Columbus, the streets were full of people singing

Of politics and poker

Robert C. Schenck

■ *Robert C. Schenck was born in Warren County and graduated from Ohio's Oxford College in 1827. He entered the Dayton bar in 1831 and soon became a community leader. He was a strong Whig, supported Harrison in the Log Cabin Campaign of 1840 and served in the Ohio legislature from 1841 to 1843. In 1844, he was elected to the U.S. House of Representatives. He served in the 28th through the 31st Congresses but did not stand for reelection after the death of his wife in November 1849. Schenck left Dayton in 1851 to serve two years as minister to Brazil.*

The Whig party was dying, and Schenck, a powerful political orator, was left without a cause until the Republican party emerged. He had met Abraham Lincoln in the House of Representatives and liked him. Schenck may have been the first to propose that Lincoln should be the Republican candidate for president. He spoke for Lincoln in many cities and was extremely effective. Most politicians expected Schenck to be part of the Lincoln administration but Schenck was not chosen.

He did, however, serve in the Civil War as brigadier general. "On the 17th of June, 1861, General Schenck was ordered to take possession of the London and Hampshire Railroad, as far as Vienna [Virginia, near Arlington]," Whitelaw Reid wrote in his book Ohio in the War. "The train was fired upon by what was known in the alarmist phraseology of those days as a masked battery. Three cars were disabled, ten men were killed and two wounded. The locomotive being in the rear, the engineer, in a cowardly and treacherous manner, uncoupled and returned to Alexandria, leaving the General with his little band in the presence of a largely superior force .... General Schenck with great coolness rallied his few men, and behaved himself with so much courage that the Rebels were impressed with the belief that a heavy force must be in reserve, and accordingly they withdrew."[11]

From that time on, The Western Empire *referred to Schenck as "the hero of Vienna." (They also called him "the great absquatulator.")* [12]

Although General Schenck's brigade led the march to Bull Run, the unit remained near the landmark stone bridge and was never committed to the battle by the Union commander, General Irvin McDowell. Schenck was ordered to guard the Union retreat which rapidly became a panic-stricken riot. "Some claimed that General Schenck saved the entire army from destruction."[13] However, The Western Empire *ran telegraphic dispatches from the field charging that the Ohio regiments had refused to go into battle and left the field in utmost consternation.*

Although the combat skills of Schenck were not overly impressive, he was promoted to major general in time to participate in another defeat at the Second Battle of Bull Run. He was struck in the right wrist with a ball but refused to leave the ground until his sword was found.

Six months later, Schenck returned to duty. Because he never completely recovered from this wound, he was placed in an administrative post in Maryland. At the time, many women of Baltimore were wearing the Confederate colors in public. Schenck recruited Baltimore's "most [notorious] women of the town," had them wear Rebel colors and greet any other women wearing the colors as "Sisters in the Holy Cause." It worked.[14]

On December 5, 1863, he resigned his commission and returned to run for political office beating "Valiant Val" only because Warren County had been gerrymandered into the Third Congressional District. (Ironically, Schenck had been particularly effective in opposing gerrymandering when he served in the Ohio Legislature.)

Schenck served in Congress from 1863 to 1871 and became chairman of the powerful Ways and Means Committee in 1867, practically running the House. With Vallandigham's support, Lewis D. Campbell beat out Schenck, and on December 22, 1870, Schenck accepted the job of minister plenipotentiary to Great Britain.

Schenck arrived in England with his three daughters in June 1871. He supposedly introduced the game of draw poker to London and wrote a pamphlet on the subject. (In a letter to Major Bickham, dated November 23, 1875, Schenck says a paragraph in The American Encyclopedia *attributing the poker pamphlet to himself is "a mean & malignment [?] use of my name. [The publisher's] lying contributor knew that I had never published a pamphlet on poker." Yet Lloyd Ostendorf has a catalog which offered the booklet for sale. The booklet may have been a fraud, someone else having borrowed Schenck's name without permission, or he may have just not wanted to claim the distinction.)

Schenck did allow his name to be used as a director of the Emma silver mine in Utah.[15] This caused a furor in the U.S. press, and when the mine failed in 1875, there was a great scandal in London as well as America.

On February 19, 1876, Schenck resigned. It was a sad ending to his long and generally distinguished public career. He became a legal advisor to the State Department and practiced law in Washington, D.C., until he died in 1890 at the age of 81.

Mary Hassett, Warren County historian, called Schenck "the greatest intellect Ohio had ever produced."[16]

TEMPORARY TROOPS: When President Lincoln called for volunteers, Dayton's men responded and many of the First Ohio Volunteer Infantry re-enlisted after their required three-month stint. Photo of Lincoln (left) was a gift from him to a Dayton family.

patriotic songs and wishing the men well.

The songs must have worked, for the three-month men survived very well. Of the men who first went to war in Companies B, C and D of the First Ohio Volunteer Infantry (OVI), none was killed, none was wounded. Apparently only one man saw action. Anton Wecher was captured at the Battle of Bull Run on July 21, 1861. He escaped. Wecher and the rest of the First Ohio Volunteer Infantry were mustered out August 8.

But the need for a more permanent army remained. Lincoln called for a half million troops, and soon Dayton had its first military camp since 1812. Camp Corwin was established two and a half miles east of Dayton. The community contributed almost a thousand blankets for the encamped army.

The first years of the war brought a series of Northern defeats. While *The Western Empire* continued its vicious attacks on Lincoln, his untrained military leaders and poorly trained soldiers, recruitment grew more and more difficult.

However, many of the three-month men re-enlisted. Eventually, Dayton provided a total of 1,888 "three-year men." Most Dayton men served in the First and the 93rd Regiments of the Ohio Volunteer Infantry.

The First Ohio Volunteer Infantry fought at Shiloh early in 1862, Chaplin Hill in October and Stone River on New Year's Eve. In 1863, they were at Mission Ridge and at Chickamauga where many died in late September.

The Ninety-third, with 200 Daytonians, represented the city's largest contribution to the Union war effort. Although the figures may not be completely accurate, they are indicative of the sacrifice Dayton paid in the bloody conflict. In Company A, five were killed in action, seven others died (at least five from injuries inflicted in the war). In Company G, ten were killed in action, thirteen died later and two died in "rebel prisons." Company I also had ten killed in action and ten more died—three were captured and died in prison, two at the infamous Andersonville. Company K lost seventeen men. Samuel B. Smith, captain of Company K, wrote about the war clearly and concisely. Smith had been home in Dayton, recovering from rheumatism and had helped his family make cider in mid-November. Knowing that a decisive battle was imminent, he returned to fight the battles of Orchard Knob and Mission Ridge, Tennessee (November 23 – 25, 1863), ten days before his leave should have been over. "My arrival was just in time," he wrote,

> as a few days after on the 23d day of November 1863 the army was drawn up just outside our works as if for review, but at a given signal the division made a rush for the Rebel intrenchments [*sic*] in our front, and one of the most important and decisive battles of American History was begun. The 93d suffered severely, but we were soon in possession of the Rebel works, having captured the 28th Alabama Regiment with its colors. In this engagement Major William Burch, commanding the 93d Regiment was killed. The works of the enemy were immediately reversed, and we lay upon our arms awaiting orders. The next morning Hooker commenced, and the movement which resulted in the Battle above the Clouds, and the capture of Lookout Mountain . . . .
>
> I well remember seeing General Grant quietly sitting on his horse but a few yards from where I was standing, by a wave of his hand give the signal, six guns were rapidly fired in succession, and the Army of the Cumberland started on its perilous undertaking. It advanced in two lines with colors flying and bands playing in the rear. When the timber about the Knob had been cleared, and our brigade had reached the open ground it was assailed by a terrific storm of shot and shell. The fire was so severe, and was reducing our ranks so rapidly, that an order was given to "Double quick" which was soon changed to "Full run" the two lines gaining the rifle pits at the foot of the Ridge at the same moment. The advance had been so rapid, the distance being about one mile, that a halt was absolutely necessary to enable the men to recover their wind. The line at the foot of the Ridge was enfiladed [*raked with gunfire*] from both flanks by the Rebel batteries, and men and officers crowded closely together in front of the captured Rebel. . .earthworks to gain from the parapet what shelter they could from the storm of grape and cannister with which they were assailed. Some minutes after the position at the foot of the ridge was gained, which it was impossible to hold, and from which it would have been death to retreat, my attention was called to the fact that the First Brigade (Gen'l. Willich) had commenced the ascent of the Ridge. I immediately notified Gen'l Hazen, who was nearby, who rising to his feet satisfied himself as to the correctness of my statement, and ordered a charge of the Ridge by the Second Brigade. . .Few if any reached the summit without stopping to rest and recover breath, although all recognized the importance of reaching the top and silencing the enemy's batteries without delay. During the ascent no lines were or could be maintained. Every soldier kept in view the colors of his own regiment, and both regiments and men contended with each other in their efforts to reach the summit. General Hazen's Brigade. . .was the first. . . .Upon gaining the summit, upon which the batteries along our flanks had turned their fire, I discovered that the enemy with considerable force were forming a line about a hundred yards to the right of the position we occupied. At that time I was in command of the 93d Regiment, (Captain Bowman, afterwards Colonel, having been severely wounded before the ascent of the Ridge was commenced). I immediately reformed by command, together with the

sixth Indiana, which was nearby, and ordered them to load. At this moment the Rebel force, above alluded to, made their appearance from behind a low hill running at [a] right angle from Mission Ridge, and separated from it by a narrow and deep ravine. My orders to load were disregarded, and the two regiments named with a fierce yell commenced to charge across the ravine, when the enemy fired a volley at random and fled down the southern slope of the Ridge.[2]

These Union victories in Tennessee, costly as they were, opened the way for Sherman to march through Georgia and split the Confederacy in half. Both the First and the 93rd fought well. Another Montgomery County man, Private Isaac James, Company H, 110th Ohio, won the Congressional Medal of Honor by capturing the flag at Petersburg, Virginia, on April 2, 1865.

The war comes to Dayton

Casualty figures mounted. The arguments of the Peace Democrats began to make sense to more and more Daytonians. And then the Confederacy suddenly advanced northwards, capturing Lexington. Cincinnati would be next. About 500 Daytonians rushed to defend the Queen City against an attack that never came.

As early as 1862, young men, such as John McCook (below), were serving in the Union Army.

As early as October 1862, Dayton had a significant percentage of her young men serving in the Union Army. To support their families while the men were away took more and more work by county officials and volunteer societies. As the war dragged on, it grew harder and harder to provide the aid required.

Replacing the increasing number of dead or crippled Union soldiers also proved extremely difficult, so the nation resorted to the draft. But no rich man had to go to war. Substitutes could be hired for $400 or $500.

The war news got better in July 1863 with twin victories at Vicksburg and Gettysburg. The tide was turning at last.

Then—suddenly—the Rebels were in Oxford, Ohio—only 35 miles away! Firehouse bells rang, and every able-bodied man was told to arm himself and be ready to take the train to Hamilton. Colonel Edward King commanded the hastily prepared militia. Morgan must have been impressed with the mobilization as he did not stay to fight. It was a good thing. In the rush to leave on time, few of the Dayton volunteers had bothered to take any ammunition.

About 150 local soldiers were in the city on furlough March 3, 1864. Approximately fifteen of them broke into *The Western Empire* office around midnight, demonstrating their anger at the Peace Democrats by scattering type all over the floor. According to the *Empire*, the mob left, "obviously intoxicated." They were addressed by Captain E. D. Badgee of the local militia who exclaimed, "Fellow citizens (hiccup) by the Great God and Resurrector of everybody, I swear I am responsible for all this. (Cheers) God d--- you, I led the whole thing. These men are under my control, (Cheers) and I am responsible. (Cheers) God d--- you, 200 average veterans such as we are worth 1,000 citizens. (Cheers)"[3]

Another attack was made on the newspaper, but supporters had arrived. Bricks—stones—then bullets. A Vallandigham supporter fired into the crowd and a father of eleven lay dying in the street.

Casualty figures and inflation dampened Dayton's ardor for war more effectively than Vallandigham and *The Western Empire* had been able to do.

Over 1,000 families needed the Relief Fund which was supposed to be $1.50 weekly—but often fell short of that amount.

But the war itself was going well for the North by the end of 1864. Atlanta fell, and December saw the end of most of the serious fighting.

The men who "contributed to the Union armies served their country honorably and well," according to Irving Lloyd Schwartz, now professor of history at Sinclair Community College. "Untrained and devoid of military background, the unseasoned soldier ultimately became a hard-bitten veteran who served on many of the most bitterly contested battlefields of the war. Had his service been less honorable it could have been justified by the mockery his motives received from the many who remained in Dayton and by the meager support given his family. In large measure the Dayton soldier redeemed the tawdry record which the city sustained during the Civil War."[4]

Recovery

"Carbo denied a hearing!"
With those uninspiring words, the huge new Turner Opera House opened act one of *Virginius* on January 1, 1866.[5] Even the choice of Edwin Forrest and his troupe to open the theater had some Dayton significance. The brilliant

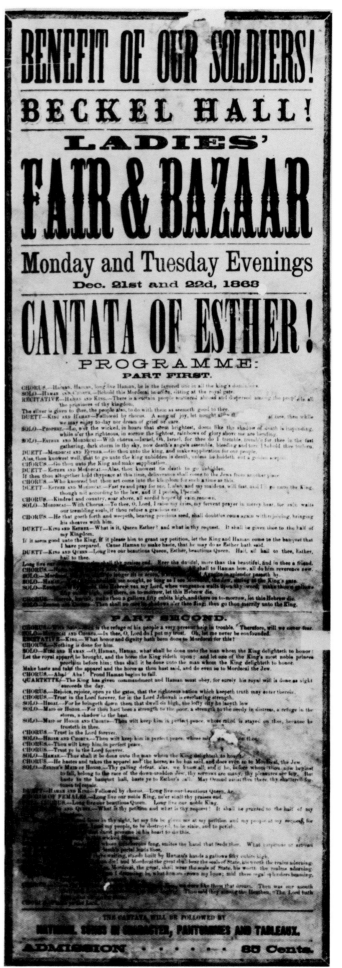

Dayton raised money for the Civil War with an evening of culture.

Brilliant actor Edwin Forrest (right) played the opening performance at the Turner Opera House in 1866. He had played Dayton before — in 1823.

American actor had played Dayton at the age of 17 in both the spring and summer of 1823.

The falling snow was quietly covering the streets as the peaceful new year began, and time, like the snow, was blanketing the city's twin traumas of war and presidential assassination.

The soldiers who had been lucky enough to return had noticed many changes. Without an ample supply of strong young workers, industry had become more dependent on power, less on labor.

There was a new market house on Wayne Avenue, reflecting the city's rapid move to the east. Barney's car works was one reason for the eastward growth. The war required railroad cars at an unprecedented rate. Initially, Barney had refused to build for the military. But after the government threatened to seize the works and operate it without Barney's help, the company decided selling cars to the government was not such a bad idea after all. Cars built near the end of the war cost $1,250 each. By 1867, the company's capitalization had increased to $500,000, and the work force was 350. Output trebled to twenty freight cars and 2.5 passenger cars a week.

Farm implement firms had grown, too. Dayton made reapers, corn planters, mule wagons, mowers and grain drills. From 1861 to 1864, Dayton men patented eight or nine inventions to improve seeding machines and reapers.

Although Daytonians did not profiteer during the war (only one wagonmaker and Barney had government contracts), all businesses had flourished. In 1864, almost 100 Daytonians had incomes of $5,000 or more.[6]

In 1866, Dayton had a flood—a bad flood. It struck in September. "There were scenes of desolation on every hand,"

wrote Robert W. Steele. "From the summit of the ridge in East Dayton there was a wide prospect of water in the valleys and broad, open pools above Bucktown. The corn in the fields. . .was standing up in seeming defiance of the floods. At the head of the hydraulic there was a wide crevasse, and from that point down to Spinning's corner, there was an indiscriminate mass of drift lumber, staves, barrels, bridge timber, shingles, hen coops, outhouses, and frame shops of every description. The side tracks of the railroad . . . were undermined, and the rails stretched across gaps in the embankments. One of the most weary scenes was that of women ankle deep in mud, collecting their scattered household treasures for the resumption of housekeeping, and the men busily engaged in fishing their effects out of the water and mud of Mad river."[7] The clean-up cost a quarter of a million dollars.

In spite of the Civil War, Dayton had grown steadily in the 1860s, adding more than 10,000 inhabitants. Yet both Columbus and Toledo grew even more rapidly, and Dayton, with its population of 30,473, was only the fifth largest Ohio city.

But Dayton did try. In 1868, the city made a massive annexation. Since the Miami and Mad rivers were the boundaries of the original purchase, separate towns had grown up wherever a ferry, ford or bridge existed. West of Dayton was Miami City, Mexico, Greencastle and Patterson. Northwest was Dayton View and McPherson Town. The annexation took in all of these areas, plus the eastern portion of North Dayton and another larger section of East Dayton.[8]

Wartime inflation led to the Panic of 1873, putting intense strain on the very new building associations. The early building associations were quite different from modern savings

An 1866 flood cost Dayton a quarter of a million dollars. The Miami River washed over the covered bridge to Dayton View (top) and made splinters of canal boats (bottom). Only the corn remained standing.

and loan associations. People deposited money until there was enough for one member to build a house. Then the loan would be repaid to the association, helping to build enough capital for a second home loan. Many early associations were work- or ethnic-group oriented. There were German associations and mechanics' associations, most with such prosaic names as Buckeye, Dayton, Miami, Montgomery, Homestead, Gem City, Franklin (there were two named for Franklin among the earliest associations), Permanent, Washington and Mutual. The first firm, however, was aptly named Dayton Building Association, No. 1.

Annexation and growth brought more need for transportation. William P. Huffman and H. S. Williams formed the first street railway. Since Huffman owned land to the east along

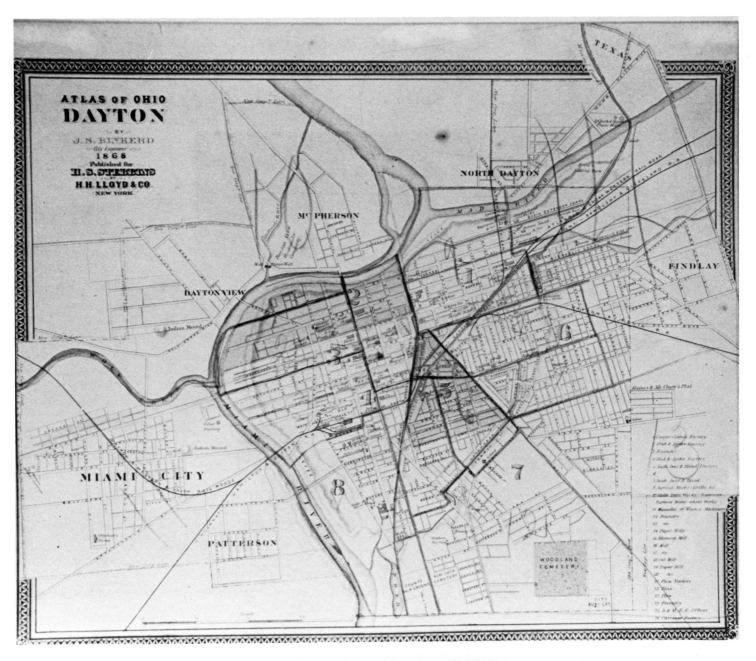

ATLAS OF OHIO
DAYTON
BY
J. S. BINKERD
City Engineer
1868
Published for
H. S. STEBBINS
BY
H. H. LLOYD & CO.
NEW YORK

POST-WAR: Dayton annexed and grew following the Civil War. The opera house (above left) as it appeared in 1889, rebuilt after the 1869 fire; a look at Main Street (below left), 1873, as seen from Fourth Street; one of the city's first street railways ran a blazing six miles per hour (left); and an atlas of Dayton (above) displayed a city with suburbs.

Roast mutton and butterine

■ *Feeding the soldiers at the Soldiers' Home required a strict regimen. Mess for the First Division was at 6 a.m., the second half an hour later. Noon and 12:30 were lunch, and 5 and 5:30 supper.*

The daily cost per man for food in 1909 was 17 cents.

The quantities of food consumed were awesome. Ham or sausage for breakfast—2,950 pounds, 800 loaves of bread, 175 pounds of "butterine." Roast mutton for lunch—2,850 pounds, 32 bushels of potatoes, 66 bushels of string beans (if lima beans: 320 pounds), 30 gallons of pickles, another 800 loaves of bread and 1,250 pies. For supper, the dried fruit weighed in at 285 pounds, or 850 watermelons, or 1,050 quarts of berries, plus 615 pounds of cookies, 800 loaves of bread and 35 pounds of tea.

Third Street and Williams owned land on the west side of the Third Street bridge, the railway ran from Williams' land to Huffman's land along Third. It was successful from the very first, even though a speed restriction of six miles an hour was imposed. A north-south line was organized in 1871 to connect Dayton View with the railway depot at Fifth Street. Although this line failed, the tracks were used by the 1875 Oakwood Street Railway which failed at once. Both lines were taken over and combined a year later into the Dayton View and Oakwood. The more successful Wayne and Fifth Street line began operation in 1871. It ran from First Street along Wayne Avenue to the insane asylum. The mules, which had to labor mightily to climb the Wayne Avenue hill, were accorded a treat on the return. They got to ride down.

The asylum had been opened before the facilities were properly completed in 1855. There were 609 inmates by 1872. Additions to the grounds made the location an excellent place for a Sunday visit.

But the real place for an evening's entertainment, a Sunday picnic or even a honeymoon was an equally unlikely location far out in the country to the west—the Central Asylum. Three street railways would eventually serve early Dayton's major tourist attraction which later would be better known as the Soldiers' Home.

EARLY CARE: Dayton took care of its wounded veterans by building an elaborately landscaped Soldiers' Home (above) and housed other unfortunates in the asylum (below), now the Dayton Mental Health Center. The Soldiers' Home provided a picnic park for area residents (right).

A home for the soldiers

T he Civil War had taken an incredible toll in casualties. The wounded men—many crippled and unable to work —needed help. The U.S. government was not quick to act but finally made plans for a number of soldiers' asylums. The largest of these was Dayton's Central Asylum.

Congressman Lewis B. Gunckel helped Dayton gain this important addition, and the land was purchased starting with 355 acres in 1867. By 1894, it encompassed slightly more than 578 acres and had cost $97,445.30. Dayton citizens contributed $20,000 towards its completion. It was blessed with excellent planning from the first. The grounds were laid out by Frank Mundt who had been landscape and architectural gardener for the grand duke of Mecklenburg-Schwerin. C. B. Davis and Charles Beck completed the landscaping.

GRAND
Pic-Nic EXCURSION

TO THE

SOLDIERS' HOME
AND DAYTON.

SATURDAY, JUNE 26, 1875.

Leaving Wellington at 5-10 a. m. Rochester **5-29** New London 5-45, Healy's Crossing 6-00, Greenwich 6-10 Carson 6-20 Shiloh 6-30 Shelby 6-46 Vernon **6-55** thence direct to Third St. Dayton, taking no passengers by the way, and arriving at 11-15 a. m. Third St. Railroad and Home Av. steam railroad have agreed to convey the party to the Home, a distance of 4 miles, and back for 25 cents each passenger. The Home is situated on the top of a hill near the center of their grounds, which contains 553 acres; 60 buildings, the finest church in the land walks, gardens, fountains, lakes, 60 deer, etc. The whole is arranged after the fashion of our finest modern cities, and has no superior. For real beauty these grounds are fully equal to Central Park, New York. No charge for admission to any part of the grounds.

NOW AT THE HOME, 2000 SOLDIERS.

Returning to the city, ample time will be given to visit all points of interest, and leave for home from the Short Line Depot at **4-30** P. M. arrive at Wellington 10.30p. m.

Tickets to the Home will be for sale on the train.

FARE for the Round Trip to Dayton, $2.25, Children under 12 years of age $1.25.

No children free. Tickets will be for sale at the stations named and by E. J. Goodrich, Book Store, Oberlin, W. D. Golding, Jeweler, New London, O. S. Griffin, Healy's Crossing, and C. E. Richardson, Provision Dealer, Shelby, from Wednesday, the 23rd, until departure of train if not sooner sold. Number of tickets limited to 400. Flavel & Gurley, Oberlin, will carry from their office, the round trip to Wellington, and connect with the Excursion Train for 75 cents a passenger.

Local rates will be charged on the train. Sunday Schools, churches, lodges, &c., all are invited. Parties of fifty or more will be furnished a coach on giving due notice to the Excursion Agent. No other excursion to Dayton this year from these points.

Robert Bloe, Division Supt, Cleveland.　　　　　　　　　　　　　　　　E. S. FLINT, General Sup't, Cleveland, O.

C. E. HEALY, Excursion Agent, New London, O.

Please Circulate and post in a conspicuous place.

THIRD STREET SITES: The covered bridge on Third provided walking space, while the brewery (right) produced a popular beverage.

Annexation brought an emphasis on education as evidenced by St. Mary's Institute as it appeared in 1875, later to become the University of Dayton.

Although the wooden three-story barracks buildings were no great beauties, the larger buildings had a beauty and style rare for the time—and for government construction. The Protestant church, built on the grounds in 1868, is believed to be the first church ever built by the U.S. government. The original hospital, begun in 1868, was almost a football field long. (Additions were made in 1909.)

The Home (the word "asylum" was eliminated in 1873) had workshops, a deer park, a small zoo, a huge library and three lakes. By 1877, there were 132 buildings.

The soldiers contributed their own money and labor to build Memorial Hall, designed for "all classes of Literary, dramatic and musical entertainments, military drills and so forth."[9] It burned only two years later, and Congress appropriated $30,000 to replace it.

Many generals paid a visit to their wounded companions at the Home. Sherman came in 1870, Grant in 1871. A hotel was built next to the train depot just inside the grounds. One street railway had a restaurant at the depot. A local man recalled that his grandparents honeymooned at the hotel, having been influenced by advertising they had seen in Indiana. In the early 1900s, the annual number of visitors was more than half a million.

But the surrounding area outside the grounds left something to be desired. "It was an unspeakable disgrace that in the early years of the Home, drinking places of the lowest character surrounded it on all sides," wrote Reverend A. W. Drury in his 1909 *History of the City of Dayton*. "To give some kind of protection to the soldiers, Gov. Patrick, an earnest temperance man, established the beer house within the Home."[10] AWOL was a more common offense than drunkenness, and no less than 1,455 rule violations were noted between mid-1908 and mid-1909. (There were 5,292 soldiers there at the time.) However, General Patrick, (governor of the Home from 1880 to 1888) was such a strict disciplinarian that Congress investigated his command, but charges were not pursued.

The Home hired professional theatrical companies for a season at a time. After the Memorial Hall fire hit and before the new hall was finished, an 80 by 100 foot tent was used for the shows. Plays for the 1880 season were *Blind For Life, Almost a Life, The Octoroon, Kathleen Mavoureen, Led Astray* and *Sea of Ice*. If not an overly ambitious repertoire, at least the price was right—25 cents for guests and only a dime for the soldiers.

A monument for the soldiers

■ To honor its Civil War dead, Dayton created an 85-foot-tall monument which was placed in the middle of Main and Water (later renamed Monument) streets. The statue originally was to have been of Columbia, but the war veterans asked that the statue be of a common soldier. A local bricklayer, George Washington Fair, one of six brothers who had served in the war, posed for a series of photographs, and the statue was carved in Italy of fine Italian marble.

The original proposal for the monument had been made by General Schenck in 1864. But it took the city almost twenty years to raise the $22,500 required.

On July 15, 1884, the veterans marched to the site and deposited a number of items, including a Bible, the 1883–1884 city directory, annual reports of most city, service and civic organizations and local newspapers. On July 29, there was a sunrise and sunset salute of thirteen guns, and one at noon of 38. There were assemblies, meetings and music throughout that day and the next.

Finally, on July 31, a parade started at ten, and the marchers went all around the downtown area in light drizzling rain. It was "a grand affair" according to historian Robert Steele.[17] "The city was ablaze with flags and banners. Exhibits of blood-stained battle flags, shots, shells and firearms filled the stores. A glass model of the monument was sealed in wine, not to be opened for 20 years."[18]

A song, "Peace to Their Ashes, Their Graves are Our Pride," especially written by Mrs. John Hancock and Professor Blumenschein, was sung (there are no reviews) followed by speech after speech. The main speech, by General Joseph R. Hawley, praised the "virtues that are or may be promoted by the military life."[19] After more speeches, including one by former President Rutherford B. Hayes, it was time for the unveiling.

Nothing happened. The sheet covering the monument would not budge. In the crowd was Clarence E. Ward, an experienced steeplejack. Ward found some ropes, scaled the shaft and freed the veil.[20]

CHAPTER FIVE

GIANTS OF INDUSTRY

Two bartenders pose outside an American institution,
"Joe's Place" — the local tavern.

AN HONEST INVENTION: Restaurant owner James Ritty (inset) had the ingenuity to devise the first cash register to keep the bartenders at his Pony House (above) honest, but failed to realize its potential. It took a tollkeeper on the Miami and Erie Canal (right) to show its advantages over a one-cent pencil.

James Ritty was a man who did not take stealing lightly. His restaurant—The Empire or No. 10 at 10 South Main Street—was selling plenty of food but not making much money. On a trip to Europe to recover from a breakdown, the mechanically skillful Ritty spent a lot of time in the ship's engine room. There, he discovered a mechanism which counted the number of revolutions the ship's propeller made.

He grasped immediately that this mechanical counter could be used to keep the bartenders of the world honest. He cut short his convalescence to build the cash register. By November 1879, he had crude working models and a patent. Soon James and his brother John Ritty had added the visual indicator of sales and a paper roll which tallied the day's sales.

Some of the first of "Ritty's Incorruptible Cashiers" were sold to John H. Patterson who had been having the same problem in stores he had opened at Coalton, Ohio.

The Ritty brothers were good inventors but poor business

operators. They sold out for $1,000. John Birch, a brother-in-law of the new owner, added a cash drawer and the famous bell. Whenever that bell rang, all eyes were riveted on the bartender or clerk. The product worked, but it did not become a success until Patterson bought control of the company.

Patterson was the son of pioneer Robert Patterson's youngest child, Jefferson. His mother was the daughter of John Johnston who had been the U.S. Indian agent near Pickawillany. (The Johnston farm is in today's Piqua Historical District north of Piqua directly on the canal.) Patterson attended Miami University, served as a hundred-day man during the Civil War and graduated from Dartmouth College in 1867.

It was a great deal of education for a toll-keeper on the Miami and Erie Canal, which was evidently the only job he could find. It netted him only $500 a year for 24-hour-a-day duty. He went into the coal and wood business on the side.

Soon he owned a coal business, complete with three coal mines, some retail goods and a general store that did not make money—until he bought Ritty's cash registers.

One evening in late October of 1883 (or so the story goes), some of the town's most prominent men were sitting around the Dayton Club when Patterson walked in and announced he was going to build cash registers. His statement brought laughter and jeers from the crowd. Shaken, Patterson wondered if his decision had been made too quickly. He offered $2,000 to George Phillips (the man who sold him control of the National Manufacturing Company for $6,500) if he would let Patterson out of the deal. Phillips refused. "Very well," Patterson said, "I am going into the cash register business and I will make a success of it." Then he added, "You will be sorry later on."[1]

Such early business anecdotes must be taken with a grain of salt. One history says the Dayton Club was not even founded until 1889, and Patterson owned a cash register company in 1883. Nonetheless, Patterson did make a success of the new business although not overnight. Since the cash register cost the tidy sum of $125 and replaced a one-cent pencil, business was slow at first. By April

1885, only 64 were sold. By the next April, Patterson had sold another 73. By April 1887, the total was up to 5,400 machines. By 1890, the number more than trebled.

Clubhouses, paper mills and foundries

The Panic of '93 hit the railroads particularly hard and one-third of the car building companies in the United States closed in 1894. Barney & Smith struggled to survive, cutting employment and even closing entirely for long periods from 1894 through 1896. But orders from the interurban companies saved them. In 1905, to insure a large supply of cheap, docile labor, Barney & Smith engaged J. D. Moskowitz, a foreign-language labor contractor. His credentials were excellent. He had already created a Hungarian colony around the Malleable Iron Works on Dayton's west side and another colony in Pennsylvania.

With his own money, Moskowitz bought land and built a four-square-block community north of Dayton's city limits on Leo Street. He erected 40 doubles with five rooms to a side for $800 each and then built the clubhouse at the entrance to the walled colony he had named Kossuth in honor of the Hungarian hero. The clubhouse held the biggest bar in Dayton and could tap a dozen kegs at once.

The clubhouse also had a bank, a travel agency (a colony resident could bring a relative over from Hungary), a grocery and a general store. It had an early form of refrigeration and electric fans, well before most Daytonians had them.

For a 55-hour week, the Hungarian worker was paid about $9, slightly less than the U.S. average. But room, board and laundry were only $8 to $10 monthly.

Barney & Smith Mfg., railway car builders, survived the Panic of '93 by providing worker colonies of cheap labor who filled orders from interurban companies. A view of the plant in 1909 shows the results (left); craftsmen designed the cars' interiors (right).

CASH REGISTERS AND CLUBS: John H. Patterson, owner of National Cash Register, with his top staff during a meeting (above). The Hungarian Club located at Moskowitz's West Side Colony (left) offered recreation for the Dayton Malleable workers.

Zimmer Spanish and other exotics

■ *Tobacco was a big operation in the late 1800s. "Zimmer Spanish" was raised in the Miami Valley and produced the "Teutonia," "Bouquet" and "Daytonia" cigars.*[10] *The cigar-makers—mostly women and children —were paid 50 cents to $1 a day.*

Only workers at Barney & Smith could live in the colony, and buying something outside brought about the employee's firing and expulsion. Brass scrip was used in place of U.S. currency. But the food was good and plentiful, there was lots of beer, and Moskowitz kept laid-off workers on credit for as long as necessary. He got the workers a day off on Easter Monday, a traditional Hungarian holiday. (After Barney & Smith closed, Moskowitz opened a retail store in downtown Dayton and was often visited by ex-members of his colony who sought his advice.)

Farm implement firms also lost importance as a major Dayton industry. Production had peaked in 1890, but payroll and gross sales dropped off by the end of the century as the marketplace moved west. The Farmer's Friend Company, Daniel McSherry and Company, the John Stoddard Company and the Woodsum Machine Company—mainstays of local industry in the '80s—were out of the farm implement business by 1910. Stoddard survived by switching to bicycles during the great bicycle craze of the 1890s. (Later, the company advanced to automobiles.)

The canal spawned paper mills from Dayton to Cincinnati. The Aetna Paper Company (later Howard Paper Mills) and the Mead Company were among the local paper and paperboard manufacturers which sold half a million dollars of products in 1900.

Foundries and machine shops required a large number of

THE MODERN FACTORY: Patterson recognized the worker as an individual, an unorthodox concept at the turn of the century. The company erected safe, well-lighted factories (upper left); such amenities as a kindergarten for workers' children (lower left); an opportunity for boys to learn woodworking (upper right); and atttractive rest areas (lower right).

workers, and they provided jobs for more than 3,000 men in 1900 and accounted for eighteeen percent of all the wages paid in Dayton.

Buckeye Iron and Brass made tobacco cutters, hydraulic presses and cotton and linseed oil extractors. Later, they became an important supplier of fire department nozzles and gasoline pump nozzles. (When the company was purchased by a Canadian firm in 1970, it was the oldest Dayton company still in existence.)

Dayton Malleable (still operating in Dayton today) was a pioneer Midwestern foundry which employed 700 to 800 men, many of them Hungarians from J. D. Moskowitz's first colony in the late 1890s.

But by 1900, the largest industry in Dayton was the "Cash," National Cash Register Company. The cash register was being used in every state and in many foreign countries as well. It had supplanted foundries, railway car builders, paper mills and corn planters because of John H. Patterson and his genius for organization.

Creating the modern factory

Patterson's success was partially the result of his unorthodox methods—at least they were unorthodox for his day. First he hired a sales force. He then told them how to dress, how to sell and when. "We teach through the eye," Patterson said, and he bought large wooden pedestals with huge sheets of paper to present his sales messages. He created the flip-chart presentation. (NCR flip-chart presentation paper is still available. The last words Patterson supposedly wrote was on one of these flip-charts, in 1922. He suggested that the United States create a separate air force.)[2]

Patterson correctly reckoned that salesmanship could be taught. "Information, protection, service, convenience, economy"[3]—they were his watchwords. He created sales contests and printed a number of publications to communicate with his sales force—techniques which led to today's modern salesmanship and sales training.

One of his first innovations was to produce an eighteen-piece direct mail program to aid his salesmen. In one of his earliest printed communications to his salesmen, Patterson showed the customer's evolution as the mailing pieces reached him. Strangely enough, the prospect reverted to a diabolically happy ape with inexplicably pointed teeth. NCR historian, H. Eugene Kneiss, has traced the origin of the caricature. The face—also used as a cash drawer handle—was the personification of a customer "happy to do business with a National Cash Register."[4]

Then Patterson took another unusual step. For the most part, owners and plant managers treated their workers as commodities, a necessary evil. And they were considered far less dependable than water power, steam—or even horses. Patterson felt differently. In 1898, the Cash was reorganized along "automatic principles." Workers—at least those schooled by the Cash—were partially responsible for their

Two nuns turned a saloon into Dayton's first hospital, St. Elizabeth's.

Caring for the sick

■ *Dayton doctors had pleaded for a hospital for years, but no church could afford to build one. In times of war or plague, tents or homes were pressed into service. The home of Mary Hess was used during the 1830 cholera epidemic, and the city had a "property" on Wyoming Street which served as a pesthouse, infirmary and hospital in the late 1860s.*

The Order of the Poor of St. Francis created the first true hospital in Dayton. Sisters Amelia and Columbia literally begged for a hospital in 1878. First it was a two-story house on Franklin Street between Ludlow and Perry. "In a disreputably dirty and wretched house, on Franklin Street, these devoted women established themselves," wrote Charlotte Reeve Conover, daughter of the hospital's first chief of staff, John Reeve. "It had been a saloon and perhaps worse. . .when it was all immaculate and cheerful, six iron beds were put up and the Sisters were ready to take care of the sick of St. Elizabeth Hospital."[11]

Two amputations were performed the first year. By 1882, St. Elizabeth Hospital moved to its present site just across the river on the west side at Hopeland Street. The new building provided 200 beds, and a large addition completed in 1903 more than doubled its capacity.

The Protestant Deaconess Society opened a temporary 37-bed hospital in a house on East Fourth Street in 1890. By 1904, Deaconess had changed its name to Miami Valley Hospital and had moved to its present location on a large hill south of downtown Dayton.

Edward Andrew Deeds was the farm boy who could make anything work.

device that could be devised, had first-class baths and locker rooms, restrooms for the women, hospitals and first aid stations, medical inspections and free aprons and sleevelets for the women."[5]

Such changes were then called "welfare." But the concept was simple: if a manufacturer served the social, cultural and economic needs of his employees, it was all to the good of his business. Henry Ford has since been credited with the concept; but Ford was merely following in Patterson's footsteps.

In the early 1900s, International Harvester Company was one of the most oppressive companies. When they decided to improve working conditions, they sent an executive to view model industries. The executive responded that there were only two companies in the United States worth emulating. One was Eastman Kodak and the other was the Cash.

In 1899, the Cash's electrification officer contracted tuberculosis and retired. Patterson needed a replacement and young Edward Andrew Deeds left his job at the Thresher Electric Company (the Thresher of Barney and Thresher) and went to work at the Cash for an $1,100 a year raise.[6]

While Deeds was at Denison College, his classmates regarded him as the hick farm boy. He once hung the mayor of Granville in effigy. He faked a phonograph demonstration by hiring a black quartet to sing through the heating pipes when the machine would not work. He also faked Xrays so that Civil War veterans could prove they had been wounded.

Soon after Deeds started to work at N.C.R., he discovered a flaw in the chimney. During repair, part of the chimney fell, incapacitating the boiler. By working all night, Deeds restored the power, and the factory never missed an hour's production.

Deeds left N.C.R. to supervise the building of a model shredded wheat factory at Niagara Falls—a great triumph for a man only a few years out of college. But when John Patterson discovered that the man who fixed the chimney had left, he hired him back. In 1903, at the age of 29, Deeds became assistant general manager of the Cash, in charge of engineering and construction.

own work. They were recognized as part of the company and as individuals. Soon factory workers were included in company publications. Mechanics in the factory were serving on factory committees with real responsibility for operations. Managers were given a good deal of autonomy, and the suggestion box was put in use by the mid-1890s.

Until that decade, factories were erected for the least amount of money in the least amount of space. That often meant cramped quarters, poor lighting and ventilation and generally poor working conditions. Patterson invented the modern factory. On the old Patterson estate south of town on high ground, he erected factories constructed to admit a "flood of light." "We painted all the machinery a light color," he wrote, "arranged hoods to absorb dust, put in every safety

Something to celebrate

Although Dayton has supported amateur sports for years, the city's love of professional sports has been an on-again-off-again affair. In 1889, the Dayton Reds were formed by six Dayton businessmen. The street railway companies also provided money since they were destined to be the winners. It cost $750 a month to field a team in 1889. Pitchers (and perhaps catchers) received $90, infielders $60 and outfielders $50.

The Dayton Reds had only one mission in life—to defeat the Springfield team. Springfield, about 26 miles upstream on Mad River, was a rival of Dayton. (Both cities were exceptionally important in farm machinery production.) When the Dayton Reds were formed, *The Journal* announced, "Dayton will sign a team on purpose to beat Springfield. It doesn't make any difference about the rest of the league. Springfield—that little hamlet east of here—is the pie Daytonians are after."[7]

It was an expensive pie. The backers lost $2,000. Apparently, the street railways did not carry enough fans to the new grandstand and "bleaching boards" on Williams Street. Dayton finished fourth in the league of six. The scores of only two games played with Springfield are recorded—Dayton tied 4-all and won 3 to 0. (Earlier, Dayton had not fared so well when they played the touring Cincinnati Red Stockings on May 26, 1870, at Binam's Park off Keowee Street. The

Dayton's new courthouse was bigger, but not as beautiful as the old, said residents who saw it go up in 1884.

Gem City team lost 104 to 9.)

As the Gay Nineties came to a close, the city began to look like a city. In 1892, at Third and Main, the first Dayton skyscraper—the Callahan Bank Building—stretched nine stories into the rarified air, dwarfing the beautiful old courthouse. Everyone agreed that the new (1884) courthouse, just next door to the north, was ugly. The Reibold Building of 1896 was eleven stories. Its ill-conceived annex followed in 1904. The thirteen-story Conover Building (1900) and the fourteen-story United Brethren Office Building (1904) joined the high-rise community. The United Brethren Building

Best little whorehouse in Dayton

■ *Pearl Street is gone now. It was only three blocks—from Wayne to East Fifth—but it was a well-traveled street. (In fact, the first paved street in the city was Fifth Street which made an easy connection with Pearl.) It was Dayton's red-light district, known as the line, and it was perfectly legal.*

The queen of Pearl Street was Elizabeth Richter, better known as Lib Hedges. She was born in Germany in 1840 and ran a saloon on South Main Street opposite the fairgrounds in 1876. Beer was a nickel—and entertainment in the back rooms cost more.

Lib was a tall, buxom redhead. She set up her younger sister (her working name was Louisa La Fountaine) in business with a red brick house (seven bedrooms on the second floor) on Pearl at Howard Street. Lib was located at 30 Warren Street less than a half-mile away.

When her sister died in 1894, Lib had her buried in Woodland Cemetery in an imposing plot topped with a beautiful statue. Louisa's will created scandal. Most of her goods went to Lib. But Moses G. Wolf, one of four hard-working brothers, was awarded a thousand dollars, her horse and phaeton and a set of harnesses as "an expression of my appreciation of uniform kindness to me."

After her sister's death, Lib moved her business to Pearl Street. Lib was a classy lady—and she expected her girls to be the same. The rooms were replete with pictures, rich draperies, vases and classical statuary. Her girls dressed in the height of current fashion—no kimonos, but frilly bespangled dresses. Coarse language was forbidden. When one of her young women passed wind during a chandelier-kicking contest, Lib entered the room with a haughty stare and demanded, "What lady done that?"

Lib's girls apparently were treated well. She opened a bank account for each of her stable and on a Sunday afternoon paraded a select few through the streets to show off her new wares to Dayton society. Her clientele included lawyers, judges and (reportedly) important politicians.

Sex was profitable. Lib apparently amassed over a hundred lots and houses in Dayton. She often sold one of them (on very reasonable terms) to one of her girls upon retirement from the trade. She supported the YMCA, YWCA and charity in general.

After the 1913 flood, a solicitor called at her door. Lib's house had been destroyed and many of her properties heavily damaged. She raged at being solicited for funds but finally calmed down. "Well," she reportedly replied, "I suppose there's others who suffered more, so I suppose I better do something for 'em. I'll give you two thousand dollars and not another goddam cent." It was one of the city's most generous contributions.

Legalized prostitution ended in 1915 (effectively increasing the number of prostitutes in town). Lib died at the age of 82 in 1923.

"Mrs. Elizabeth Richter is dead," the Dayton Daily News *reported April 12. "The funeral will be private and will be held Saturday morning at 9 o'clock at the residence. Burial will be in Woodland Cemetery. . .She was a large holder of property and owned stock in several Dayton corporations." There was no mention of Pearl Street.*

Lib was buried with her parents (she had moved their bodies to her hillside plot), her sister and three of her girls—Ollie, Mary and Lora.[16]

THE FIRST REAL BUILDING: Newcom's Tavern (left) was the city's first real structure and was saved from destruction by the historical society which moved it to Van Cleve Park in 1896, complete with demonstrations of pioneer crafts (right) to add to the charm.

was reportedly the highest reinforced concrete building in the world at that time.

The telephone had served a few Daytonians since 1879 and was catching on. The streets had been electrically lighted since the mid-'80s, and many buildings used electricity as well. Spirited opposition feared watches would be stopped by the street railway's massive currents, but electrification began in 1887. Huge gangs of workmen from both the White Line (which wanted its wires strung over North Main Street) and the Oakwood Line (which did not) contested vigorously, but electricity won.

But the street railway cars were being dwarfed by much larger interurban cars. Dayton was late with railroads but in the vanguard of interurban development. By July 1, 1896, passengers could go to Miamisburg by trolley. A little more than a year later, the interurbans headed out for Hamilton every half hour from 5:30 a.m. to 8 p.m. And Dayton finally had sewers and paved streets of asphalt, brick, sandstone and granite.

Newcom's Tavern had been the first real building in Dayton. During the ensuing years, it had been sided over and used as a grocery store. It was slated for destruction, but Patterson and the newly formed historical society saved it. It was moved to Van Cleve Park. (Later it would be moved again.)

In 1896, Dayton was a major U.S. city of 80,000 people—and it was ready to celebrate.

The three-day centennial celebration began on September 14, 1896, approximately five-and-one-half months late. The first day included formal speeches, but on the second, 11,000 school children paraded with flags and banners. Locomotive bells were rung incessantly by gangs of ringers in the courthouse.

A pageant, "Daytonia," at the Grand Opera House, capped the celebration. "Act One—Newcom Tavern" featured the arrival of settlers in Conestoga wagons, an attack by Indians, arrival of the soldiers and repulse of the savages. Then a moonlight scene of the new Steele High School, complete with trolley cars.

"Act Second—Dayton in 1841" was a scene at Third and Main, a May Day celebration in Steele's Wood, the hill behind today's Art Institute, with 150 actors performing a colonial minuet in eighteenth-century costumes.

William D. Bickham put the Journal back on a sound financial footing.

A winning family

■ *On May 5, 1863, The Journal office was destroyed by a mob as a result of Vallandigham's arrest. On May 11, a new editor arrived to revive the financially distressed paper. From then until his death March 29, 1894, William D. Bickham was Dayton's leading newspaper editor. A manager as well as an editor, Bickham put the paper on a sound financial basis.*

Bickham had five sons, two of whom were especially noteworthy. Daniel Denison Bickham pitched for the Cincinnati Reds in 1886 when he was 22. His complete major league record is won 1, lost 0. At five feet, ten inches, 160 pounds, he was not a big man, but he managed to pitch the entire game. Although he gave up thirteen hits, he struck out six, and of three at-bats, got one hit.[13] He left the Reds when his editor father called him home because baseball "was not a gentlemanly sport."[14]

In 1902, near Lake Lanao, Mindanao, the Philippine Islands, Charles G. Bickham, a first lieutenant in the 27th U.S. Infantry, "crossed a fire-swept field, in close range of the enemy, and brought a wounded soldier to a place of shelter."[15] He was awarded the Congressional Medal of Honor on April 28, 1904.

STREET SCENES: Dayton converted to paved streets in 1892 (above); and celebrated its centennial in 1896 with a three-day event which included the traditional Main Street parade (below).

ELEPHANT WALK: The circus parade offered its own special entertainment to a Dayton pole-climbing viewer. Elephants thought the Canal the perfect bathing spot during an 1899 visit (inset).

Act Three had a number of tableaux leading up to the Civil War. The last scene, billed in the souvenir program as "the most thrilling and realistic stage effect ever presented," featured 5,000 (!?!) troops—including artillery and cavalry—passing the courthouse.

Act Four was Chickamauga at sunset, "where hundreds of our Dayton boys fought in defence [*sic*] of their country's flag." Scenes included "Realistic and Sanguinary Battlefield," "Exalted Bravery," "The Hero's Death," "Visions of Mother," "The Attack," "Lincoln," "Emancipation" and "Peace."

Act Five seems to have been a reprise of the first four with "allegorical transformations" of the pioneer landing,

Hallowed ground for the gypsies

■ *Gipsy Drive and Stanley Avenue in Dayton have one thing in common. They are named for the romantic, exotic gypsies. For more than 100 years, Dayton has been sano sancto (hallowed ground) for the Stanley clan, one of the largest gypsy tribes in the United States. The Stanley plot in Woodland Cemetery—in use since 1878—holds more than 60 members of that family, including Levi and Matilda ("King and Queen of the Gypsies"), the first to be interred there. Their son, "Sugar" Stanley, had a home on Gipsy Drive. He also was a horse trader who wintered in the south and came north for summers. His sons and grandsons remained in the Dayton area, buying farms north of the city.*

In 1898, a local paper noted that the Stanley, Jeffrey, Harrison and Wilson families still spoke Romantsch, the romantic language of gypsies worldwide. At that time, most local gypsies were illiterate. By 1920, references to Romantsch and to illiteracy were no longer found in the papers, although the gypsy sense of family and gypsy loyalty were still commented on by writers.

Probably the most interesting local gypsy tale dates back to Palm Sunday 1877, when "there occurred a triple funeral, associated with circumstances of peculiar sadness." Dr. D. Berger, who related the story in the Dayton Daily Journal, *May 23, 1898, had been acquainted with the Dayton gypsies for some years. He and the Reverend David Winters performed most of the early religious services for the clan. "On one of the farms north of the city Mrs. Amelia Jeffrey died after a brief illness," Dr. Berger said. "Her husband, Thomas Jeffrey, who was in perfect health, was so deeply stricken by the sudden bereavement that he lay down and in two days joined his wife in the sleep of death. It was a case of literal dying of a broken heart. Two expensive caskets were ordered for them from another city by one of our best known undertakers. A little babe, whose birth had been the occasion of the mother's death, was laid beside her in the casket, and the three were laid to rest in the tribal burying place." Twenty-five years later, the newspapers had embroidered the tale considerably, saying that the father lay down at his wife and baby's grave, refusing to leave Woodland Cemetery, and died there two days later. The story also has a second funeral with "father, mother and babe" all buried together in a single casket.*

As recently as the 1950s, gypsies were known to have camped on the shores of Kiser Lake near St. Paris, Ohio. Since then, few references to gypsies are found locally, although the 1980 death of a "gypsy queen" in New York state was noted in Dayton as a relative of the Stanley tribe.

Steele High School.

Dayton with the first canal boat landing in 1829, Dayton in 1865, and "Dayton of today—THE GEM CITY OF AMERICA!"

The presentation was both inaccurate and melodramatic. But in one way, it was a *tour de force*. "The people who promoted and sponsored the extravaganza," according to Charlotte Reeve Conover in *Dayton, Ohio: An Intimate History*, "represented all religions, all organizations, all affiliations. Catholics worked side by side with Protestants, Jews with Gentiles. In all other interests they were divided and separate. Here it was not a question of any one concern, but of a single loyalty—Dayton. During this celebration one practical lesson was learned by those who took part in it—a lesson that was to serve them well on a future occasion of which not one of them dreamed—it was to work together for the sake of the city."[8]

Ups and downs of poetic life

In 1891, a contract was let to build a new high school. It was finished in three years, and Daytonians took pride in the medieval Richardson Romanesque Steele High School. The graduating class of '91 said farewell to Central High at Fourth and Wilkinson streets, built in 1858 on the site of the old Cooper Academy. One young man in that class literally stood out from all the rest. The writer of the class song, the editor-in-chief of the school newspaper, the president of both the School Society and Philomethean Society was black.

His name was Paul Laurence Dunbar.

His mother, Matilda, had been a slave on a Lexington, Kentucky plantation. His father, Joshua, was a Union soldier, one of the first black men to be buried in the Soldiers' Home Cemetery. Until the end of World War I, very few blacks lived in Dayton, and there was no single geographic "colored community." Dunbar's family lived on the west side. Dunbar probably attended the "colored grade school" on Fifth Street which lasted until 1887. Since so many Daytonians dropped out before eighth grade, the entire school system provided only one intermediate school from 1874 to 1886. Dunbar was the only black in what must have been the final year of the intermediate school experiment.

One of Dunbar's classmates was Orville Wright. Wright failed to complete enough credits to graduate. (Orville's older brother Wilbur had come within three weeks of graduating from the Richmond, Indiana high school.) During Dunbar's senior year in school, Orville and Wilbur printed a newspaper, the *Tattler,* for Dunbar. The *Tattler* lasted for probably six issues, only two or three of which survive. Although the established Dayton papers welcomed the

Paul Laurence Dunbar

Vengeance is sweet

When I was young I longed for love,
And held his glory far above
All other earthly things, I cried:
"Come, Love, dear Love, with me abide;"
And with my subtlest art I wooed,
And eagerly the wight pursued.
But Love was gay and Love was shy,
He laughed at me and passed me by.

Well, I grew old and I grew gray,
When Wealth came wending down my way.
I took his golden hand with glee,
And comrades from that day were we.
Then Love came back with doleful face,
And prayed that I would give him peace.
But, though his eyes with tears were dim,
I turned my back and laughed at him.

Bein' back home

Say it's nice a'gittin' back
When your pulse is growin' slack
An' your breath begins to wheeze
Like a fair-set valley breeze;
Kind o' nice to set aroun'
On the old familiar groun'
Knowing that when Death does come
That he'll find you right at home.[12]

When de co'n pone's hot

Dey is times in life when Nature
Seems to slip a cog an' go,
Jes' a rattlin' down creation,
Lak an ocean's overflow;
When de' worl' jes' stahts a-spin-nin
Lak a picaninny's top,
An' yo' cup o' joy is brimmin'
'Twell it seems about to slop,
An' you feel jes' lak a racah
Dat is trainin' fu' to trot—
When yo' mammy says de blessin'
An' de co'n pone's hot.

Tattler to their ranks with favorable reviews, the venture simply did not make money, and the Wrights could not continue printing it without payment.

Dunbar's biographers state he went to work right after graduation at the Callahan Building as an elevator operator. (Other sources say Dayton's first skyscraper was not completed until some time in 1892.) Supposedly, Dunbar wrote as he carried the businessmen of the day on his elevator and supplemented his $4 salary by doing yard work for the Rike family, owners of D. L. Rike and Company and the Rike Dry Goods Company, forerunners of today's Rike's.[9]

The elevator operator published his first volume of poems, *Oak and Ivy,* in 1892. It was modestly successful. Dunbar left town to work in Chicago at the Haytian Pavilion during the 1893 World's Fair. A year later, he published *Majors and Minors,* which attracted the attention of well-known novelist and critic William Dean Howells. (Howells had worked in Dayton briefly as a printer's devil.) His approval, expressed in a review in the June 27, 1896, *Harper's Weekly,* established Dunbar as America's leading—if not only—Negro poet.

Dunbar was constantly torn by economic pressures. His publishers wanted less straight poetry and more pieces in dialect. But Dunbar wanted to be known as a poet—not as a Negro poet. In England where he went to read and

Kissing as medicine

■ *Joe Brooks was sitting in his barber shop Thursday morning when two ladies entered, evidently mother and daughter, the younger carrying a babe....The mother of the babe said to Mr. Brooks: "I have a favor to ask of you, and, although it may seem a queer one, and you a stranger, I hope you will grant it."*

"What can I do for you, madame?" replied Joe....

"I have heard," continued the lady, "that if a colored person will kiss a baby twice in the mouth, it will assist it in teething."

Joe gave it two as sweet and resounding kisses as he was capable of bestowing, and Joseph is an expert in that direction—he has the mouth.

When this was done the mother took the child, and both ladies left the shop....They seemed to be ladies of refinement and from their actions firmly believed that caresses from the colored person would have the effect desired.

Mr. Brooks says he has heard it was good for neuralgia on older girls, say 16 to 20 years of age.

The Tattler
December 20, 1890
attributed to
Paul Laurence Dunbar

FAMOUS CLASSMATES: A school photo from 1891 shows Paul Dunbar and Orville Wright at the top of their class. Dunbar is first on left, top row; Wright is fourth from left. Wright, however, failed to graduate.

write, Dunbar showed how race prejudice (the era of lynchings was beginning) affects the victim. "It would be an inestimable blessing if a number of Negroes from every State in the Union could live abroad for a few years, long enough to cool in their blood the fever-beat of strife," Dunbar wrote in an article in the *Independent,* September 16, 1897. "Here where there is so much opposition to his development, and remember, I do not assert that [it] is always conscious and intentional, the black man practices defense until it grows into aggressions. Remove him from his surroundings, take away the barrier against which he is constantly pushing, and he will return to the perpendicular[,] to the upright."

Always frail, Dunbar probably had tuberculosis, and his heavy drinking did not help. After an attempted convalescence in Denver, he returned first to the East Coast, then to Dayton in 1903. In February 1906, Paul Laurence Dunbar was dead. He was buried in Woodland Cemetery in his mother's plot but re-interred to a choicer location in 1909.

Labor rumbles

In 1900, Dayton was a major city. It ranked 45th in the nation in population, 37th in the number of workers and 33rd in wages paid. Although it was now only the fifth largest city in Ohio, Dayton ranked third in capital investment and first in the number of patents issued.

Organized labor was not unknown in Dayton. There had been a strike in 1876 against the the *Dayton Daily Democrat* by union typesetters. (The result is unknown.) In 1895, the brewery workers' union struck Schantz Brewing, one of many local breweries, but Adam Schantz evidently soothed the situation.

Dayton's first major strike came late in 1899. The general manager of the Dayton Manufacturing Company, which made railroad car hardware, discharged seventeen employees. There was some violence, the riot act was read, and a judge ordered an end to picketing. The strike was broken.

Dayton industrialists already had an organization to protect themselves from labor problems. It was the Employers' Association, led by John Kirby of the Dayton Manufacturing Company. (It would later become the "Citizens Industrial Association of America," and still later, the NAM, National Association of Manufacturers.) The Cash was not then a member. By any standards, the National Cash Register Company was an enlightened employer. But, for all laborers of the time, hours were long and the pay was small.

In 1901, machinists at the Cash threatened to strike. The company locked out 2,300 workers for seven weeks or more. Patterson declared the Cash an open shop. Although that meant no unions, Patterson did accept a number of the workers' demands. The work day dropped from ten to nine hours daily. Wages were increased 12.5 percent, four of the strike organizers were rehired and Patterson joined the Employers' Association. But Patterson was disenchanted with both Dayton and his labor force. He had provided much for his workers—lectures, clubs, schools, libraries, a kindergarten, free baths, payment for suggestions and the best place to work in town. Instead of gratitude, Patterson felt he had been betrayed by his own hometown. He would not forget the insult.

WAR AND PEACE: In 1898, the Dayton Militia leaves for the Spanish-American War, seen off by a packed crowd. Three years earlier, Civil War veterans march in a Memorial Day parade (inset).

A CITY FOR ALL SEASONS: Winter sports on the river were not the only recreation enjoyed by Daytonians as evidenced by the young croquet players (bottom left); the Gem City Polo Club, actually a form of hockey on roller skates (bottom center); and the couple rowboating (bottom right).

TOM-LAWLER
TOM-HOBAN
ORRIE-COTTERMAN

NO-4
TAKEN-1894
OCT-1940

PETE-CAULFIELD
CHARLES-WAGNER
ADAM-DIXON

*THE PROTECTORS: Horse-drawn carriages took late nineteenth century firefighters (above) and police patrols
(below) to their destinations, but a new age was soon to come.*

CHAPTER SIX

WHERE NO MAN HAD GONE BEFORE

Wilbur Wright flew over the empty carriages of spectators during a demonstration in Pau, France, in 1909.

Wilbur and Orville Wright invented the airplane during the off-season for bicycles.

Summers with mosquitoes

Flying was not an expensive hobby in the early days; the Wright brothers built their first glider for about $15. They took it to North Carolina for testing. The machine flew more like a brick than a bird, but when in flight, it responded well to the controls.

They began to correspond with Octave Chanute, the major U.S. glider expert of the time. He sent the Wrights information on his studies, and they sent Chanute their ideas. Chanute visited the brothers in June 1901, shortly after Charles E. Taylor had joined the Wrights' bicycle firm for 30 cents an hour. Charlie Taylor opened the shop at 7 a.m. The owners arrived an hour or two later, and the store was open until 6 p.m. weekdays and until 9 p.m. on Saturdays. March, April, May and June were the tough months, gearing up for the summer bicycle season. Summers were lighter, and fall so slow the Wrights could—and did—take off.

In the summer of 1901, Orville and Wilbur tried gliding again with similar results, except the mosquitoes made life miserable. When Wilbur was to speak on the brothers' experiments at a meeting of the Western Society of Engineers in Chicago, his sister Katharine asked, "Will your talk be witty or scientific?" Wilbur answered, "I think it will be pathetic."[2]

While Wilbur was away, Orville worried. Their tests of wing surfaces had shown that the earlier experts had been wrong—seriously wrong. But who were the Wrights to criticize these eminent scientists? Orville decided that more experimentation was needed. He built a wind tunnel, and the brothers began a series of tests which proved the earlier efforts of other aviation pioneers completely false and misleading. All the theoretical mathematics used to construct them was totally wrong. No wonder the Wrights' gliders were so leaden.

In 1900, the Wrights invented control surfaces. In 1901, they invented wing design. At the Smithsonian, Samuel Langley—with tens of thousands of government dollars at his disposal—was determined to be the first man to fly. Two large steam-powered unmanned models designed by Langley had flown successfully in 1896. He had contracted for a lightweight engine which—after much work—could develop an incredible 52 horsepower. The race was on.

One night when he could not sleep, Orville made a key discovery—they needed a movable rudder not a fixed one. As would happen many more times, the other brother then improved on the idea. "We'll connect the rudder and the wings with wires to operate them together. One lever will control lateral balance. The other will keep the plane balanced fore and aft."[3]

Progress was constantly being made with the gliders. In two days, they made 250 glides. They set American records for longest distance (622.5 feet), longest time in the air (26 seconds) and lowest angle of descent (5 degrees for 125 feet). Even Professor Langley was impressed. He telegraphed the Wrights to see if he could observe some flights. But they replied that they were returning to Dayton.

They knew that next year, 1903, they would fly.

While the Wrights worked on building the airframe, they asked Charlie Taylor to build them a lightweight gas engine. Their demands were modest. Instead of Langley's 52 horsepower, the Wrights asked Taylor for four horsepower. Six weeks later, he delivered a twelve-horsepower model.

In 1903, two uneducated mechanics from an obscure hick town in Ohio invented the airplane. At least, that was what some people thought. But it was not quite true.

True, Wilbur and Orville Wright did not graduate from high school, but few people did in those days. Wilbur did know both Latin and Greek. Existing high school grade cards showed both brothers were exceptional students with scores in the high nineties. Their father, the eccentric Milton Wright, was a bishop in the United Brethren Church and had moved repeatedly before settling in Dayton in time for Orville and his sister Katharine to be born. Their mother, Susan Koerner Wright, gave Orville and Wilbur their mechanical aptitude.

The 1890 bicycle craze in America created at least two firms in Dayton. One was the large (a million-dollar payroll in 1909) Davis Sewing Machine Company, whose Dayton bicycle was known throughout the country. The other was the somewhat smaller Wright brothers' shop. They made the Van Cleve (the brothers were related to Benjamin Van Cleve's wife), the St. Clair and perhaps other models as well.

The Wright brothers had given up the printing business and seemed happy selling, then repairing and finally building bicycles in their shop at 1005 West Third Street. But in September 1894, *McClure's Magazine* ran an article about Otto Lilienthal, the German pioneer of gliding. The Wrights decided to read all they could about flying. There was not much. A letter to the Smithsonian Institution in 1889 brought a list of books, and Wilbur ordered two—one by Octave Chanute, the other by Smithsonian secretary, Samuel Pierpoint Langley, who was experimenting with powered flight.

On August 8, 1899, Wilbur made the first of the discoveries that would allow for practical control of a glider. He discovered it with a bicycle tube box. By twisting the box, Wilbur invented the concept of "wing warping," the device that presented an unequal amount of lift to the left or right wing surfaces. The Wrights tested it out with a large kite and the technique worked.[1]

WHEELS AND WINGS: The Wright brothers
were not the only manufacturers of bicycles
in Dayton. The Davis Sewing Machine Co.
was a major U.S. manufacturer of bicycles
(above), but the Wright brothers out-thought
the experts when it came to air flight,
beginning their experiments with kites, then
gliders (left).

Up and away

■ *The chilly December day*
two shivering bicycle mechanics from Dayton, Ohio,
first felt their homemade contraption
whittled out of hickory sticks,
gummed together with Arnstein's bicycle cement,
stretched with muslin they'd sewn on their
     sister's sewingmachine in their own
     backyard on Hawthorn Street in Dayton,
     Ohio,
soar into the air
above the dunes and the wide beach
at Kitty Hawk.

John Dos Passos
The Big Money

WESTERN UNION

SUCCESS FOUR FLIGHTS THURSDAY MORNING ALL AGAINST TWENTY-ONE MILE WIND STARTED FROM LEVEL WITH ENGINE POWER ALONE AVERAGE SPEED THROUGH AIR THIRTY-ONE MILES LONGEST FIFTY-SEVEN [actually 59] SECONDS INFORM PRESS HOME CHRISTMAS ORVELLE [sic] WRIGHT

Telegram to the Reverend Milton Wright, from Kitty Hawk, N.C., December 17, 1903.

They had assumed a propeller would not be a problem since marine propellers had been around for many years. They were wrong. Finally, they recognized the propeller as a rotating wing. Extensive research in their wind tunnel resulted in their own special propeller. They left for Kitty Hawk (or more precisely, Kill Devil Hills) on September 24, 1903.

Failure in plain view

Fifteen days later, Langley made his first attempt at launching a man-carrying, heavier-than-aircraft. The establishment candidate—in full view of the Washington, D.C., press corps—launched a tandem wing (one wing in front of the other) aircraft. It failed spectacularly, falling into the Potomac River immediately after the launch.

A few days later, the Wrights heard of Langley's failure. Perhaps they had a chance. A severe storm broke October 18 and put the floor of their primitive cabin under water. Nevertheless, by November 4, the "aeroplane" was ready except for mounting the propellers. But the propeller shafts broke. They sent the shafts back to Dayton for Taylor to repair. One of the replacements which arrived November 21 was cracked. Orville took the shaft home on the train. When he was returning to North Carolina, Orville read of Professor Langley's second (and final) failure. Again, the strange-looking tandem-winged aircraft catapulted from a flatboat in the Potomac. Again, it fell at once into the river. This time, the pilot Charles Manley, nearly drowned. The world said—and with some justification—"It'll never fly."

On December 14, in spite of a lack of wind, the Wright brothers decided upon a downhill test. It was not a flight, as standards for "true flying" had already been set and were

Wilbur Wright posed with his sister Katharine during a series of flights at Pau, France, in 1909.

clearly understood. A "flight" had to end up no further downhill than it had begun. The brothers' first attempt at powered flight was downhill and scarcely auspicious. The flyer took off, crashed three-and-a-half seconds later, 105 feet away from the takeoff point.

The repaired aircraft was again ready on a cold and windy December 17. The wind was 24 to 27 miles per hour and the day a poor choice for flying. Orville later admitted their "audacity in attempting flights with a new and untried machine under such circumstances."[4] Since Wilbur had won the toss for the December 14 downhill attempt, Orville was the pilot this time. And Orville became the first man to fly, bouncing up and down for a bare twelve seconds and 120 feet.

Just before noon, Wilbur made the major flight of the day, the one that proved the Wrights were right. He flew for 59 seconds, covering 852 feet.

Only nine days after Langley's hopes had sunk, the Wright brothers proved the world wrong. Langley's machine had carried a price tag of $70,000. The Wrights' machine—not counting the value of their labors—cost about $1,000.

The press was not present at the historic moment. Only five spectators from the Kill Devil Hills lifesaving station shared the Wrights' triumph. One reporter got wind of the feat and wrote a ridiculous story that only three papers (including the *Dayton Evening Herald*) were naive enough to carry. "DAYTON BOYS FLY AIRSHIP. Machine Makes High Speed in the Teeth of a Gale and Lands at the Point Selected. PROBLEM OF AERIAL NAVIGATION SOLVED."

The *Dayton Daily News* was more restrained. Its story read: "THE WRIGHT BOYS ARE COMING HOME. Norfolk, Va., Dec. 19—Orville and Wilbur Wright, inventors of the 'Wright Flyer,' which made several successful flights near here

Thursday, left today for their home in Dayton, O., to spend Christmas with their parents."

Much later, Dan Kumler, city editor of the *Dayton Daily News* admitted that the press had blown their coverage of the Wrights. "We were just plain dumb,"[5] he said.

On May 23, 1904, the Wrights invited the press to see a flight of their plane. The wind was first too high then too low. The next day, they got off the ground, but not for long, and only reached an altitude of five or six feet. The press was less than impressed. The Wrights were now flying at Huffman Prairie east of Dayton. They made 41 flights before September 7 and still had not surpassed Wilbur's 59-second flight of 1903. Dayton lacked Kitty Hawk's steady wind, so the Wrights built a derrick launcher. Then they were in business.

A. I. Root, a beekeeper in Medina, Ohio, had heard of the Wright's flying machine and drove to Dayton to seek out the flyers. He arrived to see Wilbur complete the first circular flight in history. The first full account of the Wright brothers appeared in the January 1, 1905, edition of *Gleanings in Bee Culture*.

At the end of 1905, *Scientific American* credited the Wrights with a flight of "over half a mile in a propeller-driven machine," but damned it with faint praise, saying, "the only successful 'flying' this year must be credited to the balloon type." By this time, the brothers had flown a total of more than 160 miles.[6]

A year later, within two days of the third anniversary of manned, heavier-than-air flight, *Scientific American*—after reading 60 affidavits and after months of checking—ran an editorial that set the facts straight at last. By this time the Brazilian sportsman, Santos-Dumont, had hopped into the air for more than 21 seconds.

6/17/09

THE HOMECOMING: After a triumphant showing in France, Dayton welcomed back the Wrights with a parade and church bells ringing (left); Wilbur and Orville attended ceremonies with their father, Bishop Milton Wright (above). In May 1910, Orville gave his father a seven-minute flight. The Bishop said only, "Higher. Higher."

Disaster into triumph

Europeans had been trying to fly for years. The French, especially, believed the sky was their birthright. They might, with reluctance, believe that an Englishman might fly, or Santos-Dumont, but an American? *C'est impossible.*

Wilbur arrived in France in 1908. The brothers had tried for years to sell their plane to the American government— or anybody—with no success. They were almost broke. (Wilbur called it "financial stringency.") Wilbur hoped to demonstrate—and sell—the Wright Flyer in Europe. Orville stayed home, Wilbur went to France and was greeted by the taunt of *"Le Bluff Continué."*[7]

On August 8, 1908, Wilbur called *le bluff* with a perfectly executed figure eight, landing at his starting point. European planes by this time could leap into the air, go forward a distance, then crash land. They had power, brave aviators, but virtually no control. Wilbur *flew.* Graciously, the French conceded defeat. Wilbur Wright was the hit of the continent. In France alone, Wilbur made 113 flights, 60 with passengers (the first two-man flight had been made with Wilbur flying Charlie Taylor on May 14, 1908) and logged 26 hours of flight time. One flight lasted two hours and ten minutes.

Meanwhile, the U.S. Signal Corps had advertised for an aircraft. Orville went to Washington, D.C., to demonstrate the Wright Flyer to the Signal Corps. On September 17, he took off with Lieutenant T. D. Selfridge as a passenger. Orville felt (probably correctly) that Selfridge was a spy for competitors Alexander Graham Bell and Curtiss Wright. During the flight, a propeller cracked and the plane crashed.

Orville was badly hurt; Selfridge died. But the Corps recognized the plane's potential and bought the Wright Flyer in 1909.

Shortly before the final Signal Corps' acceptance tests, Dayton welcomed their reluctant heroes with a monstrous parade on June 17, 1909. At 9 a.m., every factory whistle blew, and every church bell rang for ten minutes, the noisy commencement of a two-day celebration. There were bands, dignitaries riding in carriages, a demonstration by the Dayton Fire Department, a reception at the one-year-old YMCA building at Third and Ludlow (now the City Building) and a presentation of the keys to the city.

The second day, a Congressional medal, an Ohio medal and a Dayton medal were presented by Mayor Edward Burkhardt. Although 2,500 Dayton School children singing patriotic songs formed a human United States flag at the fairgrounds, no demonstration ever was presented to two more unwilling participants.

Dayton, hitherto known only as a producer of railway cars, farm machinery and cash registers, was on the map at last. But the Wrights did not gain such recognition everywhere. Glen Curtiss, the brilliant aviator and engineer, challenged them. Langley had died in 1906, but the Smithsonian refused to recognize the Wrights' work. The Wright brothers became bitter, even reclusive. The Smithsonian even helped Curtiss restore the Langley Aerodome and may have made significant changes in order to invalidate certain Wright patents. Lawyers fought the battles on the ground while Europe took to the air. This tragic controversy kept the United States out of the forefront of aviation for almost 30 years. More obsessed with law suits than flying, the Wrights retreated into a shell neither man would escape until death. In May 1910, Wilbur made his final flight. He died in 1912. He was 45.

Together, the Wright brothers were far more than the sum of their parts. Individually, they were good, intelligent, eccentric men; together they were the brilliant combination of scientist, innovator and engineer that was the personification of American genius at the turn of the century.

Good days at the barn

In 1904, Edward Deeds hired a young Ohio State graduate named Charles F. Kettering to help solve the problem of electrifying the cash register. The two men shared a number of common interests. Both were farm boys who had been teased by their city cousins and both shared an excitement for the future of electricity.

Deeds also had a love of another newfangled invention—the automobile. In his barn behind 319 Central Avenue, in lower Dayton View, Deeds and a mechanic built a car, the Suburban Sixty. Although it was less than reliable, Deeds felt future fortunes lay in the automotive field. Kettering agreed.

They moonlighted at the barn. Soon William A. Chryst, another N.C.R. employee (who called young Kettering "Boss" from the start) was part of the "Barn Gang."

Kettering quit the Cash in 1909 to devote full attention to developing an electric ignition system. At that time, the magneto system in operation was terribly inefficient. When the car stalled, the driver had to hop out and crank the engine to life again.

In autumn 1907, Deeds and Kettering demonstrated the system for the chief engineer of the Cadillac Company. They soon had a deal with "Uncle Henry" Leland of Cadillac for 5,000 ignition sets. There was one minor problem. There was no company to produce them—the firm did not even have a name. They subcontracted the manufacturing and promptly adopted the name Dayton Engineering Laboratories Company. It is better known today as Delco.

The ignition system appeared on Cadillacs in 1910, and the 1912 sported the newest Delco innovation, the electric self-starter. A major company was off and running. It would influence Dayton dramatically.

THE BARN GANG: In a barn behind Edward Deeds' home (below), Deeds and two other N.C.R. employees, Charles F. Kettering and William A. Chryst, invented the first self-starting ignition system for the automobile. Chryst and Kettering demonstrated the starter (right), which they sold to the Cadillac Company for its cars (inset).

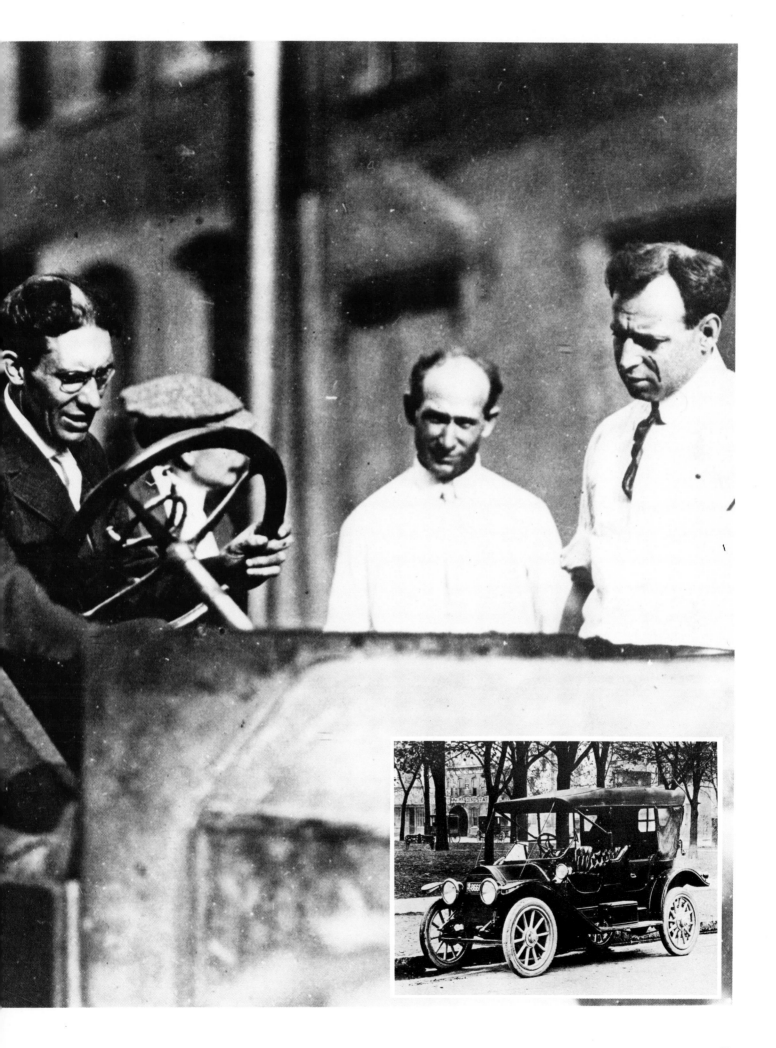

AN IDEA IGNITED: The Barn Gang's concept for a small auto part turned into big business — the Delco Company, with a room full of draftsmen (above) and a huge assembly line (inset).

N.C.R. owner John H. Patterson was an early advocate of photography as a sales tool. This remarkable picture of company employees showed who built the world's finest cash registers.

Dark days at the Cash

In the late 1890s and early 1900s, competitors were vermin to be stamped out, crushed, destroyed, eliminated. Patterson—the man who took pity on his female employees and gave them hot coffee at work—took no pity on rival cash register companies. The imitators violated N.C.R. patents. To avoid the bell, one competitor used a "cuckoo." Many were cheap, shoddy machines known as "premium" registers, given away or sold at extremely low prices by distributors of tobacco goods or other sundries in order to close a sale.

Probably as early as 1888, the Cash set out to get rid of all competition. By 1910, 153 of 158 competitors had failed. The Cash's market share had increased from about 82 percent in the late 1890s to 95 percent.[8]

Thomas Watson, who would go on to far greater fame as the founder of IBM, was one of the N.C.R. men assigned to destroy competitors. He would rent an office, preferably next door to his victim, and sell a model designed to look exactly like the competitor's model, at a cheaper price. Sometimes Watson would buy the failing company, often hiring the competitor to do to other competitors exactly what Watson had done to him.

A criminal suit was brought against Patterson and others in 1893, but it was allowed to lapse. The company continued to sue for patent violations while remaining free from Sherman antitrust action for more than fifteen years.

Patterson believed travel was the best education and often sent his executives on long trips abroad. Since N.C.R. was one of the first U.S. companies to realize the value of overseas business, it was a logical combination of business and pleasure.

In 1905, Patterson returned from a round-the-world trip with a new employee. Patterson had been ill when he left and developed a high fever near Venice. He had gone on a 37-day fast to recover in the Alps near the Italian-Swiss

border. The doctor who treated him was an associate of a diet faddist by the name of Fletcher whose "chew more, eat less" command to chew each mouthful at least 50 times was popular around the turn of the century.

The doctor told Patterson to rest and to follow the Sandow discipline in England in order to regain his strength. Eugene Sandow, supposedly the "strongest man in the world," operated a gymnasium in London. Patterson hired a physical trainer, Charles Palmer, from the gym. It proved a costly mistake.

Patterson brought Palmer to Dayton and made him the director of the department of physical culture in July 1905. It was Palmer who convinced Patterson to get the executives up and on horseback at dawn. (Deeds called this the "Kaiser reviewing his troops.") Office staff and factory workers were assembled for an hour of exercises on company time. At one of the dawn patrols, Kettering fell off his horse and was in danger of being fired since "a man who cannot control horses cannot control men."

Palmer believed that a man's character could be read in his face, so Patterson permitted the man to go around reading faces. Those whose faces lacked the right stuff were dismissed. Word of all this reached the *Dayton Daily News* and stories began to appear in July 1907, attributing the resignation—perhaps the firing—of Hugh Chalmers, then the number two man at N.C.R., to Palmer's interference. (Chalmers went on to form an automobile company and later to testify against Patterson and others.) Patterson grew furious. He, Palmer and N.C.R. sued the *Dayton Daily News*.

Tragedy struck on February 27, 1908, when C. D. Anderson, head of inventions, was thrown from his horse on one of the dawn patrols and killed. Anderson had been an assistant physical education instructor (probably serving under Palmer) before his promotion to the inventions department and was one of the most enthusiastic supporters of the exercise program. The *Dayton Daily News* had a field day. On March 2, Deeds told employees that the plant would be shut down as Patterson could not do two things at once and needed all his energies to fight the paper.

For unknown reasons, all three suits against the newspaper

RECREATION, DAYTON STYLE:
Daytonians took physical fitness seriously,
as evidenced by the swimmers at
Bomberger Park (above) in 1911, and the
tennis and croquet enthusiasts (left),
circa 1900.

OTHER AMUSEMENTS: Not all fun required physical exertion. The massive Arcade on Third (right) housed a wonderland of edibles (top), and such unusual diversions as the Bird Man (bottom).

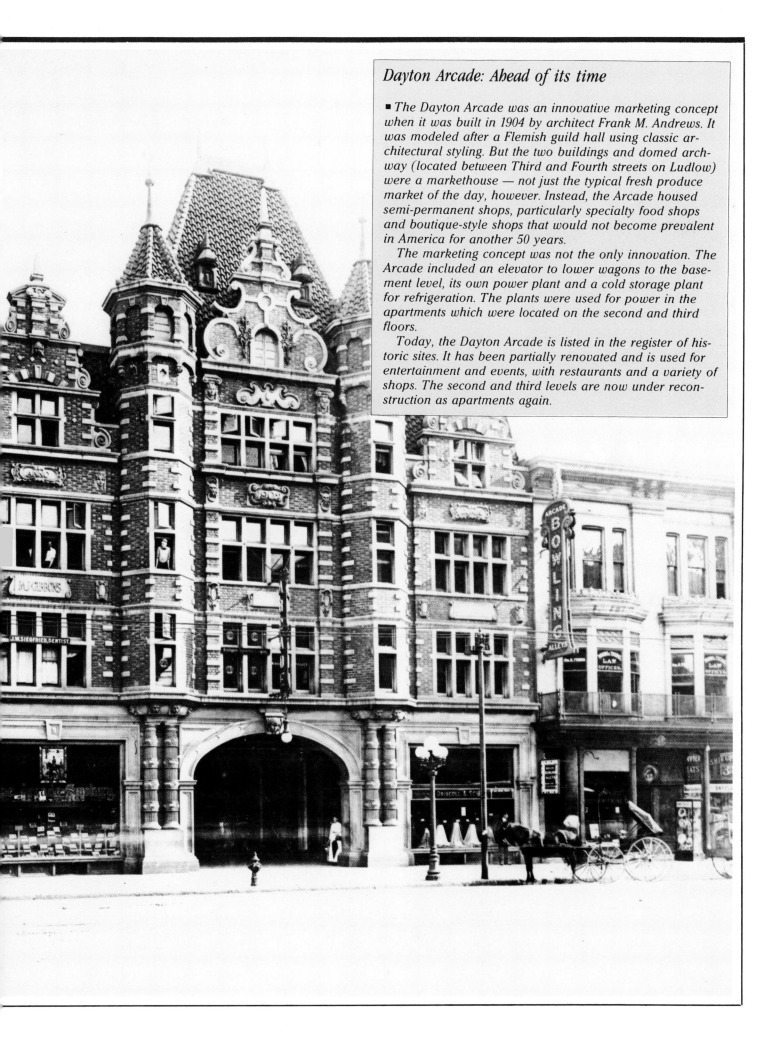

Dayton Arcade: Ahead of its time

■ The Dayton Arcade was an innovative marketing concept when it was built in 1904 by architect Frank M. Andrews. It was modeled after a Flemish guild hall using classic architectural styling. But the two buildings and domed archway (located between Third and Fourth streets on Ludlow) were a markethouse — not just the typical fresh produce market of the day, however. Instead, the Arcade housed semi-permanent shops, particularly specialty food shops and boutique-style shops that would not become prevalent in America for another 50 years.

The marketing concept was not the only innovation. The Arcade included an elevator to lower wagons to the basement level, its own power plant and a cold storage plant for refrigeration. The plants were used for power in the apartments which were located on the second and third floors.

Today, the Dayton Arcade is listed in the register of historic sites. It has been partially renovated and is used for entertainment and events, with restaurants and a variety of shops. The second and third levels are now under reconstruction as apartments again.

A scene taken in 1911 shows the wide variety of businesses that could be squeezed into a small building. Charlie Leung's Chinese Laundry and Bazaar apparently did a brisk business in post cards and photos. Note the coney island stand on the corner. Other turn-of-the-century photos show the Union Station (above right) built in 1900; and a group of workers during a break in 1901 (below right).

were dropped on April 29, and N.C.R. agreed to pay all costs. By June, perhaps earlier, the company was back at work. And Patterson even supported *Dayton Daily News* publisher Cox's campaign for the U.S. Congress later in the year.

Patterson's differences with the city (which almost led to moving the factory out of town) were serious ones. Partly because of Patterson's welfare work, other Dayton businesses were forced to offer their employees better working conditions. His innovative factories made the Cash the best place in town to work (at least for those of honest face). But the city delayed, bickered and was slow to respond to the growing factory's needs. Patterson wanted a railway siding; the city had decided to permit no more surface grade crossings. He wanted better streetcar service for his workers. He wanted the canal filled in when the state was considering canal improvements. He wanted honest government, honest police, better schools, libraries, a bridge across Stewart Street and a cooler climate. Patterson had first sketched out what Dayton should have done in a speech given for the centennial on March 19, 1896.[9] He was angry that little or nothing had been achieved in eleven years.

The threat to move the Cash paid off in 1907. The city, its

"boosters club" (which would evolve into the Chamber of Commerce) and even the newspapers came into line. The detractors of N.C.R.—the "knockers"—were silenced. And somewhere along the line, Palmer was shipped back to England.

In February 1912, the grand jury of the United States District Court of Southern Ohio handed down an indictment for restraint of trade against Patterson and 29 other company officials. The trial began on November 20, 1912, and on February 13, 1913, the jury returned a guilty verdict. Patterson and Watson were fined $5,000 plus costs and sentenced to a year in jail. Deeds and most of the others were to serve nine months.[10]

It was a time of great sadness for Dayton. By today's standards, their business tactics were clearly unfair. But the men involved did not feel themselves any more guilty than other businessmen of their day. The city was solidly behind the Cash, and the company's sales did not suffer because of the trial. But the specter of jail and the humiliation cast a huge shadow over Dayton and the men involved.

To get out of the mess, Patterson would have to walk on water. And...

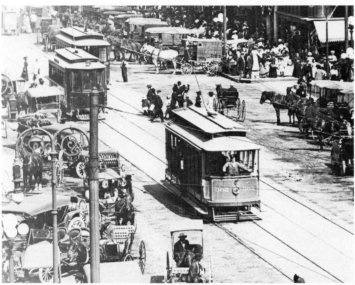

DAYTON IN 1910: A view of Dayton's Main Street as it looked near the opening of the new century (center and right); Miller's Grocery and Market (top); and workers at the Lowe Brothers Paint Factory (bottom).

THE DAYTON
SAVINGS & TRUST CO.
INTEREST PAID ON DEPOSITS.

A. NEWSALT,
THE LEADING
JEWELER

GET STYLE AT COMFORT

RED CROSS
REED SHO

REED'S S
PLEASE

Will

93

Boaters ready themselves for a rowing trip at the Phillips Boat House around 1900.

CHAPTER SEVEN

IN 1913, DAYTON HAD A FLOOD

Looking north to Dayton under water from Fairgrounds Hill during the 1913 flood.

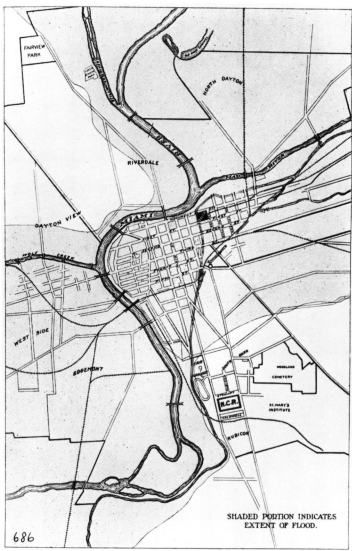

The 1913 flood encompassed nearly all of Dayton, as shown on the shaded portions of the map.

Easter Sunday in Dayton, there was a downpour until early afternoon. It rained intermittently all night, and on Monday "it seemed as if the windows of heaven had been opened," the *Dayton Daily News* reported. "There was lightning and mad rain." The storm which hit the Miami Valley had already claimed almost a hundred victims in Omaha and 25 in Terre Haute. It was one of the most powerful electrical and tornadic storms on record. Between March 23 and 27, about eleven inches of rain swelled the Stillwater, Mad and Miami river basins.

Tuesday morning, water began overflowing the levees in the north of Dayton. Rescue workers from the boat clubs in Riverdale began to help people from the area. But the seriousness was still not apparent, and few tried to leave. By 8 a.m., the levees to the south were overtopped. Then a levee broke where the Mad and Miami joined. C. R. Meyer, an N.C.R. employee, stood in the freight yards near the mouth of the Mad and watched the canal flood downtown in minutes. "Suddenly. . .the Mad River levee fifty feet [away] crumbled with a roar," Meyer was quoted in the *New York Tribune*, April 6. "A huge cataract swept the railroad yards, picking up freight cars as if they had been shoe boxes, depositing water and all in the canal . . . . A two-story house stood a moment in the path of this inrush. . .and a woman and child screamed inaudibly from a second-story window. Then

Marines delivered bread by boat from Deger's Bakery to St. Elizabeth Hospital.

■ Our brick house stood on a high stone foundation and it
didn't seem possible the water could ever get that high.
Not until it started to boil up out of the sewers and rush down
the street in a wall of five feet high—not until then did
we think it could happen. The water rose on the bricks of the
house next door to us at the rate of a brick a minute.
It came into the house, and from the second floor we watched
as it came up the stairs, step after step covering our red
Brussels carpet. On the second floor it covered the beds and
we took refuge in the attic.
Dayton Journal Herald, *March 22, 1958*

Hundreds of dramatic rescues were effected by boat as flood waters rose as high as second-story windows.

the house toppled over, mother and child disappeared from view.... The infuriated water then burst into every street which the canal intersected—Monument Avenue, 1st, 2nd, 3rd, 4th, 5th, all the principal east and west business and residential streets, in fact. It was this flank movement which more than anything else plunged Dayton into a panic."

Thousands of people were trapped. There were 300 men, women and children who spent four nights in the Beaver Power Building at Fourth and St. Clair. There were 400 travelers trapped with one box of chocolate creams in the Union Station. Katherine Kennedy Brown (later an Ohio Republican committeewoman) was marooned in her home at the northwest corner of Keowee and Webster streets in North Dayton for five days. In Cannon Street, waters rushed and tumbled, flooding most houses. Only one stood higher than the others and offered residents a chance of escape. They fashioned a boardway of thin curtain stretcher poles placed side by side and delicately inched their way across the dangerous waters.

There were hundreds of dramatic rescues. Eighteen-year-old Ethel Clare, whose home on Madison Street was devastated, rescued eighteen people from second-story windows with a raft built from household debris. The "newsy" at the Phillips House corner (who needed a tricycle to get around) took to the water and rescued 87 people by boat. Joseph Dowling, superintendent of Memorial Hall, saved two elderly women who lived in the house next to him on Norwood Avenue; he secured a board from the wreckage and laid it across to their windowsill. But it was not long enough, and he leaned out, placed himself face downward with the board upon his neck to make a bridge for the women to cross to safety. Alfred and Carl Anglemyer, two west side youths, saved over 200 people in their canoe.[1]

One stirring newspaper account regaled rescue efforts of "the well-known colored ball player," W. G. Sloan. Sloan reportedly commandeered—at gunpoint—a steel-bottom boat from "a selfish owner at the handle factory." He was credited with saving 317 people in 68 hours of continuous work. But Sloan remains a mystery. The Negro league, of which Dayton was a part, did not exist in 1913, and there were supposedly no blacks on the regular ball team. Furthermore, the handle factory is also unknown.

Death was everywhere—but life continued on. Children arrived even in the very midst of the raging waters. Mrs. Forrest Kuntz bore twins in a boat while being rescued from her Lehman Street home. Mrs. James Gebhart gave birth to her fourth child during the first night of the flood.[2]

Homes of the rich and poor sheltered victims, and everyone shared whatever they had left. "When Mother got home late that night," Katharine Houk Talbott wrote in her diary, "she found three hundred people in our house, old and young, frightened, miserable, and—until they had reached Runnymede—cold and hungry."

The Dayton View area was particularly outstanding, arranging food and a place to sleep for more than 500 women and children on the first night. Frank Reisinger, an undertaker, mobilized his horses and wagons and aided the

■ *7:30 [March 25, 1913] Arose—breakfasted—water had already broken down back and side cement wall—nearer and nearer it came. Now it is on the walk by the house. Shèry and I flee to the cellar and begin shoveling coal into all recepticles [sic]—carrying it up into the kitchen—now dumping it in kitchen—now dumping it on kitchen floor—next canned goods and now the water is entering the cellar—hurry with the canoe. The boys (Charlie, Brookie, and Shèry) smash a window and push it out. Now I rush upstairs, order the boys to take up the rugs, furniture, typewriter, books— now the tiffany [sic] glass—every piece is upstairs except piano. Now we heap clothes-baskets with books. . . .*
Diary of Katherine Kennedy Brown

poor of Dayton without regard of race, creed or nationality. He ordered 110 coffins from nearby Richmond, Indiana, and offered them to the poor.

And then came the fire

If Dayton was little prepared for the flood, it was less prepared for the fire which started in the Burkhardt and Rottermann Drugstore which stood on the northwest corner of Third and St. Clair streets. It spread rapidly, ultimately burning large parts of two city blocks. Hundreds were trapped downtown but managed to escape. The south side of Third Street was swept by the conflagration, the flames advancing eastward as far as St. Clair Street. "The sight caused by the explosion of combustible contents of tanks," said J. L. Wilds, quoted in a *Boston Herald* article, "although of grave significance to us, was magnificent."

The people trapped in the Beaver Power Building at Fourth and St. Clair drew up water from the street in buckets, stored it in barrels and threw it on the building to extinguish cinders as the block between Third and Fourth burned.

In the Ball Candy Company factory on Third Street, 130 girls emptied 300 candy pails and formed a bucket brigade to fight the flames. They were finally rescued by Ed H. Thompson of Cincinnati, who, with E. J. McConnell and three others, made the first trip into the burning district in a motor boat.

"The water was rising very rapidly at the rate of about one inch a minute," recalled Harvey Kirkbride. "About two o'clock in the afternoon the walls of the drug store on the corner fell. This being only about seventy feet from our building, we thought it best to move. We climbed to the fourth story by means of a ladder, crawled up through the hatch to the roof. We found that all the people in our square had done the same thing. Our building being the first one of the four story buildings on the square, we did a good deal of rescuing of people in the lower building between us and the corner, who had also crawled to the roofs....There were five women, one boy about twelve years old, and twenty-two men....The highest stage was reached at twelve o'clock Tuesday night. This was eight feet and eight inches on the floor of our building. This meant about eleven feet on Third Street....About three o'clock in the afternoon of Wednesday, those in the front of the store looking out of the window, noticed the fire which originated in the drug store on the corner of Third and St. Clair Streets. There was a high wind blowing from the north and east which fanned the fire and it was only a matter of a few minutes until the two buildings on the corner were ablaze. Everybody went to the roof...We all moved west over the roofs to the last one of the four story buildings which was occupied by Rauh & Sons Company. There we went down through the hatch and down the stairs to the second floor, leaving the building from the rear window. By climbing around on low roofs, soaked with water, we got into the Beckel Building, occupied by the Fourth National Bank, which is on the corner and just a block from where the fire started. It was very cold and there were but few of us who had wraps or overcoats. Nearly every one wore blankets taken from the Chas. Cooper Company.... The fire walls seemed to have no resistance whatever but I learned later that it traveled along the cornice from building to building and the strong wind moved it right in and flames would curl around the walls, break the windows and

■ *I [a crippled newsboy who got around on a tricycle] was awakened at 4:30 in the morning by the distress whistle of the Platt Iron Works....I then thought of my motor boat, and not having time to install the motor, I quickly tied a rope to it, and as the water raised to the second story I fastened it to the shutter while I made seats of ironing boards. My folks... and my neighbors, Mr. and Mrs. Smith, embarked. Leaving my oldest brother, Herbert, on the roof, and using brooms for paddles, my youngest brother, Walter, and I paddled up the swift current on Webster Street to the Hart Street landing.... Seeing a man and a woman on a railroad watchman's shanty, who had to swim to get there, we went to their rescue. Not far away was a woman and five children in a cottage garret. [They] crawled through the chimney to the roof and slid down to the boat....I saw a man in a tree, wet through, almost exhausted. We got him. Having a boatload we landed them in safety....We got five women, three of whom were bedridden, and five children, out of cottages, and landed them to safety. We...then pulled three women and seven children to safety.... We reached Webster Street through much difficulty and a great risk, for at one time we were washed down by the swift current onto a telegraph pole, and almost lost control of the boat. We got Herbert. On the way back we got five women and their children to safety. Going to Keowee Street again we got five women and eleven children to Hart Street landing. Walter and I were wet to the skin and chilled by this time. We... were told by a friend...to go to his house. I was carried to this place by two men, Walter tugging behind...we were unable to sleep. We could hear the cries and shouts for help, and see water, when we shut our eyes. After having a little rest we felt refreshed, but both had bad colds....Penn happened to have a girl's tricycle which enabled me to get around, as mine was in the water at home. Edgar and I went to the edge of the water to see if I could find my boat. We found it, and insisted on going in it because there were men around who didn't know how to handle a boat. We got in and went to the Webster school after two sick people who needed medical help....We got ten women and children from the flat to safety....We got eleven more from the flat to safety. We then went to Kiser Street and had to tear a roof off a house to get a woman and child out. Going across the street we got a woman and three children. Next door we got a woman and two children. We landed them all to safety. We rescued for eight hours this day until we were cold, wet and tired out.*
Dayton Daily News, *April 29, 1913*

then the suction would draw the flames in. We thought it best to move north on Jefferson Street toward the river, as we would gain higher ground by going in that direction. We left the Fourth National Bank Building, crawled over the roof of the Traction Depot, into a side entrance of a building and traveled north on the cornices to the Sims Building on the corner of the alley....The current was strong so that it was impossible for any one to swim. By means of a rope we got the women across the alley with food provisions and water. The men followed. We reached Gronewald Bindery from the window in the south side and again made our way north passing from building to building around the cornices. Where the cornices were not on a level, we stretched a rope from window to window as a hold, and where they were unusually dangerous we stretched two ropes and the women crawled between them. When we reached the Johnson Printing Company, we were able to walk with perfect ease, the cornice being wider. We passed through a printing establishment to the rear window and then by means of a ladder reached the low roofs of our buildings and entered a residence on Second Street. Of course, as we traveled from the bank building north, all the places being occupied

The Lowe Brothers Paint Store was among the buildings in the two city blocks destroyed by the raging fire which followed the flood.

and everybody wishing to reach safety, there were about seventy-five who were in this residence . . . .We had been nearly six hours and had traveled two and one-half squares."

The flames spread to residential sections as well. A man and wife were trapped on a roof with their two babies. Although the adults could jump across to another building, they were afraid to throw the children across. According to *Leslie's Illustrated Weekly*, the man rushed back through a trap-door into an upper room of the burning building, reappearing with hammer, nails and a blanket. He nailed one end of the blanket to the eaves of his roof, jumped across, nailed the other end to the opposite roof's edge and then called to his wife to roll the babies across. She did so, and he caught them in his arms. The woman jumped to safety as the flames demolished the building.

"Such a night 12, 1, 2, 3 o'clock—terrific fear—a storm raging without," wrote Katherine Kennedy Brown in her diary. "Will the rain never stop—and yet see the fires. Coal cars on the railroad are burning—the heart of Dayton seems one awful blaze. Morning—the house is cold—the smell of oil comes from downstairs. We have watched and counted the steps all night in the hall to see how the water

■ *Several of us were on the third floor of the hotel, when we saw a trolley car loaded with screaming passengers tossing about on the top of the torrent. Just after it passed us the car became wedged between an electric light pole and the Y.M.C.A. building, which is just across Third Street from the Algonquin. It looked as if everybody aboard the car would be drowned and we were powerless to help them.*

Then, suddenly, a boy jumped from a window of the Y.M.C.A. into the stream and started for the stranded conveyance.

He had a rope tied about his waist, the other end of which was made fast to the Y.M.C.A. Building. He hadn't taken more than three strokes, however, before the current caught him and threw him aside. He tried again, but got so exhausted they had to haul him back to the window.

Pretty soon another youth started on the same journey, but failed. All together five of the young men tried before the last one managed to get the rope tied to the trolley car. Then in the next two hours every person in the car climbed along the rope to the Y.M.C.A.

Joseph B. Reichmann, president, Platt Iron Works, quoted in New York Herald, *March 31, 1913*

is moving—nine steps out of water only, and so for hours. The whistles downtown are blowing every little bit. What signals are they giving? How they jar. Do they mean that the water is rising? Everyone is praying—walking the floor. The fires still rage in the distance."

Saving the city

But one company was prepared not only to salvage itself but the city as well. Monday, March 23, 1913, the N.C.R. built cash registers. On Tuesday, John H. Patterson declared the N.C.R. was out of business—or so the story goes. The business of the Cash would be to try to save a city.

Only a smoothly running organization could have even approached what occurred. Patterson clearly envisioned the calamity facing Dayton and prepared to handle all contingencies. He sent motorcycle messengers south to buy food. He ordered his woodworking shop to build boats (and coffins) and, within a few hours, some very ugly and ungainly boats were coming off the line every six or seven minutes. No handcrafted yacht ever looked as good to so many Daytonians as the 275 rowboats N.C.R. built. The factories were strewn with straw, and thousands were housed in them. A tent city on factory grounds served company employees whose homes were inundated.

Patterson told his New York employees to organize and send a train filled with relief supplies. The first train left Wednesday night, another on Thursday, a third on Friday.

The cash register works was suddenly transformed into hotel, restaurant, hospital, printing plant and whatever was needed to save lives. Salesmen, brought into the Cash for a meeting and left with nothing to do, walked the telephone wires into the city to save lives.

When the press arrived, beds and sandwiches were available; muddy clothes could be cleaned and pressed overnight without charge. Arthur Ruhl of the *Outlook*, in a superbly-written account, compared the Cash to one of those "sanitary socialistic Utopias pictured by H. G. Wells."[3]

Although there were many cases of heroic public service during the flood, Patterson was known as the man who saved Dayton. His quick thinking and his immediate concern for the prevention of disease saved hundreds of lives.

When government officials reached Dayton, they reportedly told him, "We can do nothing more than you have already done." His old enemy, James Cox, then governor of Ohio, made Patterson an Ohio colonel for his services. President Wilson offered to pardon Patterson for his antitrust conviction, but Patterson refused since he firmly believed he was innocent. Later, the government dropped the charges.

The aftermath

After four days of fire and flood, the rivers receded, leaving behind a stinking mass of mud coating the city. Dayton was a mess.

To the children, it was an event. "My brother caught two catfish in the cellar," resident Fred Stroop remembered.

But it was more serious to the adults. Martial law was administered by Brigadier General George H. Wood of the Ohio National Guard who happened to be in Dayton at the

OUT OF THE MUD: Daytonians searched for belongings (top) while militia guarded against looters (above); a horse was killed by the wreckage of the Fifth Street bridge (above right); while rescuers set up refugee camps and other safe areas (far right). At least one business, Elder & Johnston, remained open to aid in the aftermath (right).

time. He declared martial law on his own authority[4] and sent three volunteer militiamen with a telegram to Governor Cox in Columbus. Firemen Nee and Huesman made it. First Sergeant William Harris did not. On April 16—more than three weeks later—the body of Sergeant Harris was found in the mud of the canal.

"Father sent to the country and got enough hay to cover our garage floor," Katherine Talbott wrote. "Fifty to sixty militia men slept there until better quarters could be found for them."

Out-of-town correspondents invented stories of looters shot after drumhead court-martials, but no one was shot during the period of martial law. It was lifted May 6.

"Virtually the only certainty about the Dayton flood death toll is that it did not turn out to be nearly as great as was early anticipated. . . .An estimate placing the number of Gem City deaths due to the 1913 flood at 300 or more seems too high, even if based upon a calculation including all deaths in which the deluge played a major role regardless of time lapse."[5] It was probably less than 100.

But the business of cleaning up was immense. "Apr. 10—rain—rain—rain," wrote Katherine Kennedy Brown. "I go in phaeton with M'Gee behind lame horse (just recovering from two days and nights in water up to his neck and no food) to town."

"Mud, mud, MUD," Al Foose wrote in his *Memoirs*. "The water eventually left our basement, but there were about 6 inches of mud all over the floor. This I had to shovel up into buckets and toss out the basement window. . . . It was a good thing that I went back early, because I was able to take a broom and sweep out the mud while the water was still on the floor. Thus, I got rid of the mess, at least on the first floor."

"At present the city's problem is its mud," wrote Miss Marot of the Marot School. "We are buried in tons of sticky mud. I have calculated that in our house alone we have one hundred tons. In this, as in most houses, are plastered and buried dishes, silver, books, chairs, furniture. Every drawer is glued with mud, within and without. People put the hose through their pianos, onto their upholstered furniture. We ooze at every pore. The back yards are full of mud—the front yards, steps, sidewalks, streets, basements. Men wade above their knees in mud."

"The water mark upon the houses will disappear," wrote one Daytonian in her diary, "but the water mark upon the people—upon the men and women and children who survived the experience of Tues., Wed. & Thurs. of the last week in March 1913 will go to the graves with them; and yet that mark might have been deeper. Some men who have been made poor will never be rich again. Some family circles that have been broken will never be full again, but the city as a city will recover & hide her scars beneath a rebuilt city."

"The most authentic data as to the losses sustained were secured by the Dayton citizens' relief committee after a careful investigation of all interests and personal inspection of 2,164 residences in the flooded zone."[6] Total losses exceeded $73,249,000, including such items as loss to public property, public utilities, building damage, furnishings, stock and fixtures, automobiles, wages, contracts, rents and animals.

Hundreds of companies had been severely damaged by the flood. Some never recovered. Barney & Smith, already in receivership by 1913, was badly hurt. Some of its teak and mahogany lumber reportedly ended up down river in New Orleans. The company lingered on for a few years at partial capacity, and the buildings were auctioned off in 1921.

Remember the promises made in the attic

Although Patterson's health was not good (he was almost 70), he worked feverishly during the next few months. On April 20, 1913, he called a meeting to unite the Miami Valley to end the problem of flooding forever. He proposed a flood prevention fund of $2 million. The fund, a voluntary gift from those who had suffered most, was supported by the rich and the poor alike, under the slogan, "Remember the promises made in the attic." Adam Schantz Jr., son of the early brewer, gave $160,000 on behalf of the Schantz family. Twenty-three thousand Daytonians subscribed a total of $2.16 million.

An unprecedented and bitter conflict began. On the advice of Ed Hanley, a Democratic "boss" of Dayton, Deeds had

THE BOAT BUSINESS: In the flood's aftermath, N.C.R. stopped building cash registers and began building boats which served as home for many (top and center); Dorothy Patterson, John H.'s daughter, supervised a soup line at the company's kitchen (above) to feed the homeless.

NEVER AGAIN: Daytonians pledged $2.16 million to end the flooding of their city (below); it led to the Ohio Conservancy Law. The Dorothy Jean, a conservancy district steamboat (above), floated in the Great Miami River carrying crew and, apparently, a few sightseers.

already acquired the services of Arthur Morgan, one of the country's leading flood control engineers.

Deeds and Morgan asked John A. McMahon to prepare the legal portion of a complex piece of legislation for the Ohio legislature. The Ohio Conservancy Law was introduced into the Ohio legislature by Representative Victor Vonderheide of Dayton on January 16, 1914. On February 17, Governor Cox signed the act.

But there were serious problems.

In order to prevent flooding, Morgan had called for the creation of large dams on the rivers merging near Dayton. The bulk of those who would suffer from the flood control project were the people least likely to be flooded.

Farmers, whose land would be flooded by the dams, were violent. One who promised to kill Deeds was visited by the Dayton industrialist and converted to the cause of conservation.[7] To dramatize the creation of the conservancy district, Deeds contributed a handsome building on East Monument Street. The first floor was to contain historic exhibits of the flood and the conservancy. (Although part of the first floor has been converted to business, much remains exactly as Deeds intended it, a museum open to the public.)

The plan involved the building of five earthen dams: one north of Piqua at Lockington on the Miami, a second at Taylorsville near Vandalia on the Miami, a third at Englewood on the Stillwater, Huffman Dam on the Mad River near Dayton and Germantown Dam on Twin Creek south of Dayton.

There were also railway relocations and river channel improvements in Piqua, Troy, Tippecanoe City (now Tipp City), Dayton, West Carrollton, Miamisburg, Franklin, Middletown and Hamilton.

The flood had come early in 1913, and it was late in 1917 when more than $24 million in 5.5 percent bonds were sold

Five dams were needed to halt the flooding — one at Taylorsville, shown (above) under construction in 1921.

to finance the project. On January 27, 1918, construction began. Finally, in 1919, the last major legal obstacle was overcome by a Supreme Court ruling.

More than 70,000 properties along 110 miles of river frontage were assessed for the improvements. Only 2,000 appealed, and perhaps 150 cases went to trial. The assessments approved in August 1917 totalled almost $28 million. The people and companies lived up to their commitments. Even in the Depression, the delinquency rate was only three percent.[8]

The project was completed a year ahead of schedule in the summer of 1922. There have been minor floods in the area since, mostly in the low lands north of Dayton near El Dorado. Some flooding occurs south of town as well, but Dayton has *not* had a disastrous flood since 1913.

CHAPTER EIGHT

BUILDING A CITY

A small group gathered to show off the Dayton Public Library book wagon in 1923.

ohn Patterson had determined that Dayton should be a better city even before the flood. What he wanted was a city free—at least on the surface—of politics.

In September 1912, Ohio voters agreed on the "Home Rule" amendment, which allowed the cities of Ohio to choose their own form of city government. Although designed to be nonpolitical in nature, it was clearly political—Republicans favored the new plans; Democrats and Socialists opposed them.

Although Dayton was primarily a Democratic town and the Socialists were strong in 1912, the Republicans won. The Republicans put up Patterson, Deeds, Rike-Kumler's president, Frederick Rike, and two lawyers, Leopold Rauh and E. C. Harley. The N.C.R.-trained leaders of industry utilized all their techniques of salesmanship to convince the city. (By an overwhelming majority, the electorate of Dayton today still prefer the somewhat autocratic city manager form of government to the "strong mayor" government.)

The Republican citizens' Committee of Five was expanded to a Committee of 100. From this group, fifteen were chosen to run in the election of May 20, 1913. The goals of the committee were simple, and the citizens' committee led by Patterson won. They formulated a plan of city government

which was overwhelmingly approved.

The plan called for the election of five city commissioners at large. (The Democrats wanted more commissioners, elected by district.) The five commissioners were to choose and hire a city manager.[1]

The idea that such a campaign was nonpolitical was a joke. It was the citizens' committee versus "Boss Hanley's" Democrats and the Socialists[2] (the same boss Hanley who loyally supported the conservancy district).

In the election of November 1913, five city commissioners were chosen. George W. Shroyer (with the most votes) became mayor. The other members were A. I. Mendenhall, John McGee, John R. Flotron and J. M. Switzer. They selected Cincinnati's city engineer, Henry M. Waite, to be Dayton's first city manager.

What Dayton did was to adopt a professional and business-like concept of city government. A city manager would be responsible for day-to-day operation of the government, much as a general manager is responsible for the daily maintenance of a business. Des Moines and Houston had formerly adopted this form of government. While it has proved generally free from politics, it does have flaws. Since the commission members and the mayor are "part-time," only a wealthy person or a person subsidized by an employer

Dayton adopted a businesslike form of government when it named Henry M. Waite (inset) as its first city manager.

can perform the job and still support a family. But the system has worked surprisingly well.

Dayton's first city manager, Henry Waite, was both vigorous and effective. He held open meetings, was easily accessible to all, established parks Daytonians still enjoy today and set up the beginnings of sound, businesslike government which made Dayton a model city during the 1910s.[3]

Dayton goes to war

In 1914, when Europe went to war, Dayton's estimated population was 123,794. But the number of people with one or both parents born in foreign countries or born out of the country themselves was very high—about 39,400. Of the five newspapers in town, two were German. The 1910 census showed that Dayton's largest foreign populations were German, Hungarian and Russian. The large number of Germans played an important role in Dayton's war efforts when America entered the conflict on April 6, 1917.

Many Daytonians adopted an exceptionally vocal peace stance before U.S. entry into the war, and local Germans purchased German war bonds. A modest effort, largely in the churches, attempted to boost patriotic fervor as America's involvement in the war became inevitable.

Dayton was called the "city of a thousand factories." Although there actually were less than 600, Dayton was a powerful industrial town. The auto industry augmented railway cars, cash registers and a host of metal-working firms.

Probably because of the Cash, and the related industries which had been built up to support and augment it, Dayton offered high technology for the day. Working men could handle close tolerances with ease. Management was efficient, and both cost and quality control were integral to city industries.

The Miami Skating Rink, on Main Street between First and Second, served as a recruiting station at the start of World War I.

The Old World comes to the New

■ *Dayton's industry attracted hundreds of immigrants from foreign countries, according to a 1917 report by Alice M. Doren, secretary of the YWCA immigration and foreign community department.*

Moskowitz's Hungarian Colony in North Dayton housed 500 to 600 Hungarians and 100 Rumanians. To the west of the colony lived five-sixths of the Poles, two-thirds of the Bohemians and Lithuanians and most of the Dutch, Greeks, Italians, Turks, Croatians, Bulgarians, Russians and Serbs.

In West Dayton, west of Broadway and north of Third Street were 6,000 immigrants. Two to three thousand were Hungarians. There were also Rumanians, Poles, Greeks, Macedonians, Serbs, Croatians, Bulgarians, Turks and Russians.

In East Dayton, on East Monument, East First, Second and Third streets were more nationalities, most of them Catholic.

The Russian Jews congregated in South Dayton east of Brown Street in the neighborhood of Wyoming Street and Wayne Avenue where two Orthodox synagogues were located. Most of the 4,500 Jews had arrived before 1912.

A small colony of Syrians lived at South Brown and Hickory. Edgemont housed a small colony of Austrians and some Italians; but for the most part, Italians were scattered throughout the town.

Foreign students made up only about four percent of school enrollment—low considering the large total numbers—only 716 in grades one through twelve.

The library tried to accommodate the variety of languages. One-sixteenth of the library's 85,000 volumes— 5,200 books and periodicals—were in twenty languages other than English.

WARPLANES: Before America entered World War I, the Dayton Wright Airplane Company sought contracts with Europeans. Ship No. 1000 (below) as it appeared ready to "take off" for France; factory workers (bottom left) formed a pool of skilled labor second to none; a woman sewed fabric for the plane's frame (center); and a plane in its actual takeoff state, dismantled and crated for transport by sea (right).

When contracts came, employment rose dramatically.
Pratt Iron Works employed more than 450 people before the
summer of 1917. By November of 1918, 2,500 were on
the payroll.[4]

Early in 1917, the patriotic youth of Dayton tried to enlist.
In just thirteen days, the army enlisted 346 men, but it was the
draft which provided the bulk of Dayton's contribution.
In spite of parades and churchly admonitions, most Daytonians
did not rush forward. Blacks in Dayton did. By 1915,
blacks were probably second only to Germans as the city's
largest minority group. They formed Company C of the Ninth
Battalion, Ohio National Guard.

The elite of Dayton formed a military unit at the Engineers'
Club and became Battery D, Second Battalion, 134th Field
Artillery, 62nd Field Artillery Brigade, 37th Division. They
reported for duty at Triangle Park on July 15, 1917. (The
bridge that crosses Stillwater River at that point is the
Battery D Memorial Bridge.) Members of Battery D did not
distinguish themselves in action upon their arrival in France
almost exactly one year later. They did not suffer a single
battle fatality. Two men were killed when a round exploded
prematurely; the only other death was caused by lightning
before Battery D left for Europe. They were, however, in
action, and their *esprit de corps* was remarkable. A French
officer commented on the 134th, "I marvel at the combative
spirit of this regiment. Are all American regiments like this?"
The group did have the chutzpah to publish a book of their
military adventures called *Cease Firing*. Soldiers in World
War I were more polite than those following. They called
complaining about the army "crabbing."

Perhaps 1,500 Daytonians volunteered for service, and about
5,000 men were drafted. Many saw front-line action. St. Mary's
Institute (today the University of Dayton) had an active
ROTC program, and at least 519 served in the war. Thirteen
were killed.

But dodging the draft was rampant even though the papers
carried lists of the guilty. A surprise raid (mostly at "saloons,
cabarets, poolrooms, depots, amusement parks, theatres

MARCHING HOME: Dayton's boys returned home in style with a Main
Street parade (above); a group of doughboys from Battery D show their
delight in the war's end (below right); and a view of McCook Field in 1920
(right).

and other public places")[5] netted 1,100 men without registra-
tion cards. There were incidents in Dayton which could
have been acts of sabotage. Within three weeks, the Dayton
Glove Factory, Coca Cola, the Victory Theatre and the
Dayton Fan and Motor Company all burned. An employee of
Dayton Wright Airplane Company was arrested for stealing
airplane plans. A trunk loaded with dynamite and cartridges
was found in Union Station.[6] Anti-German feelings forced
the end of German schools.[7]

The winter of 1917–1918 was a bitter one, with January's
mean temperature only 15 degrees. Coal was scarce, and
some businesses and schools closed. Dayton led the state in
the theft of coal.

When the United States went to war, the nation needed a
man to coordinate the procurement of military aircraft.
The choice was Edward Deeds who took the job in August 1917.

A year earlier, Deeds had formed the Dayton Wright
Airplane Company with Kettering and the two Talbotts, father
and son. The senior H. E. Talbott was a pioneer engineer
known for his bridges. He and his wife spent months crossing
the frozen wastes of the Canadian tundra building railroad
bridges. In Dayton, he built the Main Street bridge which
had withstood all that the converging Miami and Mad rivers
could bring against it.

Deeds may have built the first private landing field in the
United States at Moraine Farm south of town. Orville
Wright contributed his name and his experimental expertise
to the company. Formed before America's entrance into

WWIV1

■ *Kettering worked on a secret weapon during World War I, an aerial torpedo. For security reasons, the project was called "the bug." The bug was a cheap aerial flying bomb designed to be built of non-vital materials. The 40-horsepower engine was made mostly of cast iron, the fuselage of plywood and the control surfaces of muslin and brown wrapping paper. The weapon was a simple one. A small railway track and a retrievable carriage launched the flying bomb. An "airlog," a small rotating vane which drove a subtracting counter (shades of the cash register!) counted off the miles. When the pre-set number of miles was counted down to zero, the engine was cut off, the bug went into a dive which tore off its wings, and the bomb crashed and was detonated. If this sounds familiar, it is because Kettering's bug was a crude predecessor of the V1 buzz bomb of World War II.*

The first test of the bug was a comedy of errors. On the evening of October 1, 1918, the bug was readied. But a mechanic who noticed that the airlog was turning in the winds decided that its unwinding would curtail the flight prematurely and tied the counting mechanism down with his handkerchief.

At 5:15, the engine was started and warmed up. The bug took off but climbed far too swiftly. It stalled and came within six feet of crashing. Then it took off and began to climb in wider and higher, then still wider and higher, circles. Kettering must have wondered why the bug did not crash as it was supposed to do almost at once. At 10,000 feet of altitude the test crew lost the bug.

It was almost midnight when a farmer near Xenia complained that a plane had crashed in his fields. The story goes that Kettering told the farmer the bug's "pilot" had bailed out; and he even got one of his staff (fortunately dressed in flight gear) to pretend to be the unlucky flyer.

Despite the somewhat tainted inaugural flight, later tests proved the bug to be a potentially successful weapon, and 20,000 were ordered. An assembly line at "South Field," Moraine, was set up and MIT students were trained to launch the bugs. The Armistice ended the need for the bug, but similar devices were tested throughout the '20s and '30s. Apparently, just as Europe went to war in 1939, the U.S. decided against pilotless bombers, and the buzz bomb became a German, not American, weapon of war.

---

the war, the company sought—and obtained—contracts with the warring powers of Europe, especially Russia, as did many other industrial companies in Dayton.

In Washington, Deeds (by then an Army colonel) immediately set up Dayton as an aviation center. He ordered the Dayton Wright Aviation Company to produce the "warplanes" America needed. The United States authorized over $1 billion for aircraft, including the Liberty engine, which was to be built by auto makers in Detroit.

The plane the United States had chosen to build was the De Havilland 4. Its friends described it as a bomber or observation craft; its enemies called it a "flying coffin" because of an exposed fuel tank in front of the pilot. It was certainly not up to European combat standards.

But the United States and its allies had agreed that the United States would build training, not combat, aircraft. And although fewer got to the front than desired, the aircraft did perform well as a trainer. The Liberty engine saw little real action in the war, but was an excellent creation and performed brilliantly in the 1920s. Liberty engines were used in the first trans-Atlantic flight and the first flight around the world. The Delco ignition proved itself thoroughly reliable.

During the war, at the instigation of Gutzon Borglum, a prominent sculptor (later he would sculpt the presidential statues on Mount Rushmore), an investigation was made of Deeds and U.S. aircraft production. President Wilson asked Justice Charles E. Hughes—the man Wilson had defeated in the 1916 presidential election—to head the investigation. "The evidence with respect to Colonel Edward A. Deeds,"

Hughes recommended, "should be presented to the Secretary of War to the end that Colonel Deeds may be tried by court-martial."[8]

The charges against Deeds were—in part—that he owned stock in the Wright Airplane Company, that he sent the Talbotts confidential information useful to the company and that the company profited excessively. Although the Attorney General agreed with the recommendation of the Hughes report, new hearings produced a report exonerating Deeds; and the Colonel was honored, rather than court-martialed. Deeds had divested himself of interest in the company by giving his shares to his wife (a practice neither uncommon nor illegal in those days). His telegrams to the Talbotts are ambiguous, rather than damning, and while the profits and salaries—for both Talbotts and Kettering— were high, they were certainly not unprecedented. It is also fair to add that sculptor Borglum had an axe to grind. His unconventional aircraft design—the fish—had been turned down by the government. Borglum, an enthusiastic KKK member, was obsessed with the idea that Deeds was really a German agent.

The relative failure of American aviation in the war was a combination of American technology lagging behind Europe and the relatively short period America was at war. The aircraft board, the Dayton aviation industries and the Detroit automobile firms created a highly technical working industry in less than one year. Yet development of a successful aircraft takes time (as World War II would prove).

Dayton industry generally performed honorably and well during the war. The Cash cut cash register production 75

percent and proceeded to supply the war effort with aviation parts, tripods and fuses. The Davis Sewing Machine Company made fuses, bicycles and sewing machines for the U.S. Balloon Corps. At the close of the war, Dayton was well on its way to becoming a tank manufacturing center, courtesy of the Maxwell Motor Car Company.

At the end of the war, Dayton boasted McCook Field (the first inner-city airport in the United States), production facilities second to none, a tie-in with automobile manufacturers and a pool of skilled labor.

This, and the large influx of both blacks and Appalachians during the period, set the stage for modern Dayton.

Ohio runs for president

The youngest of seven children, James Cox was born in Warren County in 1870 and moved to Middletown at the age of 15 to continue his schooling.
He became the Middletown correspondent for the *Cincinnati Enquirer*. Once, when a train wreck occurred, Cox

COX FOR PRESIDENT: A Main Street parade (above) celebrated the nomination of former Dayton newspaper publisher Gov. James M. Cox as the Democratic presidential candidate; his running mate was Franklin D. Roosevelt (below), but the pair lost to another Ohioan, Warren G. Harding.

PEACE ~ PROGRESS ~ PROSPERITY

FOR PRESIDENT
DEMOCRATIC NOMINEE
JAMES M. COX

FOR VICE PRESIDENT
DEMOCRATIC NOMINEE
FRANKLIN D. ROOSEVELT

1920s Potpourri—Dayton Daily News

1920   *No unsolved murders for an entire year.*

1921   *Maxwell car production not expected to reach 300 or 400 a day for some time.*

A charity drive nets a quarter of a million dollars; John H. Patterson gives $137,500. He has already given Hill and Dales Park to Dayton and helped found the Community Golf Course. (Patterson claims a working man needs a golf course more than his employer.) Mrs. H. G. Carnell (Frank Patterson's widow) is another major contributor.

Colonel H. E. Talbott dies on a Miami, Florida, golf course.

Arthur Morgan leaves the Conservancy District job.

Dr. Franklin I. Schroyer uses radium for the first time in Dayton as a treatment for cancer.

1922   *May 7. An era ends when John H. Patterson dies. One hundred ninety-two stills are confiscated in 1,165 raids.*

1923   *January 3. Dayton bans Fatty Arbuckle movies.*

A helicopter is successfully tested at McCook Field.

A new flight endurance record is set at McCook Field by John Macready and Oakley Kelly.

June 20. Eugene V. Debs speaks at Memorial Hall. The socialists are a major force in Dayton politics for a brief time, even contributing a socialist history, Biography of Dayton, *by Joseph W. Sharts.*

November 25. The Dayton Daily News *publishes purportedly the largest paper ever printed in the United States—twenty sections, 256 pages. Radio listings are a major part of the newspaper.*

1925   *March 2. A con man posing as a U.S. inspector is royally entertained at the Soldiers' Home.*

Barney & Smith's properties are sold for $452,761.61. (Six of their buildings still stand, just off East Monument Street.)

William Stroop, tobacco farmer and merchant, and John Kirby of the Employers' Association die.

1926   *January 18. Frederick B. Patterson explains a complex stock option to N.C.R. employees. If N.C.R. makes three dollars per share, the company will remain in the hands of the Patterson family. If not, the command passes to those who own the stock.*

April 10. John Macready fails to set an altitude record and resigns. He is replaced by Lieutenant James Doolittle. Three days later, ground is broken for the new Wright Air Field.

May. Workmen start to tear down the Phillips Hotel.

June. Construction begins on a $20-million Delco-Light plant.

Early Dayton boasted several auto firms, including the Dayton Motor Co. which produced the Stoddard-Dayton, shown (above) in 1910.

1927   *February 1. Aimee Semple McPherson visits Dayton. A month later, Dayton bans Sunday dancing.*

May. Daytonians subscribe more than $20,000 to Mississippi flood relief.

June 22. Charles Lindbergh, fresh from his triumphant trans-Atlantic fight, is guest of Orville Wright in Dayton.

September. A $100,000 fire at the Dayton Country Club kills many polo ponies.

October 1. Fredrick Ohmer dies. The Ohmer Fare Register Company which manufactures fare recording registers for street cars and interurbans was founded in 1849.

October 2. The cornerstone for the University of Dayton Library is laid.

Three million dollars is given to Antioch College in nearby Yellow Springs by Charles Kettering. Kettering, the once-poor farm boy, especially appreciated the cooperative system at Antioch where a student worked one semester then went to school the next.

■ *A number of automobile firms were located in early Dayton. Nearby towns also produced automobiles, most notably the Westcott (manufactured in Richmond, Indiana, and Springfield) which lasted from 1897 to 1925.*
Unfortunately, Dayton's attempts did not last long, and the industry drove on up to Detroit.

One Dayton car, the Custer, ran on electricity, and two youngsters tried out a pint-sized model in 1927.

Automobile	approx. year begun	approx. year ended	Manufacturer
Thresher (electric)	1900	1900	Thresher Electric Co.
Stoddard-Dayton	1904	1912–13	Dayton Motor Car Co.
Speedwell	1907	1914–15	Speedwell Motor Car Co.
Courier	1909	1910	Courier Car Co.
Stoddard 20	1911	?	Dayton Motor Car Co.
Stoddard Knight	1911	?	Dayton Motor Car Co.
Dayton (electric)	1911–12	1915	Dayton Electric Car Co.
Mead	1912	1912	?
?	1914	1918	Dayton Motor Truck Co.
Arrow	1914	1914	M. C. Whitmore
Darling	1915	1918	Darling Motor Car Co.
Apple	1915	1917	Apple Automobile Co.
Custer (electric)	1915	1921	Custer Specialty Co.
Spencer	1921	1922	Research Engineering Co.

ran to the telegraph office and handed the operator an old newspaper to transmit, tying up the lines until he finished his report. Then he had his story transmitted, and the *Enquirer* got a scoop. Soon the man who was called by a colleague "the best reporter and the worst writer in southwestern Ohio" was working full time for the paper in Cincinnati.[9]

Cox went to Washington to serve as private secretary to Paul Sorg, the Middletown millionaire who had won a special election in 1894 succeeding George Hauk, who had died suddenly. Cox enjoyed politics, but he also enjoyed journalism. With a loan from Sorg, the 28-year-old Cox returned to Ohio and bought the failing *Dayton Daily News* for $26,000. At that time, there were three afternoon newspapers in Dayton, but the *Cincinnati Post*'s Dayton circulation exceeded all local papers combined. Cox soon purchased a Springfield paper as well.

In 1908, Cox ran for the U.S. House of Representatives. No one believed he had much of a chance. But a scandal against his major opponent made Cox an easy victor. He served two terms competently but without particular distinction.

In 1912, Cox ran for governor and won. Cox was a progressive. From 1912 to 1914, he supported consolidated schools, prison reforms and—after Dayton's flood—the Conservancy District. All were unpopular. Even when he was told the Conservancy would defeat him, he continued to promote it vigorously without flinching. He was defeated, but he bided his time and was reelected governor in 1916. A third term in 1918 made him a national figure in Democratic politics, in spite of strongly anti-Cox sentiment among the German voters of Ohio. (Cox had believed in eliminating German schools in Ohio. Although the U.S. Supreme Court disallowed Ohio law forbidding German schools, bilingual education in Ohio was effectively terminated.)

In 1920, Cox sought to follow Woodrow Wilson as president. On the first ballot at the San Francisco Democratic convention, Cox had 134 votes, third among 22 candidates. The leading candidate was William C. McAdoo. By the twelfth ballot, Cox surpassed McAdoo. The lead swung back and forth, but on the 44th, Cox was nominated. His

running mate was Franklin D. Roosevelt.

Cox's opponent, Warren G. Harding, campaigned by sitting on his front porch in Marion, Ohio, while Cox stumped the country. No Democrat could have won in 1920. The country was tired of Democrats, tired of Wilson's "internationalism" and afraid of the League of Nations. It elected Harding, also an Ohio newspaper publisher, by an overwhelming majority. Even Montgomery County went for Harding by a convincing 46,493 to 38,433 vote.

Cox purchased newspapers in Florida and Atlanta and began an empire of radio—and later television—stations, which included WHIO, WHIO-FM and WHIO-TV.

In 1932, Roosevelt succeeded where Cox had failed.

Cox died in Dayton on July 15, 1957, at the age of 87. His autobiography dwells at length on one achievement of which the usually modest Cox was inordinately proud. It had nothing to do with political victories, social reforms or business successes. He made the first eagle ever on the fourteenth hole of the LaGorce golf course in Miami Beach on March 8, 1932.

Dayton is a GM town

Early in 1918, Dayton had more than 400 industries. Machinery and castings was the largest group, dominated by the huge Platt Iron Works, one of the country's leading producers of munitions. During the war, Dayton produced seven types of aerial bombs varying from twenty pounds to two tons. There were 125 such machinery firms, including Dayton Malleable, already 52 years old at the time. Reynolds and Reynolds, also founded in 1866, was the oldest among the 47 paper and printing firms. City firms employed 45,000 people, and at least 25 percent were women.

The 1920s started badly. Gearing up to fuel the flames of war left overbuilt industries and more workers than the peacetime economy could absorb.

The Fifth Street market (above) in 1926, and the Third Street market (below) in 1920.

TRIANGLES 1919

STANDING: STORCK, MGR. ROUDEBUSH -REESE - AL.CLARK - WINSTON -THIELE -CUTLER-STOECHLEIN -HOUSER - DELLINGER - PARTLOW - TALBOTT, COACH
SITTING: ON - YERGES - ABRELL - MAHRT, CAPTAIN - FENNER - KINDERDINE - TIDD

TRIANGLES	51	TIGLES	14	TRIANGLES	0	TRIANGLES	0
NORDYKE-MARMON	0	CLAND PANTHERS	19	PANHANDLES	6	MASSILLON	0
TRIANGLES	28	TIGLES	26	TRIANGLES	20	TRIANGLES	21
PITCAIRN QUAKERS	0	CII CELTS	0	PINE VILLAGE	0	PANHANDLES	0

Scummy Says Slingin' Sammy Second

■ In 1916, the Triangles started playing professional football in Dayton. According to Si Burick, Dayton's nationally-known sports writer, the Dayton Triangles were charter members of the original professional football league in the United States—the American Professional Football Association. When it was formed in 1919, the cost to join the league was a whopping $25, and the teams included Akron, Canton, Columbus, Dayton and Rochester. The keys to the Triangles' early success were two men—the manager, Carl "Scummy" Storck, who would later become president of the National Football League, and the team's quarterback, Al Mahrt, whom Storck believed was better than Slingin' Sammy Baugh, early football's most famous passing quarterback.

Mahrt, who had been—somewhat prematurely— declared dead in the 1913 flood, was an all-around athlete. In 1914, he completed a 70-yard touchdown pass for the University of Dayton—a record which lasted 45

years. But his brother Lou, who played for the Triangles in 1926 and 1927, surpassed that. Lou Mahrt (practicing law today in Dayton) achieved a world record of 72 yards (62 from scrimmage). "But," says Lou, "my passes were long, high arcs. There was always a crowd waiting for the ball. Al's passes were 'rifles'—they nearly knocked down the receivers." Al left football to become an important executive for Mead Paper in Chillicothe, Ohio.

The team, somehow, missed being a part of the NFL, formed in 1922, but the Triangles survived as a pro team until 1929.

It may have been the Depression that did in the Triangles, or perhaps their 1929 record—0–6.

What did a player make on the Triangles' team? Superstar Al made about $150 a game in the team's earlier years. Brother Lou made $300 (most team members made $100 to $200), but Lou had to perform as coach, captain and quarterback.

Two major technological advances were the talk of the town. One was radio, whose major impact was felt in the middle of the decade. The other was the automobile.

The auto industry wanted Kettering, the innovative genius who had made the automobile a reliable means of mass transportation. They got him. June 1, 1916, the "Barn Gang" was bought out by United Motors Corporation (later GM) for $9 million.[10]

After the flood, Delco became a major industry. Delco begat Delco-Light, an important, if short-lived, industry. Kettering had once promised his mother an electrically-powered home, and he invented the electric generator which Delco-Light produced. By raising expectations of rural customers on isolated American farms, the company increased the demand for rural electrification. But the 1921 depression was especially hard on farmers (prime market for Delco-Light), and rural electrification eventually put Delco-Light out of business. Its sales manager, Richard H. Grant, an ex-N.C.R. executive, would later prove vital to both GM and Dayton.

By 1920, GM was struggling to stay alive. Sales had slumped badly from about nineteen percent of the market in 1909 to nine percent in 1916. Although the share of market

CARS AND MORE: Dayton bombed as an auto producer (above), but still found itself a place in the auto industry, helping to bolster General Motors subsidiaries such as Frigidaire (below).

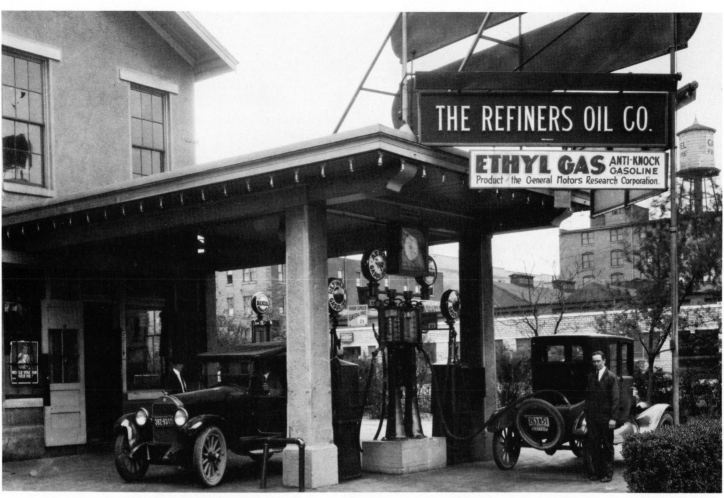

FOR LOVE OF WHEELS: Like all America, Dayton loved the automobile. The Refiner's Oil Company sold America's first gallon of ethyl gas in 1923 to a Dayton motorist at a Sixth and Main street station (above). Ethyl was developed for Kettering by the hard-working chemist, Thomas Midgley. The first open-air parking lot was adjacent to the Fourth Street bus station (below).

ROARING '20s: Dayton enjoyed itself during the post-war era at the 1924 Fourth of July regatta at Island Park.

He brought the world 3-D

Andrew Sheets Iddings

■ *Andrew Sheets Iddings, born October 18, 1880, was named after his grandfather, Dr. Andrew Sheets, an eccentric inventor-dentist, whose "Sheet's Writing Fluid" (a bottled India ink) was packaged and sold from his dental office.*

Members of the Iddings family had been lawyers in Dayton since 1804. Andrew and his brother Daniel continued that tradition. Although an excellent lawyer, Andrew is better known for his vacations.

Iddings was an explorer—more importantly, he was an explorer-photographer. Beginning his travels in 1891, he soon had a reputation for quality pictures and interesting narratives.

In 1908, Iddings was hired by the Keystone View Company to be chief of photographic staff. For eleven years, he traveled all over the world taking thousands of glass plate stereographic negatives which he carefully waterproofed, packed and shipped to Keystone.

The paraphernalia he lugged was awesome—a six-foot wooden tripod, a cumbersome Folmer & Swing stereoscopic camera, an extra set of wide-angle lenses and plenty of glass plates. Six double plate-holders enabled him to make twelve photographs per case. Each case had to be protected against damage. Iddings' greatest difficulty was changing plates in the holders. He was always housed in the royal suite of the city's best hotels— with no darkroom. *"He would either change plates lying on the floor underneath all the bedding, writing a consecutive number on each one, or in a standing position in a portable wardrobe with the door closed."*[14]

In 1912, the National Geographic *carried a series by Iddings on the Balkans. In June and July 1916, The* Journal *ran "Our Neighbors in South America" as its Sunday feature. In 1919, soon after the armistice, Iddings was sent overseas by the U.S. government to photograph the postwar devastation. Many of his photographs became the first audiovisual material used in America's classrooms.*

Although his association with Keystone ended as he became more involved in law, Iddings continued to travel regularly. In 1951, at the age of 71, he went on a six-month photographic safari in Africa. Film taken on that trip was shown to the prestigious Explorers' Club. (He had been a member since 1912 and continued until his death.)

Iddings never married. Eccentric in his latter years, he was always willing to talk of his exploring. After he died on May 14, 1974, hundreds of priceless glass negatives were found in his attic and donated to Wright State University. They included photos of the Wright brothers' homecoming parade taken in 1909.

increased slightly, GM was on the verge of financial collapse by the end of 1920. But moves had already been made to get the company going again by hiring Kettering and Grant.

Frigidaire, acquired by GM in 1919, was dumped into Grant's organization. Kelvinator dominated the market, and Frigidaire was simply a bad product (with worse distribution) that nobody wanted in a time of serious economic depression. Within four years—by the time Grant left Dayton for Detroit—Frigidaire dominated the appliance industry. Grant's new assignment was GM's other weak sister, another poor product with bad distribution that nobody wanted. Its name was Chevrolet. It had joined the company in 1918. In 1924, Ford outsold Chevrolet more than four to one. By 1928, Chevrolet sold 65 percent more than Ford.

In 1923, GM founded Inland Manufacturing which had evolved from the Dayton Wright Airplane Company. Its basic product was steering wheels, produced by laminating and curving wood in much the same way propellers and aircraft parts were formed.

That same year, Moraine Products Division was formed to manufacture Durex bearings. In a space of about four years, Dayton had the nucleus of Delco Products, Delco Moraine, Frigidaire and Inland. Dayton was a GM city.

The white sheets of Dayton

By 1921, Americans were worried about their jobs. America became more provincial. U.S. immigration laws were tightened, severely restricting the influx of foreigners, many of whom were eastern European Catholics. There were "Red scares," and the country seemed in a state of uneasy and constant change.

The Ku Klux Klan offered solidity. According to a speech in nearby Ada, Ohio in 1923, the Klan upheld "Christian teachings, white supremacy, protection of pure womanhood, just law and liberty, closer relationships of pure Americanism, upholding of the states-rights, separation of church and state, freedom of speech and press, closer relationships between capital and American labor, preventing the causes of mob violence and lynchings, preventing unwarranted strikes by foreign labor agitators, prevention of fires and property destruction by lawless elements, limitation of foreign immigration, and law and order."[11]

Jazz age local

■ No one knows how many local bands were playing regularly in Dayton during the Jazz Age. James May, local booking agent, and the Dayton chapter of the American Federation of Musicians remember at least 21—Jake Barbee, Johnny Becker, Charles Buddi, Dick Burrows, Paul Cornelius, Cliff Curtner, Harold Grenamier, Clarence Doench, Chuck Helwegan, Michael Hauer, Hugo Kies, Lonnie King, Paul Kleinke, Henry Lang and Cliff Perrine.

There was also the Harmony Four with Jack Shetterly as leader, the All Ohio Band led by Joe Sheean and two pit bands that played the local vaudeville houses— Nelson Anderson and Armand Guarrini. The Piqua band under Les Shepherd played Dayton regularly.

HOODED "KONCLAVES": Little information exists about Dayton's involvement in the Ku Klux Klan, although it was one of the nation's strongholds for the organization in the 1920s. A female gathering of the Klan (right); and Knights at a rally (below).

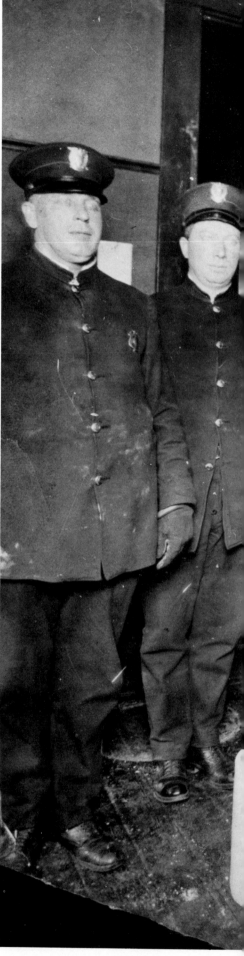

HOME BREW: Police proudly pose with a still taken in a raid during Prohibition (right); a drinking customer shortly before Prohibition went into effect (above); one victim of the law was a Dayton brewery, which also produced a non-alcoholic sparkling water (below).

Bootleg raid

■ *In 1934, the Dayton police conducted their largest liquor raid in nine years. Following a tip, they hit the house on West Second Street where "Fat" McCrosson and Lonnie Carmer had been slain the year before in a liquor war. But they found only two pints and one gallon jug in the basement. They were leaving when Michael Brayn said, "It's mine. Take me." Suspicious, the officers investigated further and found 504 gallons in the garage. Suddenly, a car drove up. The driver panicked at sight of the police and ran. The car was packed with cartons, six gallon-jugs per carton. It was the biggest haul since 1925 when someone flagged down a truck on its way to Hamilton and discovered it filled with bootleg whiskey.*

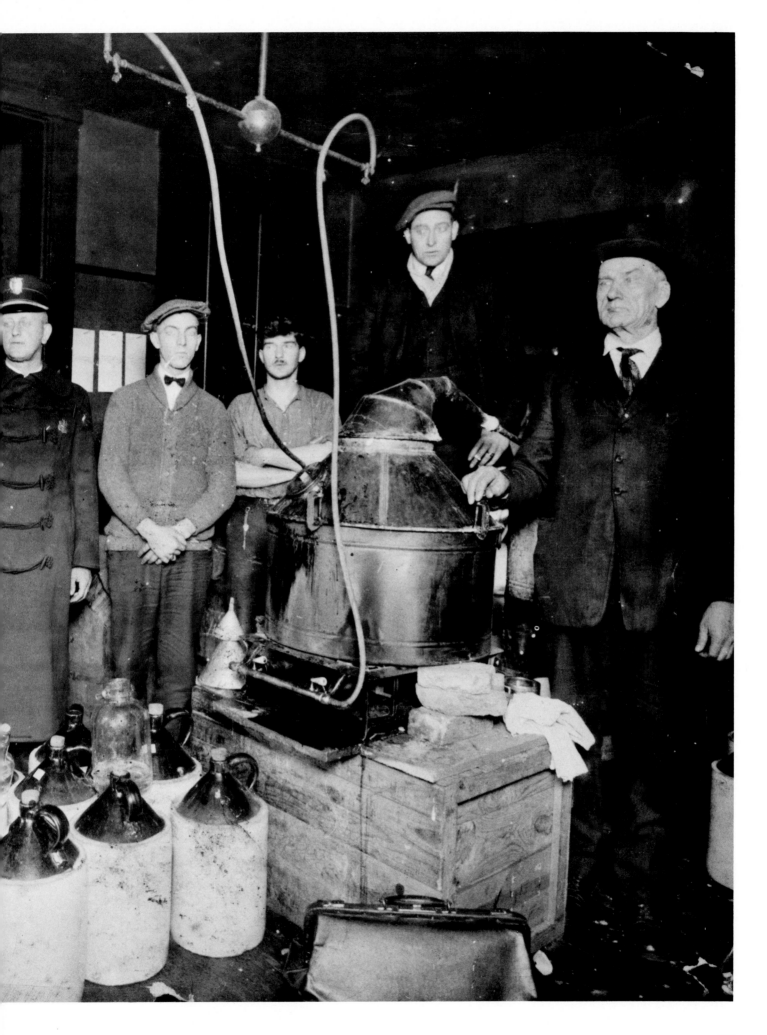

The Klan even converted ministers to its cause. Every Protestant minister in nearby Middletown (where KKK activity still exists today) was supposedly a member. By 1923, the Klan was strongly entrenched in the Dayton-Springfield area and around Columbus, perhaps with as many as 300,000 members statewide.[12]

Members were expected to support other members in business dealings. Booklets were published (in Columbus, at least) listing "approved stores." Jews, Catholics and the few blacks running businesses were excluded.

There is little information on the Klan in Dayton although it was one of the Klan's largest strongholds. On a percentage basis, Indianapolis, Dayton, Portland (Oregon), Youngstown, Denver and Dallas were said to be the "hooded" capitals of the nation. Dayton's total membership between 1915 and 1924 was estimated at 15,000. The population of Dayton in 1920 was 152,229. An official in the Montgomery County sheriff's office was a Klan member, as were some "high police officers," and at least one county commissioner. In late 1926, J. W. Richardson was head of the Montgomery County KKK.

In 1924, the board of directors debated whether or not to allow the Klan to assemble at the fairgrounds. Finally deciding that freedom to assemble was of prime importance, the board allowed the Klan to rent the facilities.

A 1926 rally had 1,500 hooded Klansmen, twelve bands and 25,000 spectators. On September 25th, the temperature dropped seventeen degrees, and it poured rain. The Klan managed to get a rebate from the fairgrounds because of the weather.[13]

But by then, the Klan was declining rapidly. There were less than 34,000 Ohio members, and a year later, less than one-tenth of that. Membership did increase briefly in 1928 to oppose Catholic Al Smith's campaign for the presidency. The Klan's effectiveness was essentially destroyed by bad money management, graft and scandals. (In Indianapolis, D. C. Stephenson, head of the Midwestern Klan, killed his mistress.)

The ridiculous, the sublime

In 1920, the United States decided to try Prohibition. There was little left to prohibit since Congress had outlawed production of anything other than beer and wine in 1917 and had lowered the alcohol content of beer to 2.75 percent early in 1918. Prohibition immediately cost the United States about a billion dollars a year—half in federal, state and local taxes. Prohibition also increased the number of criminals and police and increased graft, drinking and ingenuity. Home brew was made everywhere. An estimated 60,000 gallons of industrial alcohol were converted to synthetic liquor in 1926. The rich, of course, never suffered. An amazing number of Americans "died" in Cuba, and the returning coffins gurgled.

In 1920, there were 44 arrests for drunkenness in Dayton. In 1930, 2,525 went to the workhouse for drunkenness and for transporting liquor. One local victim of Prohibition was Adam Schantz's brewery. Long a major Dayton firm, in spite of its major money-maker, "Lily Water," a local purified water, the brewery failed in 1920.

Little is known of Dayton women before the '20s. By then, women began to play an undeniable role in the city.

Julia Shaw Patterson Carnell believed the city needed an art museum. She helped open one at St. Clair and Monument streets in 1920, with a grand total of three permanent exhibits. In 1927, she offered Dayton a beautiful building to house the art treasures. The Art Institute, in Italian villa style, was begun in 1927, finished in 1930. Julia Carnell paid all the operating deficits of the institute until her death in 1944.

Julia Carnell provided Dayton with its Italian villa Art Institute and paid its operating deficits until her death in 1944.

CHAPTER NINE

THE GREAT DEPRESSION

WPA workers rebuild Decker Street in a 1934 project.

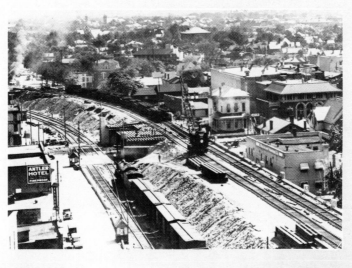

599

Despite Black Friday, Dayton completed the elevation of its railroad tracks to move passengers and freight more easily (left), although there was soon not much to move. The B&O passenger train was the last to pass on the ground-level tracks (below) in 1931.

In 1929, Dayton saw itself as the center of the United States, a typical fast-growing manufacturing community with plenty of money to spend. The population was about to exceed 200,000, and the urban population center of the United States was located within 34 miles of Dayton. Greater Dayton had 521 manufacturing establishments employing 50,446 people at total annual wages of nearly $86 million. The city had the largest per capita building and loan association investment in the United States. The new Biltmore Hotel, with its opulent lobbies and adjoining garage for 300 cars, was opened on November 16, 1929.

Dayton This Week, the "official civic weekly," was chock-full of advertisements for places to go and things to do. A season membership at the Community Golf Club cost $5; and streetcar rides were only 5 cents. Membership at the club was up. Marathons of all kinds were big. There was the National Marathon and Endurance Carnival, a dance marathon at the Eagles' Auditorium on South Main Street. Dayton claimed world records for dance marathons and for radio-listening marathons.[1]

But October's Black Friday did not go unnoticed. "The stocks I held I had bought on margin," Al Foose wrote. He had been in New York City on the floor of the stock market with his broker when the crash occurred. "I had bought four or five stocks in hundred-share lots, and I watched the house of cards fall around me. . . .It was impossible to know what was happening, even right there on Wall Street, as the ticker tape was running several hours behind. I was wiped out completely. . . .It didn't do any good to cry. . .everyone was in the same boat. Anyone who was in the market at that time sustained tremendous losses. . .and we were getting into a hole, as we could not secure enough volume of business to meet expenses. . . .There were weeks when we could not meet the payroll, and it looked as though it was only a matter of time until we would have to close up shop."

Except for individuals like Al Foose, whose capital was so closely tied to the stock market, 1929 and 1930 were not so bad as they might have been. The city went ahead and finished elevating the railroad tracks to move passengers and freight more easily. The Dayton police department even took delivery on a new high-powered armored car to protect bank money deliveries.

But it was not long before there was very little to deliver to banks, and a number of banks were no longer open to accept money. The Dayton Savings and Trust closed its doors. The Mutual Building and Loan Company—one of the oldest building and loan companies in Ohio—had to close. When Dayton's largest bank, Union Trust, failed on Halloween in 1931, Dayton knew the Depression had arrived.

In 1931, the community chest fell $98,000 short of its goal, and the city budget of Dayton included $500,000 for relief. "Before 1931, the city had been carrying on various kinds and amounts of work which contributed to the health and well-being of the citizens of the community through the Welfare Department of the city; but relief had never been experienced to any large degree before."[2] By 1939, the cost of relief exceeded the total cost of operating the city government. In an attempt to find the money for relief, the city reduced personnel by eliminating the positions of safety director, legal aid attorney, the city engineer and building director.

Newspapers of the day reflected changes that became commonplace. The Junior League collected food for the needy. Frigidaire advertised a meter purchase plan—"buy a Frigidaire for 25 cents a day." The meter was attached to the refrigerator and once a month a representative came to collect. A Dayton vigilance committee was formed in January 1932 to protect banks from rumormongers. The *Dayton Daily News* ran free want ads for those seeking jobs. On New Year's Day 1932, five job openings were advertised for men, only one job for women.

Keeping active

I t could have been worse. Sports were still exciting. Bob Kepler, a Dayton boy, became the Ohio amateur golf champion by defeating another Daytonian, James Barrett ("Scotty") Reston. (Reston survived the Depression to become bureau chief for the *New York Times*.)

One of Dayton's more colorful sports teams was named after organizer and manager Howard Ebbert "Ducky" Holmes. The Dayton Ducks minor league baseball team was organized in 1931. The team managed to survive the Depression, but, like many other organizations, it was suspended in 1942 because all the players were drafted. Many Ducks players lived at the Biltmore Hotel for $1 a night and the agreement that they would be on call to help the night detective quell any disturbances. George Servis, owner of Servis Restaurant on First Street, also gave the players discounts. The Ducks soon had their own field—Ducks' Park (later Hudson Field) on West Third Street.

Holmes was a real character. "Big Quack" ran a grocery store during the off-season, but baseball had been his real love since he began as a minor league catcher in 1901. Never successful in the major leagues (five weeks with the

One of Dayton's more colorful sports teams was named after organizer and manager Howard Ebbert "Ducky" Holmes.

St. Louis Cardinals in 1906), he managed and umpired all over the Midwest until he started the Ducks. He once managed a game with hand signals from atop a light pole after being ordered out of the park. Ducky Holmes died in 1945 before the team could be re-assembled after the war.[3]

Dayton's Virginia Hollinger put Dayton on the map as a tennis city. Unseeded in 1933, she advanced to the finals of the Women's National Indoor Tournament, where she was trounced 6–1, 6–0. The next year, she came back with a vengeance and won easily, becoming the first Daytonian to make a showing in a national tennis tournament.

Sports helped Daytonians weather the Depression. In fact, parks and city recreation facilities and classes outside school were well attended. "Enforced" leisure became commonplace. Inland Manufacturing, as did many other large companies, organized teams for employees. The company also had an orchestra, and land was available for employee gardens.

The city knew only too well that gardens were needed. In 1932, 42,292 persons applied at the city-state employment service. Of that number, only 4,084 were hired. Expenditures for relief groceries alone amounted to $631,157.44. Total city relief expenditures were $672,416.63. This included clothing, shoes, stoves and furnishings. Direct relief predominated, although some departments began work relief— recipients received groceries in return for work, usually in park maintenance. The relief gardens, sponsored by the city, soon grew until they totalled 2,945 plots in 1935. That year, 200,000 pounds of green beans, 250,000 pounds of tomatoes and 95,000 pounds of turnips were harvested. Value of the gardens was estimated at $51,525.

"I almost got down on my hands and knees and begged for a basket of groceries," Charles Cross said. "But I couldn't get any help because I had my savings, even if I couldn't get to them. They'd let you have it in dribs and drabs—$5 or $10 a week. At that I was luckier than some."[4]

KEEPING BUSY: The new Central Bus Station was completed during the Depression (top); the city devised numerous projects to keep people working, including a training course for domestics sponsored by the Young Woman's League (bottom).

The Depression had its high points, such as the feats of Amelia Earhart, shown (above) with Ray Brock of WSMK.

Dayton gets help

Beginning in 1931, large tax delinquencies compounded the city's problems. In 1933, delinquent taxes amounted to $3,167,148. Collected taxes were only $2,312,676. By 1935, delinquent taxes totalled $8,762,000.[5] "No Money On Hand to Pay City Teachers Next Tuesday," was the *Dayton Daily News* headline January 19, 1932. January 30 found the library expecting to close. Tax levies failed routinely. Some bond issues were passed, enabling city government to limp along. (There were no new street lights and 600 existing bulbs and globes were removed in order to save money.) Salaries in scrip were common for government employees.

All county schools closed intermittently except the Oakwood school system. It would have closed, too, but the teachers continued to work without pay.[6]

The ends never meet

■ *Times were hard during the Depression, families were large and jobs scarce. The* Journal *for May 23, 1937, printed the budget of a family of seven children and two adults:*

Item	Monthly total
Food	$ 43.40
Milk	6.16
Rent	17.50
Gas/electricity	5.00
Furniture payment	8.76
Washer payment	5.00
Clothing	11.00
Fuel	6.00
Water	1.50
Insurance	2.00
TOTAL	$106.32

Since the father worked whenever possible, he averaged $20 a week or $80 a month. That left a deficit of $26.32 per month.

In 1930, Dayton became the second city in the United States to utilize the Federal Surplus Commodity Food Stamp Plan. For each dollar the welfare recipient spent on red stamps, the U.S. Government contributed 50 cents in blue stamps. The stamps were redeemable for surplus food.

The Civil Works Administration (CWA) initiated 45 projects in 1933, the PWA (Public Works Administration) and WPA (Works Project Administration) followed. Such work relief not only helped alleviate the massive unemployment but also provided park improvements, bridge and street repairs. The Diehl Band Shell in Island Park was a WPA project.

Johnson Flying Service at Vandalia sold its airport to Dayton, and CWA improved and added runways. The home of aviation finally had its own airport. Wiley Post left the Dayton airport July 2, 1933 on the first leg of his record-breaking round-the-world flight in his plane the "Winnie Mae" and cut 22 hours off the previous record.

Homesteading—the agrarian self-sufficiency movement—was an early '30s dream. Daytonians developed the first locally sponsored subsistence homestead community to receive federal funds. After appraising several available properties, in mid-April 1933, a local homesteading unit committee purchased the farm of Dr. Walter Shaw, a 160-acre tract four miles west of Dayton on the Dayton-Liberty Road, one-half mile south of Route 35. The original plan was to divide the farm into 35 three-acre tracts and to use the remainder for common parks, roads, pasture, tilled fields, orchards and woodlands.[7]

The members were drawn primarily from the unemployed middle class and were to become totally self-sufficient. Though "bread-winners" could continue to work in the city, weaving and other crafts were expected eventually to supplant outside income. The farmhouse on the Shaw property was remodelled, and government loans obtained.

By December 1935, there were only twelve families left. The earth, stone or cement block homes they had started were never completed. What began as a pilot project for hundreds of other homestead units across the country fizzled out despite $500,000 of government funds and ample government advice. The government of Ohio purchased the property for development as an urban living experiment.

At least three relief factories were begun in the 1930s. A garment factory in the Comer Building on Apple Street employed 50 relief workers who cut and sewed raincoats and windbreakers; the Gem City Stove Company employed 84 relief workers making cooking, heating and laundry stoves. A mattress and comfort factory, employing 34, was located at Linden and Davis streets. Output from these factories was distributed as additional relief.

By 1934, the relief situation was complex. With so many agencies involved, mix-ups did occur. In late 1934, three bachelors, each on "single" relief, pooled their living in one apartment. They soon had accumulated 542 extra cans of food which they turned over to the city. The city subsequently listed them as a family for welfare purposes. In April 1935, Charles Dixon was arrested for "fleecing people for money" to find jobs. A truck driver, he offered the unemployed jobs driving for his company. He would extract $1.50 to $4 from the individuals and then disappear. Naturally, there were no jobs.[8]

Although there were fewer unemployed white-collar workers, they also had fewer job opportunities. Some managed, as did Al Foose, on a shoestring business. "I had a number of customers in various bars throughout the city. I loaned each customer a warmer, which was placed on the bar, and it automatically maintained the heat at just the right temperature to keep the hot tamales warm. I worked

The unemployed lined the streets in 1934 outside the Montgomery County Relief Administration office, a scene photographed many times over in similar places nationwide.

at this for about a year and was making a living but not a very great amount of money. In addition to the hot tamales and chilie [*sic*], I used to buy turtle soup made by the Snell Company of Piqua. I bought this turtle soup in case lots, No. 10 tins, and sold it to various bars."[9]

There were some white-collar relief jobs—taking census for unemployment or Montgomery County schools, canvassing door-to-door describing WPA home improvement, surveying water valve locations, building property lines and sewer plans or inventorying public property. And then there were the WPA arts projects.

The fine arts come to town

Franklin D. Roosevelt established the Federal One Federal Arts Project in 1935. Locally, little mention was made of writers' projects. Harlan Hatcher, the Ohio Writers' Project director, distributed most of the writing jobs in and

One-two-three-one-two-three

■ *Generations of young Daytonians learned real dances—the two-step, the waltz, even the foxtrot. Botts Academy of Dancing had opened before the flood. They survived the '30s by reducing tuition fees by one-third. The male shortage in the '40s was difficult, but the '50s were a dance teacher's delight. White gloves were necessary for young ladies, and young gentlemen asked a lady to dance, then returned her politely to her place. Botts finally lost to urban renewal in 1957. The graceful Pollack House, home to Botts for so many years, became the Board of Elections office and was finally moved from Third Street to its present home on Monument Avenue.*[14]

around Columbus, although an index of fine arts projects was compiled in Dayton.

Seigfried Weng, director of the Dayton Art Institute from its opening in 1929, was appointed the state's art project director.

To qualify for the Treasury Relief Art Program (TRAP), an artist had to be on relief. In some areas, artists applied for relief merely to be eligible for the projects. In Dayton, there was only one case where the rules may have been bent a little. Max Seifert, a retired Dayton art teacher, lost his life savings of $8,000 in the crash. He was employed to do a series of easel panels of Montgomery County trees. "The paintings gave comfort and pride to the closing days for a fine old couple," wrote Weng. "Perhaps we made the little job last a little longer than its tangible results merited? I don't think so."[10] Nineteen local artists completed pictorial maps for Dayton schools, murals at Dunbar, Greenville and Oakwood high schools, fountains and pools, wood carvings, lithographs and easel paintings. Robert Koepnick, dean of area artists, had three sculptures in the TRAP project. He was among the ten percent of non-relief artists hired by TRAP. The weekly wages began at $55 (unskilled worker) and went up to $94 for a professional. The artist furnished his own materials, although the Dayton Art Institute did provide studio space.

The music project was patterned under the same rules as the art project. The Dayton committee held open auditions for the WPA orchestra. Conductor Alfred Hein led the orchestra in "more than 600 music-appreciation concerts in the public, parochial, and township schools to an audience of 50,000 school children and parents."[11] Summer concerts in the parks were also initiated. A dance group of "all colored musicians"[12] was directed by Wilson Higginbottom. (Although not a WPA project, the 60 members of the Dayton Civic Harmonica Band were also performing locally.)

Theater did not fare as well. Although the WPA hired two professionals—Garland Gaden and Alfred Charmon—the theater season was limited to a group of plays presented

...AND DANCE: The Schwarz Sisters, Hermene and Josephine, during a 1938 performance.

Photo by — Jane Reece

Red Devil 126 of the Cincinnati & Lake Erie Railroad demonstrated it's 100-mile-per-hour prowess as one of the finest interurban designs, in this highly publicized race with an airplane, recorded by Pathé newsreel cameramen in July 1930. The interurban won convincingly.

Great idea at the wrong time

■ *Thomas Conway Jr. was an unlikely railroad man. He had been a professor at the Wharton School of Finance, and his outside consulting work led him into the tottering world of interurban traction companies. Soon he wanted a company of his own, and after a successful effort in Chicago, he arranged to buy the desperate Cincinnati & Dayton Traction Company. He changed the name to Cincinnati, Hamilton and Dayton when he bought the line in early 1926.*

Conway improved the track work, purchased new cars, lowered labor costs and constructed an impressive new car barn in Moraine near the Delco-Light factory. On June 22, 1927, he arranged a dramatic burning of seven of his oldest cars in a Moraine field. Twenty-five thousand Daytonians watched—and ate Conway's free popcorn and ice cream.

In 1928, Conway acquired two more moribund interurban companies, and CH&D became one of America's largest traction lines. It ran from Cincinnati to Dayton then to Springfield where one line went east to Columbus and the other north to Toledo.

Conway ordered new high-speed lightweight cars from the Cincinnati Car Company and began improving track work to permit the cars to operate at maximum efficiency. The Red Devils proved to be one of the finest interurban

designs—and they were fast. To demonstrate their speed, Conway arranged a highly publicized race between Red Devil 126 and an airplane. Pathé newsreel cameramen were there to record the event July 7, 1930. Although the race was clearly rigged, the interurban won convincingly, probably hitting 100 miles per hour as it ran from Dorothy Lane south to about where West Carrollton is today.

Soon the Red Devils were operating on one of the longest interurban lines in America—the 277 miles between Cincinnati and Detroit (Toledo to Detroit on a leased line). Travelers could leave Cincinnati at 7:30 a.m. (or Dayton at 10:50 a.m.) and be in Detroit by 5:15 p.m. There was even an overnight run for a time. The weekend round-trip fare was only $6.60.

But the Depression took its toll. The Toledo-Detroit run ended in 1932 when the Michigan interurban line failed. Renamed the Cincinnati & Lake Erie Railroad (C&LE), it was a leader and innovator in handling freight which most traction lines ignored.

In spite of excellent management, the automobile and the Depression killed the C&LE in painful stages. Hamilton was the last of the long-distance runs to fail—in May 1937. On September 27, 1941, the final run from Third and Kenton to Moraine was completed. In 1947, the traction lines' bus operation was purchased by Greyhound.

CAMP TOWNS AND CUES: Many Daytonians found themselves living on a reduced scale in such places as the Island Park Trailer Camp (above), but still able to enjoy their enforced leisure with cultural activities — Morton Da Costa (left) was "The Man Who Came to Dinner."

at the Soldiers' Home. The first attraction was *G-Men*, which ran for two weeks in February 1936. Perhaps competition from the Wright Players and the Phoenix Players— a repertory group of professionals including Morton DaCosta —was too much for the WPA group.

The turning point

In 1934, the president of a local bank had committed suicide on the links at Moraine Park Golf Club. Local fear of more bank closings was averted when Kettering once more appeared on the floor of Winters Bank, as he had done in 1924 when the bank had had financial problems. Even the possibility of his capital was enough. Although 13,622 were still seeking work by 1936, jobs were opening up, and some of Dayton's industries were back to a full work week. The bank holidays of 1933 were past, and even the faltering savings and loans were beginning to release some funds.

The lion which today overlooks the Art Institute grounds once served as mascot to the former Steele High School, closed in the late '30s.

Debts incurred by the city's bond issues still had not been paid (and would not be until the middle of World War II). The housing market was still depressed. (Photographer G. K. "Dutch" Biel ice-skated in unfinished basements during the '30s. Dozens of unfinished foundations still remained in one East Dayton plat.) The Island Park Trailer Camp, opened in the late '20s as a tourist camp and used through the Depression for relief housing, remained a trailer camp. (It was not dismantled until after World War II.)

Employment in GM plants rose to 22,500 in 1937, and N.C.R. had 6,000 full-time workers. Wright Field, once down to a three-day work week, was back to full-time and hiring. Even so, there were still 10,500 on relief rolls that year. It was not until the United States geared up for war that the ghost of unemployment was exorcised.

No more bread lines, no more coal being picked from the railroad tracks. Influenza epidemics were down. The 1936 polio epidemic (47 stricken, twelve dead and twenty paralyzed) seemed a thing of the past. Society pages listed posh parties, the Dayton Country Club reopened its dining room and began to consider expansion instead of soliciting free memberships.[13] In place of sheriff's sales, the newspapers advertised Noritake china (service for eight, $15.95), and help-wanted ads appeared regularly.

The biggest news in town was the final game in the Stivers–Steele high school football rivalry. Steele won 13 to 0, and Stivers missed its last chance to paint the Steele lion with the orange-and-black tiger stripes. Steele was no longer to be used as a high school. The lion was moved to the Art Institute grounds where he stands today, overlooking the city. Dayton was back to normal.

Professional fund-raiser Miriam Rosenthal showed personal involvement in charitable causes by acting as foster parent to two World War II evacuees from war-torn England.

Saint Miriam

■ *Miriam Rosenthal was born in the country of Lebanon in 1901, her father an itinerant peddler with a pack on his back. She lost her first job as a reporter because the* Dayton Herald *no longer wanted to employ women reporters. James Cox hired her for the* Dayton Daily News *as a reporter and lovelorn columnist. Eight years later, in 1932, she set up her own public relations firm. Asked why she started a risky business in the worst of times, Miss Rosenthal replied, "I needed more money to save for my old age."*

Miriam Rosenthal and Associates ran most of the fund-raising drives in Dayton for the next 30 years. The Memorial Hall renovation, Sinclair College building fund, the new Montgomery County Library building community chest drives, University of Dayton expansion—she masterminded them all. UD named Miriam Hall for her. They called her their "Jewish saint," to which she replied, "It's sacrilegious."

Rosenthal managed the Dayton Philharmonic for 24 years, during which time she brought in most of the touring theatrical and musical productions which visited Dayton—including grand opera. In the '40s, she opened a New York office to accommodate her burgeoning booking business and became one of the best-known impresarios in the United States.

During World War II, she cared for two sisters for a period of four years, perhaps the only unmarried person in the United States to take in evacuees.

When Miriam Rosenthal died April 3, 1965, the newspapers were filled with the outpourings of a citizenry who recognized a great loss.

CHAPTER TEN

KEEP 'EM FLYING

Among the ships launched during the war was the SS Julia P. Shaw, named for the donor of the Dayton Art Institute.

ARSENAL OF DEMOCRACY: Wright Field (above) doubled its size to meet the war effort, and President Roosevelt inspected the progress (inset) along with Orville Wright and Roosevelt's one-time running mate, James Cox. Women went to work on the assembly line to produce war ammunition (far right).

By 1940, Dayton could see the light at the end of Depression's dark tunnel. Although the population increase during the '30s was only a modest five percent, the 210,718 inhabitants of Dayton, plus 7,652 in Oakwood, had finally exceeded the $100-million mark in industrial payrolls. Dayton's 432 factories produced 750 different products, many of them war-related, and America became the "arsenal of democracy" well before her entrance into the war. Wright Field was planning to double in size by adding a two-mile-long runway and a $2.5-million wind tunnel. One plane being tested in 1940 was the B-17 C bomber. Daytonians followed Joe Louis on radio and in the newsreels as he bested the "bum-of-the-month." They hummed "Chattanooga Choo-Choo" and clap-clap-clap-clap—"Deep in the Heart of Texas." President Franklin D. Roosevelt, in his unprecedented run for a third term, beat Wendell L. Willkie in spite of the unpopular draft signed into law just preceding the 1940 election.

Although producing arms for England and Russia developed many jobs, it also brought a series of shortages—coal, oil, paper, matches, silk stockings (parachutes), tin cans. Sugar was scarce and so was booze, since alcohol was used in making gun powder. Beer became the national drink. Dayton's draftees were reduced to drinking 3.2 percent beer at their local PX. Beer had been about twelve percent. Soldiers complained that the weaker brew tasted like a mixture of kerosene and dishwater, but they drank it anyway.

Dayton's association with aviation was reflected in the local newspapers' comic strips. "Flying Jenny" was a somewhat overweight blond pilot who would soon be shooting "Japs" both in the air and on the ground. There was "Smilin' Jack," and Daytonian Milton Caniff's "Terry and the Pirates." Other favorites included "Li'l Abner," "Mary Worth," "Abbie 'n Slats," "Napoleon and Uncle Elby," "Little Orphan Annie," and "Henry." (Annie and Henry have grown no older, but Mary Worth has grown younger.)

At the movies, Dayton watched Gene Autry and Roy Rogers. "Citizen Kane" hit with the impact it still retains. Daytonians laughed at Hope and Crosby in the "Road to Zanzi-

bar" and drooled over Rita Hayworth. Young girls swooned over Frank Sinatra who, with Harry James, had defected from Benny Goodman's band.

A day of infamy

On December 7, 1941, 360 Japanese planes bombed Pearl Harbor. Congress declared war against Japan the following day, and Germany and Italy joined Japan against America on December 11. Almost all the world was at war.

One of the first things Dayton did was to prepare for an air raid. Both New York City and the West Coast had air raid warnings in early December of 1941. In Dayton, Hessel S. Knight was appointed air raid warden and Jane O'Dell was chief fire watcher.

The National Cash Register became the first Dayton plant to win a Navy "E" flag denoting excellence. Frigidaire and Delco products also won their "E" in 1942. They produced munitions and precision instruments. As industry geared up, the housing shortage grew worse. Many homes were converted to boarding houses in both Dayton and Oakwood (60 in Oakwood alone). The Army Air Force took over Steele High School, Borchers' building, the telephone building and a number of garages. Empty buildings downtown were used by the Quartermaster Corps.

Scrap drives became common. Tin cans were requested. (Daytonians were supposed to remove both ends, place the ends in the can, then step on the can to flatten it.) Sugar sales were frozen, and schoolteachers became the rationing agents. In early May 1942, all Americans went to the nearest school to be issued ration books—one for each family member. Hoarders were asked to confess, and many did. The sugar ration was eight ounces per week per person (when available), later increased to twelve ounces. People who used sugar in their coffee found it easier to cut down when coffee became rationed in November. Rubber was in shortest supply, and citizens were asked to turn in any of their excess tires.

Retail price ceilings were imposed on May 18. Dayton was designated a war area and rents were frozen.

Gas rationing was complex. Drivers received stickers to buy gas. An "A" sticker was for pleasure, worth five gallons a week. "B" was for commuters and was based on the commuting distance (they also got an "A" sticker). "C" stickers were for salesmen, delivery people and others who used their car for work and were almost unlimited. "E," for emergency vehicles, clergymen, reporters and photographers, was also largely unlimited. To save more gas, the speed limit was set at 35 mph.

The government asked a lot from its citizens. It asked citizens to buy war bonds and war stamps, give blood, grow victory gardens, save cans, paper, cooking fat, toothpaste tubes and tin foil, learn to spot enemy aircraft and grow milkweed (for stuffing life jackets). Every man between twenty and 45 was registered in mid-February of 1942, and those 45 to 65 registered in late April. If a man was not fit for military service, he was expected to work in an essential job. Women were recruited in record numbers for both military

From Britain with love

■ *"In the early summer of 1940, France fell and a German invasion of England seemed likely, there was a sudden rush to try to have children sent abroad,"* Anthony (Tony) Bailey wrote in America, Lost and Found. *"The government set up the Children's Overseas Reception Board, which received two hundred and eleven thousand applications in less than a month. . . . The cost of passage, rail tickets, and escort fees would be twenty-four pounds. . . . We wore our life jackets and carried our gas masks in little cardboard boxes on cords hung around our necks."* Anthony Bailey was one of the British war evacuees who eventually landed in Dayton. He was 7 years old at the time, and he stayed four years with the Otto Spaeth family in Oakwood. At least two other English children spent the war years in the city; Valerie and Geraldine Holder were wards of Miriam Rosenthal.

"In Dayton, twenty-five cents a week pocket money gave us the wherewithal for a pack of Juicy Fruit gum, a Baby Ruth bar, and a roll of caps, which I used in a toy .38 automatic, stamped "Special Detective," Bailey continued.

"For lunch at the Spaeth's we generally ate soup and a sandwich: a peanut-butter-and-jelly sandwich or a bacon-lettuce-and-tomato, which, with lots of mayonnaise, on rye bread, remains for me one of the glories of American cuisine. . . . I wasn't conscious of any real shortages, though there were apprehensions of some in 1943, when sugar, coffee, and meat were all rationed, and the local weekly paper, the Oakwood Press, headlined an editorial 'Famine Looms in America.'

"There were the well-known blocks through which Tony S. and I zigzagged to school; the newspaper route we shared; and the trolley-bus line out to the Far Hills movie theatre, where on Saturday mornings we watched such films as "Viva Cisco Kid," with Cesar Romero, and "Shooting High," with Jane Withers and Gene Autry. . . . To reach the city, downtown, we went by trolley, bus, or car, crossing through the land of the National Cash Register Company, where small steam locomotives called 'stubbies' shunted freight cars from one factory building to another. Downtown was a regular gridiron, made interesting by small alleys subdividing the blocks and by certain buildings among the rest that had a surreal prominence for me—many of them with columned fronts, like the courthouse and the post office. We knew the whereabouts of WING, the radio station that brought us the adventures of Jack Armstrong; and the Rike-Kumler Company, where we went on shopping expeditions and once, in May of 1944, to see a real P-40 fighter plane, which was being exhibited on Rike's ground floor."

Bailey and the Holder girls returned to their homes in England after the war. But all kept their ties with their Dayton "families." The Spaeths moved to New York in 1948. One of the Holder girls is now a grandmother; Tony Bailey is married with four daughters, but the 1940s in Dayton remain his memories—and his gift to America.

and war plant jobs. The Navy WAVES took over N.C.R.'s Sugar Camp. So-called "non-essential" occupations found few workers.

Stars fell on Dayton to encourage war bond sales. Ilona Massey, Fred Astaire and Hugh Hubert came in September 1942. Bob Hope and Tony Pastor did network radio broadcasts from Dayton a little later.

WHIO radio organized a fox hunt, New Year's Day 1944, to eliminate the foxes which had been eating farmers' crops. Three thousand men, women and children—armed with clubs and baseball bats—surrounded eight foxes southeast of Centerville. Six of the eight escaped.

In 1943, Dayton industrial payroll was over $210 million—an incredible growth. If jobs were easy to find, transportation was not. In October 1943, Bill Bickham wrote his father:

New York

Dear Father—

I am still hoping to pay you a short visit two weeks from now. . . . There are plenty of hurdles to cross however. I tried to reserve a berth on a Penna [Pennsylvania RR] Train for Friday the 29th and was told no space on any train that day. Apparently the . . . trains are reserved solid for military and war production priority folks. Our traffic manager knows how to get them and thinks he can find a berth for me. He says Dayton is one of the hardest places in the country to get to by train these days. . . . It would be nice if I could bring you a pound of butter and a big roast of beef, but we can't get it any more. . . . Chicken and chicken and Nucoa [margarine], and once a week some lamb and a little butter.[1]

Aircraft parts and aircraft development were Dayton's major contribution to the war. Of war orders between June 1940 and October 1943, $378.9 million were for aircraft, $361.7 million for ordinance and only $99.1 million for all other manufactured war goods. Supplies, such as food, accounted for the remainder.

In January 1944, the United States admitted it had tested a "new jet-propelled plane" in 1942. Orville Wright was quoted as saying he believed it "never could compete with the conventional motor-type."

Carrying on

Newspapers brought the war home sharply. There were lists and pictures of local servicemen, and a soldier back from the war usually rated an interview. Few days passed without one or more young faces pictured beneath "Obituaries." Friday, January 21, 1944, was typical: "John T. Webster, fire controlman third class, USN. Missing in action since November, 1942, believed killed. PFC Harry B. Hunter, Mediterranean Theater, MIA. Lt. James R. Carnaham, European Theater, B-24 pilot; MIA."

One missing-in-action story had a happy ending. Lieutenant Harry G. Zavakos, a fighter pilot and ex-University of Dayton athlete, was shot down somewhere in China and reported missing. He was found by the Chinese and slowly moved across the countryside to return to his unit. (Surprisingly, the Chinese kept feeding him fried chicken, sometimes twice a day, during his travels across China.) His brother, Lieutenant Frank Zavakos, was one of the 74 UD students killed in the war. (At least 1,832 students served in World War II.)[2]

Liberal was a Dayton-based supermarket chain begun in 1921 by immigrant Abe Schear who started with a "Groceteria" Mack truck. In a full page ad on January 27, 1944, Liberal Markets explained how to use ration points wisely, adding that they had generous supplies of unrationed foods. Bacon was 35 cents a pound, smoked ham 33 cents, hamburger 25 cents. A quarter would buy two bunches of broccoli, while two bunches of carrots cost only 15 cents. A 25-pound bag of flour cost $1.25 and a 100-pound bag of potatoes $2.98. (Liberal had as many as 47 stores before its demise in early 1981.)

Daytonians worked hard and played hard, too. Only a few weeks after Pearl Harbor, Dayton had a Soldier's Service Club at the Christ Church parish house. It soon moved to what had been the former Municipal Building gymnasium. By 1943, a Linden Center Service Men's Club was started to serve the 700 black servicemen from Patterson Field. (Patterson Field, which had opened in 1931, was named for Stuart Patter-

Stars descended on Dayton to promote war bond sales, including such big names as Hope, Astaire and band leader Kay Kyser and his orchestra for a war bond rally at Leslie L. Diehl Municipal Shell.

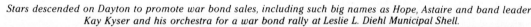

Dayton typified the "good news from home" as major contributors of aircraft parts and development.

son, a test pilot who died at Wilbur Wright Field in 1919. It was composed of the old Wilbur Wright Field and the Fairfield Air Depot. Wright Field was farther east.) Dayton's civilian black population soared. The city's 1944 annual report indicated almost a 50 percent increase since the 1940 census.[3] To care for civilian war workers and military personnel, the Federal Public Housing Agency built 1,075 housing units in Dayton in 1944. Private builders handled another "334 family units for White occupancy and 39 units for Negro occupancy." The major projects were Hebble Homes in Osborn (now Fairborn, 320 units); McGuffy Homes, Kiser and Webster streets (220 units); Skyway Park, Air Service Command (564 units) and Harshman Homes, Riverside (364 units). Homeview and Lakeview, both on Lakeview Avenue, provided 240 units for blacks. In addition, 200 permanent and 60 temporary units were added to the DeSota Bass complex. (The first units of DeSota Bass had been finished in 1939; it was one of the first public housing projects in the United States.) Hundreds of dormitory accommodations—also segregated—were available for single women near the airfields and in town.

For lively entertainment, Dayton provided a swinging downtown night life. Stage shows augmented the movies at three RKO Theaters—Loews', Keith's and Colonial. Lantz's Merry-Go-Round, on Main Street south of Fifth, brought Red Skelton, Eddie Fisher and Stepin Fetchit to town. Big bands played Dayton often, and dancing was usually available at the big downtown hotels—the Biltmore, Van Cleve, Gibbons or the Miami.

Wright Field tested many of the combat aircraft used in the war, and Daytonians grew accustomed to seeing planes overhead not found in the *Aircraft Spotters Guide,* including the strange, awesome Flying Wing.

In 1927, Katherine Houk Talbott had built Runnymede Playhouse for her family's social and cultural activities. Sometime during the early war years, the predecessor of the Atomic Energy Commission was using the building in which the Monsanto Corporation conducted atomic energy research. When the outraged Oakwood government found out in 1948, it forced the United States to buy the building from the Talbott Corporation and tear it down.

With the Normandy invasion on June 6, 1944, and the capture of Rome only two days earlier, Hitler's fate was sealed. But many would die before the war was over. In the *Dayton Daily News,* January 14, 1945, casualty lists included five killed, five wounded, five missing and sixteen taken prisoner.

At home, the labor shortage was so acute there was talk of drafting men for civilian jobs. In January, 4,951 essential jobs were open, with 602 classified as critical. A severe coal shortage caused Dayton theater owners to reduce their outside lighting, and the city furnished trucks to move available coal to customers. Cigarettes, coffee, soap and butter practically disappeared from local stores. But Dayton was thinking ahead. The city was making moves to acquire the army-built Vandalia airport after the war. And it was acquiring land to straighten both Stewart Street and Wolf Creek.

VE Day was May 7, 1945. F.D.R. had not lived to see it; he had died on April 12. Two down (Italy and Germany), a jubilant America cried, one to go.

Dayton enjoyed "Meet Me in St. Louis," "National Velvet," "Spellbound" and "State Fair" at the movies and read *Forever Amber, Stuart Little* and *Lord Hornblower.* They sang "One Meat Ball" and "Chickery Chick Che-la Che-la," while the war continued in the Pacific.

STEIN, TONY: Official report, Congressional Medal of Honor

■ *Rank and organization: Corporal, U.S. Marine Corps Reserve. Born: 30 September 1921, Dayton, Ohio. Accredited to: Ohio. Citation: For conspicuous gallantry and intrepidity at the risk of his life above and beyond the call of duty while serving with Company A, 1st Battalion, 28th Marines, 5th Marine Division, in action against enemy Japanese forces on Iwo Jima, in the Volcano Islands, 19 February 1945. The first man of his unit to be on station after hitting the beach in the initial assault, Corporal Stein, armed with a personally improvised aircraft-type weapon, provided rapid covering fire as the remainder of his platoon attempted to move into position. When his comrades were stalled by a concentrated machine gun and mortar barrage, he gallantly stood upright and exposed himself to the enemy's view, thereby drawing the hostile fire to his own person and enabling him to observe the location of the furiously blazing hostile guns. Determined to neutralize the strategically placed weapons, he boldly charged the enemy during the furious single-handed assault. Cool and courageous under the merciless hail of exploding shells and bullets which fell on all sides, he continued to deliver the fire of his skillfully improvised weapon at a tremendous rate of speed which rapidly exhausted his ammunition. Undaunted, he removed his helmet and shoes to expedite his movements and ran back to the beach for additional ammunition, making a total of 8 trips under intense fire and carrying or assisting a wounded man back each time. Despite the unrelenting savagery and confusion of battle, he rendered prompt assistance to his platoon whenever the unit was in position, directing the fire of a half-track against a stubborn pillbox until he had effected the ultimate destruction of the Japanese fortification. Later in the day, although his weapon was twice shot from his hands, he personally covered the withdrawal of his platoon to the company position. Stouthearted and indomitable, Cpl. Stein, by his aggressive initiative, sound judgment, and unwavering devotion to duty in the face of terrific odds, contributed materially to the fulfillment of his mission, and his outstanding valor throughout the bitter hours of conflict sustains and enhances the highest traditions of the U.S. Naval Service.[6]*

• • • •

On December 16, 1948, Corporal Stein's body was returned from Iwo Jima for burial in Dayton.

Dayton provided a swinging night life for war workers. Famous names came to local hotels and stage shows augmented the movies at the Colonial Theater (above), at Ludlow and Fifth streets.

The "Little Monster"

■ *In addition to M-30 carbines, Inland Manufacturing made the prototype of the "Saturday Night Special." Called the "Little Monster," it was a one-pound pistol that cost about $2 and was designed to be air-dropped to resistance fighters in Europe. Walt Disney designed the package and the non-verbal instructions.*

On August 10, 1945, Japan—suffering from two atomic blasts and a chronic oil shortage—sued for peace. On August 14, at 7 p.m., Eastern War Time, the war was over.

Coming home

Unlike earlier wars, World War II had required the services of all Americans, rich or poor, educated or uneducated. Those who had not gone to war had made money—in amounts beyond their wildest Depression dreams. A subsistence farmer of $1,000 a year suddenly made $4,000 or $5,000 on a Dayton assembly line. Servicemen returned home to a different America. How was anyone to keep

them down on the farm, now that they had seen Paris, Buchenwald, the South Pacific? The war had been fought by civilians, and they had changed.

By law, the serviceman's old employer had to rehire the ex-GI and keep him on the job for at least one year. But many servicemen had learned the advantages of an education through the great meritocracy of war. The military had demanded leaders so quickly, they created them of any likely material, regardless of background. A sharecropper's son was as likely to be promoted as anyone. And when he returned, he need not remain a sharecropper any longer. There really was an American dream available to all. And it could be obtained through the GI Bill. Colleges were flooded with serious-minded students. The University of Dayton, nearby Miami University, Miami-Jacobs Business College and Sinclair College (grown out of a YMCA school project) were jammed with returning GIs.

The war was over. There were a record 5,229 marriages in Dayton in 1946, as well as 4,075 divorces. Life was new, it was exciting. It was a time for new beginnings. Americans were ready for anything and everything—and Dayton was ready to do its share of the building.

In 1947, industry in Dayton was booming, unemployment almost unknown. Dayton was the seventh city in the nation

The Soldiers' Monument eventually created a bottleneck for the increased traffic of the post-war era. In early 1948 it was moved to Riverview Park.

and first in Ohio in number of automobiles per capita. The Dayton Municipal Airport, with its 1,700 acres, had become the largest city-owned airport in Ohio. GM employed 40,000, and N.C.R. had 14,500 employees—6,500 more than before the war and 2,500 more than during the war. Maxon Construction was busily rebuilding Guam for the U.S. Navy, and Monarch Marking had 30,000 customers in one year. Two printers of business forms—Reynolds and Reynolds and Standard Register—reported sales increases of about 25 percent. Wright and Patterson Field employees cranked over $2 million into the economy every two weeks (although employment was down from 19,300 in 1946 to 15,802 in 1947). Acme Aluminum Alloys was making the machines that gave America "Bubble-Lites" for Christmas trees. And meatless days at local hotels ended early in January 1948.

There were other changes. The last streetcar ride on the Third Street line was Saturday night, September 27, 1947. The Soldiers' Monument at Main and Monument had become the most serious traffic bottleneck according to Dayton police officials who viewed it from a blimp. Early in 1948, the monument was moved to Riverview Park, shortly after Fred Eichelberger, city manager for 26 years, retired.

Dayton was saddened when Orville Wright died on January 30, 1948, of a heart attack. He did not live to see the original Wright Flyer returned to its place of honor in the Smithsonian's National Aeronautics and Space Museum. Another major Dayton figure, George H. Mead, resigned as chairman of the board at Mead.

Harold Stassen and Robert A. Taft came to town in 1948 seeking the Republican nomination for president. Dewey won. Then Harry S. Truman made a number of whistle stop tours across the nation, especially in Ohio, and beat Dewey.

But the incredible production and booming economy could not hold up. A strike at the Univis Lens Company had pickets fighting 150 police near the plant on Leo Street in late July 1948. Soon, 1,200 National Guardsmen moved in to keep order. The recession began to take effect late in 1948. It was intense but short-lived. Daytonians, paying one-half of one percent income tax, noticed the improvement in 1950.

The school system was jammed with the first of the war babies. Daytonians were listening to Gene "By Golly" Barry and Symphony Sid on WING radio. Barry's theme, "The Honey Dripper," was available on transcription only, not a regular recording, and demands from the area almost forced its commercial release. Bandleader Stan Kenton first heard The Four Freshmen in Dayton, probably in 1950, and helped launch their career.

Suburban flight

The Korean War began in 1950 and—after a bloody exchange of all-out offensives—became a static war, lasting until 1953. It was at this time that all America, and especially Dayton (with the Strategic Air Command bomber operation at Wright-Patterson), felt atomic war was inevitable. The cry of "build your own bomb shelter" was heard throughout the land. In 1954, Dien Bien Phu, Vietnam, fell to the Communists. As the defeated French left the country, the United States began overt, if low-key support,

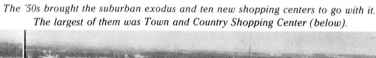

The '50s brought the suburban exodus and ten new shopping centers to go with it. The largest of them was Town and Country Shopping Center (below).

Downtown renovation at the Chemineer Building.

of South Vietnam. Americans liked Ike. Colleges were full of the silent generation. The space program provided an exciting diversion from day-to-day living and maybe, just maybe, the Russians' lead in space could be overtaken after all.

Dayton was doing so well that few people could see the problems which were beginning to emerge. They were the problems besetting almost all U.S. cities.

There was flight of citizens to the suburbs. And business followed the people. Between 1948 and 1954, downtown retail sales rose only 6.1 percent, but in the outer areas, sales were up 56.3 percent. The automobile, which had made Dayton rich, was beginning to make it poor. In 1946, the trackless trolleys and motor coaches of the city's transit lines carried more than 66.4 million riders—in 1952, 47 million and, in 1957, only 33.5 million—about half the number of the previous decade.

Although Rike-Kumler and Elder-Johnston, the leading department stores, announced that they had no plans to build outside downtown, Arthur Beerman had seen the wave of the '50s. As early as 1947, he built the first shopping mall (actually a suburban business concentration) called McCook's on Keowee Street. He soon had three more—Northtown, Eastown and Westown. Between 1950 and 1958, ten suburban centers were erected with more than 150 stores and over 10,000 parking places. In 1956, the handwriting on the wall should have been clear—J.C. Penney, a traditional downtown retailer, located its store far to the south in the Town and Country Shopping Center on Stroop Road. When the center opened about 1950, there was far more country than town. Five years later, Town and Country got its "town." It was named Kettering, and the new town honored Charles F. Kettering with a celebration in July 1955.

Pre-war and wartime urban housing projects had contributed to ghetto development with blacks concentrated in

Famous Daytonian Jonathan Winters began his career by winning a talent contest at a local RKO theater.

the near west side and in lower Dayton View.

Dayton had passed its first urban-renewal bond issue just after the war. The city's earliest urban renewal project eliminated the area Lib Hedges had made famous and also set up a government area from Third to Second Street and from Ludlow to the river. The first of the government projects was the Safety Building, at Third and Perry, completed in 1953. The whole urban renewal concept of the '50s was to tear down Dayton in order to save it.

But the flight from the city had begun, and downtown was in trouble. Hotel dance bands dropped from fifteen to six or fewer members. All but one hotel discontinued weekday dancing. Movie business in downtown theaters began to decline. Ansel Winston, manager of the three RKO Theaters, blamed television, neighborhood theaters and that new American phenomenon, the drive-in. Winston's total receipts in 1948 had been $2.324 million. In 1954, they dropped to $1.828 million. The King Cole restaurant continued to thrive, but restaurants, too, began to move away from the city center. The Pine Club, a Dayton landmark, was successful in spite of its location, size and lack of advertising. (Even in the '50s everyone joked that nobody really knew if the food was as good as everyone said, since the two-hour wait in the bar made it impossible to tell.)

That's show biz

In the mid-1940s, a chubby teenager lost his watch at one of the RKO theaters which was holding a talent contest. Since the contest prize was a new watch, it may have inspired the young man. He won with impressions of a Joe Louis fight and—complete with sound effects—the Indianapolis Speedway. The budding comedian was Jonathan Winters, a direct descendant of Dayton's first bank employee.

In 1945, McCall Corporation's printing operation, which moved to Dayton in 1923 to be closer to the U.S. population center, embarked on an $11-million plant expansion on McCall Street. James McCall had begun as a pattern maker in 1870 and published a monthly publication promoting his patterns. Soon, his advertising piece became a woman's magazine, then a major publishing venture, reaching a circulation of over three million by the early 1900s. In 1929, McCall's added *Redbook*. A year later, the company was printing *Popular Science Monthly*. By 1952, more than three million magazines a day were printed at the Dayton plant. In 1955, 52 national publications reached America via Dayton.[4]

In 1951, Dayton went to New York. The "Cinderella Kids" of the University of Dayton, coached by Tom Blackburn, went to the National Invitational Tourney (NIT). The basketball team—with Daytonians Monk Meineke, Junior Norris and Chuck Grigsby—made it to the finals before being beaten by LaSalle. But UD, and Dayton, had tasted big-time college basketball. UD would win the NIT in 1962 and 1968.[5] In 1967, Dayton's basketball team reached the finals of the NCAA Championship, losing to UCLA.

In 1951, the Dayton Indians Class-A baseball team won the Central League title, but the team, which had played in Dayton for four years, did not return in 1952.

Barry MacKay moved to Oakwood in 1950 and played tennis with anyone who was foolhardy enough to take on the young teenager. His most formidable opponent was his older sister, Bonnie, who achieved national prominence in 1950, winning the national girls' junior doubles title. Barry

SPORTS SPECIALS: The "Cinderella Kids" of the University of Dayton made it to the
N.I.T. in 1951 and lost, but came back to win in 1962 and 1968 (above). Tennis champ
Barry MacKay (below) moved to Oakwood in 1950 as a teenager,
and went on to win through the '60s.

NEW AIR AGE: The runway at Cox Airport as it appeared in 1957 (top);
and XB-70 being examined by tourists
at the Air Force Museum (above).

credited Mack Hummon, the Oakwood tennis coach, with starting him in his competition winning streak. Barry won the state championship twice while in high school and the national collegiate championship his senior year at the University of Michigan. He represented the United States on the Davis Cup team four times and won the National Indoor and Clay Courts title in 1960, the year he was rated the number one amateur in the country. He turned pro in 1961 and continued to play professionally until about 1966.

Management of the huge Memorial Hall Theater on First Street decided to let John Kenley have a go at live theater for the summer of 1957. Kenley knew Daytonians wanted to see stars, particularly television stars. He brought them, and he did well—so well that Kenley's rent was raised dramatically, and the showman said thanks, but no thanks. A succession of other entrepreneurs tried to follow in his footsteps. Although some seasons were successful, it

was not what Dayton wanted. After two years of no summer theater (1964 and 1965), Kenley made a triumphant return. He has been successful ever since.

Dayton was enamored of all travel. In 1953, the National Air Show came to Dayton for the 50th anniversary of flight. By 1956, Dayton boasted of 8,262 traffic lights. In 1958, auto deaths dropped to only 24 (perhaps because of 145 new traffic lights), and airline passenger traffic from Dayton exceeded railroad traffic for the first time.

Dayton was first of Ohio's largest cities in terms of weekly industrial wages. An average Daytonian earned $101.21 a week, while Columbus and Cincinnati workers only earned between $83.21 and $85.18.

At the end of the '50s, although the threat of all-out war still was strong in the public mind, Daytonians looked forward to more of "business as usual."

It was not to be.

CHAPTER ELEVEN

NOTES FOR FUTURE HISTORIANS

The Wright brothers' flights at Kitty Hawk brought the beginnings of a new age for Dayton.

While new stores sprang up, old landmarks sometimes went down, such as the Beckel Hotel, (here in 1913) which burned in 1964 while in the death throes of demolition.

Returning Korean War veterans could find good buys in Chuck Huber's Huber Heights, the "biggest all-brick community in the United States." For $385 down, a man could buy the three-bedroom Highlander (with garage) for only $11,995. The four-bedroom Suburban was only $3,000 more.

Although Dayton had grown slightly in the '50s (262,332), the surrounding suburbs had grown much faster. In 1960, Kettering had almost 55,000 inhabitants, Fairborn 19,453 and Vandalia 6,342. Employment dipped slightly in 1960 from 1959 levels, but unemployment was still less than four percent, lower than most Ohio cities.

Rike-Kumler planned a suburban store but also prepared to expand its downtown operation on the site of the Miami Hotel. Late in 1961, Arthur Beerman began a running feud with Rike's, possibly because he felt the long-established firm had an unfair commercial advantage. Beerman's and Elder's merged in 1962 and planned a new suburban store.

The Dayton-based Gallaher Drug Store chain of 55 stores was sold in 1963. The Beckel Hotel, while being demolished the next year, burned, as did the Plantation Country Club. R. Stanley Laing was named new president of N.C.R. Gentile Depot (named for Don Gentile, a World War II ace from Piqua) became the

Defense Electronics Supply Center. (Daytonians soon shortened the name to "Dessy.")

It was the era of the "blue laws," an effort to close stores on Sundays, especially those in suburban areas. The owner of Woody's Supermarket in West Carrollton was sentenced to ten days in the workhouse for blue-law violation. The owner of the Far Hills Theater in Oakwood received a six-month sentence for showing an obscene film.

Late in 1960, a TWA Super Constellation outbound from Dayton was struck by a United DC-8 in mid-air over New York City, and a number of Daytonians were among the 134 killed. The State Highway Department approved an interstate bypass east of Dayton in 1962, and the never-ending saga of I-675 began. The Aviation Hall of Fame was founded that year. It was first located at the Biltmore Hotel. (In 1973, it would be moved to the Convention Center.) The first two inductees were Orville and Wilbur Wright. Milton Caniff was commissioned to do all inductees' portraits.

Sports kept Daytonians entertained. Kettering diver Sam Hall won a silver medal at the 1960 Olympics, and early in 1961, UD was involved in a point-fixing scandal.

But sports was not the only entertainment. Local and national politics piqued Dayton's interest. Both John F. Kennedy and

Phil Donahue, whose show has become the bright spot in the day to millions at home, developed his wide-eyed yet skillful questioning technique with Dayton radio and TV talk programs.

The Boy Next Door

■ In Centerville in the early '60s, on one side of the street lived Erma Bombeck, whose career as a columnist was just beginning. On the other side of the street lived a brash young WHIO radio newsman, Phil Donahue. Donahue moved to television to anchor the eleven o'clock news, but he continued a radio telephone interview show called "Conversation Piece." Donahue quit WHIO in 1967 and became a salesman for the E. F. MacDonald Company, one of Dayton's two major sales incentive companies. He had been vaguely unhappy in broadcasting, but personal selling seemed worse. When WLW-D offered him a chance to do a show similar to "Conversation Piece" on television, he was ready.

He started off, on November 6, 1967, with a blockbuster; his guest was the famous atheist, Madalyn Murray O'Hair. From the first, Donahue was the wide-eyed, slightly naive, small-town Catholic boy in awe of his guests. This was his great skill, along with his ability to ask exactly the questions his viewers would like to ask— or would ask if the viewers had done their homework as well as Donahue and his staff.

The show prospered in Dayton and slowly acquired a network of 38 cities. But it could grow no further. The producers felt Dayton could not attract the caliber of guests required for a major television talk show. It was moved to Chicago, and "The Phil Donahue Show" has grown into one of the most successful syndicated shows on television today, winning Emmys for best host and best show.

Columnist Erma Bombeck began parodying the problems of housewives while still among those caught in the wash-a-day world of Centerville in the '60s.

Mark Twain going down!

■ A "low water dam" on the Miami River raised the water level in the first step of the river-front development. In 1976, a local entrepreneur floated a small, passenger-carrying "steamboat" on the stream. When the craft developed engine trouble, its CB crackled, "Mayday! Mayday! The Mark Twain is going down for the third time!" The Miami was all of three feet deep at the spot.

Dayton's river-front development provides a new measure of enjoyment to residents.

The unrest of the 1960s brought trouble to Dayton. Workers (above) went out on strike against the Rockwell Corporation in 1966.

Richard Nixon solicited votes with personal appearances in the city in 1960. Don Crawford became the city's first black city commissioner. Another young city commissioner told friends he was about to get inside information on the numbers racket, then he disappeared on August 2, 1962. The police began a frantic search. Officials and media soon discovered his baby-sitter was also missing. The commissioner was found in Knoxville, claiming amnesia.

Another President, Lyndon Johnson, campaigned for reelection in Dayton in October 1964. Barry Goldwater had visited Dayton earlier. In the 1964 election, Rodney Love upset Congressman Paul E. Schenck who had represented the city for thirteen years. Schenck had the support of self-made multimillionaire L. M. Berry whose "Yellow Pages" business was one of Dayton's outstanding successes. In November 1965, David Hall was elected mayor and contributed the memorable quote, "This is the greatest thing since Ex-Lax."

Herbert Starick resigned as city manager, and Charles Whalen, a UD professor, defeated Love as U.S. congressman in 1966. Whalen was a very liberal Republican and an exceptionally popular candidate in the Third Congressional District. No Democrat could beat him; his only difficulties were in the primaries and party meetings where well-financed, conservative Republicans tried and tried to unseat him.

Trouble in River City

Like most large cities, Dayton had its frustrations. In January 1961, United Fireworks had its fourteenth blowup in its 26-year history. (A dozen men were killed between 1934 and 1959.) In 1964, the FBI picked up a 67-year-old sniper who had been firing at Wright-Patterson planes because they made too much noise. People who had lived in town during the Cuban missile crisis of late 1962 when Strategic Air Command bombers were at a high stage of alert understood the sniper's concerns though they did not sympathize with his methods.

Early in the 1960s, a barber in Yellow Springs, Lewis Gegner, attracted national attention by refusing to cut a Negro's hair. Sit-ins, even riots, in the town followed in later years, until Gegner retired in June 1964. But it was only the beginning of racial difficulties. A time bomb had been ticking on the near west side as Dayton blacks felt they had waited patiently (some out-of-town black leaders said "docilely") for help with their problems. On September 1, 1966, Lester Mitchell, a black man, was shot outside his West Fifth Street home, apparently by a white man in a car. A major riot followed, destroying a

Racial difficulties troubled Dayton as well as other American cities. A major riot destroyed several city blocks in 1966, and in 1968 (above) blacks and whites marched in tribute to Martin Luther King Jr.

number of blocks in the most deteriorated portion of the ghetto. Police arrested more than 130 people, and the National Guard was called in. By the time President Johnson spoke at the fairgrounds on September 5, most of the guard had been released. Although the west side was "cool," racial relationships were strained.

A speech by H. Rap Brown in 1967 added fuel to the tensions. Blacks patrolling the west side wearing white hats managed to keep things quiet. But when Robert Barbee, a black field investigator for social security, was shot and killed by a policeman who thought Barbee's pipe was a gun, disturbances broke out. White students at Roth began a week-long boycott of the high school, and the schools were in frequent racial turmoil. Voters rejected a bond issue in November, probably as a result of the problems.

Dr. Wayne M. Carle came to Dayton in late February 1968 to run the racially troubled school system. On March 1, Dunbar High School fans—angered when their basketball team was upset by Beavercreek—jammed the floor. A Beavercreek player was stabbed, and one fan suffered a heart attack and died in the disturbance.

In November 1969, voters turned down a school tax levy. The Dayton School Board was controlled by the conservative SOS (Serving Our Schools) Party. The war between Superin-

Exceeding the criteria

■ *In the late 1950s, doctors and scientists at Wright-Patterson Air Force Base were given a strange assignment.*

"We'd like you to pick some astronauts," the government said.

"Fine," replied the doctors, "but what is an astronaut?"

Finally, it was decided that astronauts were something like test pilots, only more so. A number were recruited and tested. The criteria were arbitrary, such as height (since Mercury capsules were small, shorter men were preferred) and age. When the list was released, one name was missing.

The government came back. "Nice job, but we have a problem," they said. "You've given us some fine Air Force and Navy pilots, but there's no Marine."

"Oh, there was a Marine Corps pilot who did very well on the tests," the doctors replied. "He even holds a coast-to-coast speed record. He's just a bit too tall and a few months older than our cut-off date. We think he'd make a fine astronaut."

The astronaut was John Glenn.

The Popcorn City

■ *Airline personnel call Dayton "The Popcorn City," because of Wileswood Country Store. Founded in 1966, the store grows its own popcorn in northern Ohio and pops between 100 and 200 pounds a day. Some ground crews refuse to work on aircraft if the flight crews do not return with Dayton popcorn. An Englishman was told if he failed to buy Dayton popcorn he had not really been to America. Sales have been made to popcorn-hungry vistors to take as far away as Japan and Afghanistan.*

PROTEST FOR PEACE: Demonstrators hold peace rallies in 1972 on the court house lawn (top); and at Wright-Patterson Air Force Base (bottom).

tendent Carle and SOS could be counted on to fill five inches of newspaper space and two minutes on television daily.

Higher education was expanding. Ohio State and Miami agreed to open a branch university in Dayton early in the '60s. The branch later became Wright State University. In 1966, Deeds Park was sold to Sinclair to expand the college. Public outcry forced the city to save the park, and urban renewal land to the west of the business district was found for Sinclair.

There were more troubles. The popular police captain, Russ Guerra, whose traffic reports on WHIO radio had made him a household word, was shot and critically wounded by a robbery suspect. (Guerra is now a state representative.)

Dayton had a flood in May 1968—the worst since 1959—and two people died. Kettering had a tornado the following May, with 25 people injured and thirteen homes destroyed.

The city had passed its population peak and was beginning to decline as suburbs grew around it. The bedroom communities bled the inner city of business and industry, providing little in return. There were 26 planning and zoning commissions in the county with practically no coordination between them. There were few parks or playgrounds in the suburbs, fewer industrial sites. The lack of industrial space forced land costs up, discouraging any company considering the area as a plant location.

As citizens put stronger demands on their government for services, federal money became available. But the city—particularly the central business district—was drifting into

decay. Dayton joined the U.S. Model Cities program but received far less money than it had hoped. A central business district study was produced in 1967— its key element a Courthouse Square renewal project. City Manager James Kunde immediately began work on the idea.

Two area landmarks disappeared in 1967—the Union Stockyards in Dayton and a pilot atomic power project in Piqua. A major downtown project, Winters Tower, was begun in February 1968, and that year, Dayton was declared America's cleanest city.

Some of Dayton's most prominent citizens died in the '60s. Edward Deeds died in July 1960; Frank Tait of Dayton Power & Light (DP&L) in 1962 and Tom Blackburn, coach of UD's basketball team, in 1964. A new generation of leadership was running the businesses and the city. Robert Oelman took over the Cash after S. C. Allyn retired. Marj Heyduck, the *Journal-Herald*'s woman's editor and "Third and Main" columnist, died in 1964. (She and Erma Bombeck—"Our Gal in Centerville," later "Our Gal in Bellbrook"—were two of Dayton's favorite columnists.)

Two Dayton men gave their lives in Vietnam to save their fellow servicemen. On August 18, 1965, Marine Lance Corporal Joe C. Paul deliberately placed himself between enemy fire and five wounded comrades to allow them to be evacuated. Critically wounded, the 19-year-old continued to fire until he collapsed. Army Specialist Fourth Class Joseph G. LaPoint Jr., was a medical aidsman. During a helicopter assault on

QUIET, PLEASE: Students still hit the books as evidenced by the libraries at Wright State University (top), and the underground facility at Sinclair College (bottom).

161

June 2, 1969, LaPointe crawled directly in front of an enemy bunker to give first aid to two wounded men. Even after being shot at least twice, he continued to help until a grenade killed all three men. Both Paul and LaPointe were awarded the Congressional Medal of Honor posthumously.

In 1972, City Manager Kunde warned that Dayton was on "the critical edge" in the struggle to strengthen downtown. But that year, a lot of things began to happen. The Convention Center opened in January, and the Regional Transit Authority took over the City Transit Company. Sinclair's modern campus and the Montgomery County Building across the street were both designed by Edward Durrell Stone. The Winters Tower, Dayton's tallest building, opened.

The new president of N.C.R., William A. Anderson, was brought back from Japan to overhaul the company. (By 1974, it was no longer National Cash Register nor N.C.R., but simply NCR.) Anderson immediately began a dramatic changeover from mechanical cash registers to electronic point-of-purchase terminals and sophisticated computers. Two thousand men were laid off, and the 12,000 skilled workers on the mechanical assembly lines could see the writing on the wall. By 1974, NCR workers with twenty years of seniority were being laid off. Still, NCR began to build its world corporate headquarters in the city. A new sideline—the encapsulated liquid crystal material used in mood rings—created a fruitful market in 1975.

Frigidaire workers were also in trouble. Competitive appliance firms had much lower labor costs, so the employees accepted a 30-month wage freeze. Continued inflation, poor car sales and sugar prices up 300 percent did not help the city. DP&L was short of natural gas and began applying restrictions. Don Huber began to build Newfields, a complete "new town" development near Trotwood. Although imaginatively conceived, it was begun at the wrong time—federal funds dried up, and the project later failed. By 1975, unemployment had reached seven percent.

Another tragedy struck close to home as a tornado slashed through Xenia on April 3, 1974. Dayton and Wright-Patterson AFB responded at once. The tornado wrecked a train, cutting the town in half. Officials from Xenia, Dayton and surrounding communities all pitched in. Paramedics and firemen from the Dayton area rushed to the scene and provided quick relief to the citizens of Xenia on the Dayton side of the train's derailment.

Racial unrest continued. A black man fired a shotgun into a car, killing a white man and wounding the man's wife and daughter. Later, a white "hit-and-run killer" roamed the west side in his car, wounding five blacks in five separate shooting incidents. By 1973, a new homicide record was set with 104 murders. Civil rights advocate, W. S. McIntosh, was shot and killed trying to prevent a jewelry store robbery on Main Street. A white patrolman was also slain by the black robbers, and the city moved closer together to mourn the senseless loss of both men.

In 1973, James McGee became the first black mayor of Dayton (and one of the first black mayors of any major city). The SOS won big at the school board election, and Wayne Carle moved on, replaced by the more conservative John B. Maxwell. By the next year, school enrollment had dropped from 49,028 to 47,031, and the system had become more than 47 percent black.

On September 19, 1976, Dr. Charles A. Glatt, who had come to the city to plan Dayton's school desegregation, was shot and killed in Dayton's Federal Building. Glatt had done a job even his political enemies admired, and his loss was a sad one. His killer, Neal Bradley Long, was later identified as the west side "hit-and-run killer" of 1972.

SIGNS OF THE '70s: James McGee became the first black mayor of Dayton in 1973 (left); three years later Bicentennial celebrants marched past Rike's parking garage (above). The decade saw more landmarks go, such as the State Theater in 1971 (right).

Tax abatements proved the key to Dayton's Courthouse Square development.

A new lease

Not all news was bad, however. The rivers were being cleaned up and returned to the people with bikeways and walkways. Bused school desegregation had begun without the tragedy and trauma of many northern cities. Pat Roach became the first elected female commissioner. UD received accreditation for its law school, and Wright State was ready to start its first medical school class in 1976. The SOS chose William E. Goodwin as its spokesman, and the gruff, plain-speaking man proved to be a major local television personality.

Stouffer's Dayton Plaza Hotel was under construction despite a general construction strike. Dayton pulled Stouffer's into the city through a combination of government and business cooperation, including federal monies and tax concessions. The controversial concessions were tax abatements which proved the key to the Courthouse Square development as well. Stouffer's opened in 1976.

And that was the year that everything seemed to come together for Dayton. In Courthouse Square, the new Dayton Power and Light Building opened, as did the Elder-Beerman Department Store. Arthur Beerman, who died in 1970, had started Dayton's first suburban store and fought many downtown improvements with an impressive array of lawsuits. Yet

DAYTON RECREATIN': There is always something to see in Dayton, whether at Courthouse Square (top left and right); under the dome at the Arcade or on the walkway above Ludlow Street (center left and right); or in the Oregon Historic District (bottom left and right).

campaign to attract additional business is the Metropolitan Life Insurance Company regional headquarters which opened a handsome new business campus south of the Dayton Mall in 1976. Metropolitan proved to be a loyal Dayton booster, even producing a Dayton song—"Great 'n Dayton"—which has been recorded and played on local radio and television.

Key to a functioning downtown is transportation. Federal funds and a Montgomery County tax levy have enabled the Regional Transit Authority to provide a viable alternative to automobile transportation. Convenient bus schedules and modern; if jerky, equipment (contrasted with high automobile parking costs and escalating gas prices) made RTA's "countrywide" services an instant hit in 1980. Average ridership in early 1981 was 62,000 per week.

Dayton's aviation heritage was revitalized with a huge air show at Cox International Airport, source of America's most famous airport popcorn. The Air Show of 1976 became the Air Fair in later years and is one of the premier air shows in America. Promoters are striving to make it an international showcase second only to the Paris Air Fair in France.

Dayton is a typical midwestern city—and typically it grew in the '50s and '60s. Then it began a gradual decline. The population of Dayton proper dropped again in the unofficial results of the 1980 census to just slightly over 200,000. Although the suburbs have enjoyed rapid growth and the total area a slow, steady increase, in recent years Dayton has dropped from the 44th to 50th largest U.S. market. (Some statisticians

it was Beerman's corporation that made department store history by building the first new downtown store in any major American city in more than ten years. (In 1969, Beerman arranged to feed a traditional Thanksgiving dinner to any Daytonian who had no other plans for the day. There was no test of need—being alone was enough. After his death, the Arthur Beerman Foundation has continued the tradition.)

The old Burns-Jackson area (now Oregon Historic District) was also a visible success. Portions of Dayton View were being repopulated—in large part by college professors who preferred the "front-stoop society" of urban life to the "back-yard community of suburbia."

In the early '60s, the Dayton Area Progress Council was formed. The membership is composed of the chief executive officers of major Dayton area businesses. Immediately there was some public outcry that this was a return to the corporate paternalism of the early 1900s. But the council believed that federal money alone would not solve area problems; business leadership was needed, too. The council meets for two hours on Saturday mornings to hear presentations from government, industry, education and the arts. It tries to avoid politics—there are no official pronouncements—but it does take stands.

It has supported such projects as Stouffer's, Courthouse Square, Arcade Square, Oregon Historic District and the Daytonian Hotel restoration. The most visible result of its

Workers got an aerial view of downtown in 1976 as they prepared to place the last steel beam on the Mead Tower.

use slightly different criteria, but the trend is clear.)

To counter this, Dayton has produced its own standards of measurement. In the "90-minute market" (places accessible from the city center in 90 minutes), Dayton ranks as the tenth largest market in America. More than four million people are in Dayton's 90-minute market. Recently, Dayton has been touting its 90-minute air market. Within 600 miles of the city are 62 percent of the population, 65 percent of U.S. businesses and 75 percent of all employed workers. Of the top ten 90-minute markets, Dayton ranks first. The other top ten markets—such as New York, Chicago and Los Angeles—are more hindered by seacoasts and national boundaries.

The message has gotten across. Emery Air Freight is building a major regional air freight center in Dayton. Other transportation-related companies also have selected the city as a regional center, including General Motors which is building a huge diesel engine and truck plant.

Another ace up Dayton's sleeve is water. Dayton's underground Hamilton River can produce water for generations. And because wages have increased elsewhere at a faster rate than in Dayton, the city has become more competitive in both the skilled and semi-skilled labor market.

The greater Dayton area is the home of eleven banks and eleven savings and loan associations. There are seven hospitals, including the Veteran's Administration Center (formerly the Soldiers' Home), a children's hospital and a hospital specializing in osteopathy. There are six schools in the Dayton area offering degrees—Wright State University, Air Force Institute of Technology, United Theological Seminary, University of Dayton, Sinclair Community College and the Kettering College of Medical Arts, as well as a number of business and technical schools.

The Dayton Gems boasted six IHL championships during their years in the city.

"Beautiful Hockey!"

■ Dayton's most successful professional sports team was the Dayton Gems, an International Hockey League team which played in Dayton from 1964 to 1977. But their history really began in 1938 when Edgar "Lefty" McFadden arrived in Dayton to play baseball with the Dayton Ducks. McFadden was the force behind the Gems, and wherever six or more people were gathered together, Lefty was there to promote the team. The original owners earned their investment nine times over—during McFadden's ten years, he produced six IHL championships.

The Gems played in Hara Arena far north of town, and Lefty had to cajole, challenge, embarrass, bribe and threaten the fans to get them to show up. One year, the Gems had 5,100 of the 5,600 seats in the arena sold as season tickets.

But, after McFadden left in 1974 to help form the Washington, D.C. Capitols, the team began to struggle. They disbanded in 1977. Many Gems players, mostly Canadian, liked what they found in Dayton and decided to stay. Many other players went on to the ne plus ultra of professional hockey—the National Hockey League. Guy Trottier did both. A veteran hockey player when he arrived in Dayton, Trottier was called "too small" for the International League. After scoring an unbelievable 74 points in one year in Dayton, he moved to Buffalo to the American Hockey League where he was declared "too small" for the AHL. All Trottier did was to lead his team with 52 points. He moved up to the National Hockey League where, "too small" for the NHL, he scored 40 points (anything over 30 points is a superstar). Trottier currently lives in Dayton, as do former Gems coach, Warren Back, and goalie Pat Rupp.

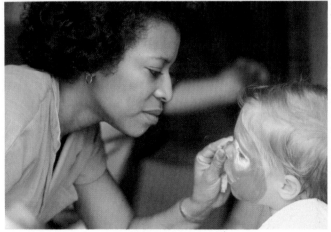

FESTIVALS AND TOURNAMENTS: Dayton is a ball — at the Hydrobowl (above); at the River Festival (below left); at Spring on the Farm (above right); or cheering the kids at the Special Olympics (right).

The dance in Dayton

■ *In September 1937, the Experimental Group for Young Dancers was organized by dancers Josephine and Hermene Schwarz. Always an independent company, the group held annual auditions for members. The first years were difficult. The company grew slowly, performing on the Dayton Art Institute stage, in living rooms, on 4-by-80-foot runways, in schools and on the massive Memorial Hall stage.*

The name of the organization has been changed several times to reflect the company's growing professionalism. In 1956, the Dayton Civic Ballet became a charter member of the Northeast Regional Ballet Festival Association.

The Dayton Ballet now consists of a fully professional touring company and the apprentice company. The second oldest regional ballet in the United States, it is fortunate that, for the past ten to fifteen years, male participation has been much greater than in most regional ballets. The new director, nationally-known dancer and choreographer Stuart Sebastian, began as a student at the Schwarz School. Dayton Ballet has a reputation for quality that reflects "Miss Jo" and "Miss Hermene's" original purpose—to prepare local dancers for professional work.

The renovation of the Victory Theatre in the early '70s provided the Dayton Ballet with a much-needed auditorium with a good floor. Using the theater as a base, the ballet continues to grow, and Dayton enjoys some of the best dance in the United States.

BOATS AND BASKETBALL: Eastwood Lake is home of the Hydrobowl, a center for championship power boat racing (above); the University of Dayton's basketball squad offers fierce competition worth following (right).

A time for leisure

But Dayton is not all work. Dayton boasts eight baseball diamonds, 99 softball diamonds, 32 bowling centers, 38 public pools and swim clubs, six public and nine private golf courses, 85 public tennis courts and six indoor clubs, three outdoor and three indoor skating rinks and 60 volleyball courts. There are miles of public bikeways, and Vandalia hosts the Ohio and Grand American Handicap Trap Shooting championships.

Although there are no professional sports teams in town, Cincinnati is not far away, and on a per capita basis, Dayton reportedly supports the Cincinnati Reds better than Cincinnati does. Local college and high school teams provide a high level of competition, especially in basketball. Amateur softball (Dayton was once a major center of fast-pitch softball), football, soccer and rugby thrive.

Musical groups include the Dayton Ballet, the Dayton Philharmonic Orchestra (and the Youth Philharmonic), Dayton Opera Association, Dayton Contemporary Dance Company, Dayton Music Club, Daytona Chorale, Music Under the Stars, Dayton Community Concerts and the world class barbershop group, The Sweet Adelines.

Although there is no full-time professional theatrical company in Dayton, there is the long summer season of Kenley productions at Memorial Hall, touring shows at the magnificently refurbished Victory Theatre (some recent shows have been produced locally by outside professional groups), and dinner theater. Some shows brought to Dayton by local impresario James Bridges are theater or musical theater.

Dayton has some of the finest amateur theater in the state and has won far more than its share of Ohio theatrical competitions. The prestigious Theatre Guild—Dayton's oldest amateur group—owns its own building and wins most of the competitions in spite of other strong local groups. Both Sinclair and the University of Dayton have active theaters. Wright State has an exceptional program and offers a fine arts degree in theater.

For painting and sculpture, Daytonians visit the Dayton Art Institute, one of the finest art museums in any city of Dayton's size. And for arts and crafts, there is the River Bend Art Center.

The area has four excellent museums. Three are small but important. The Montgomery County Historical Society, located in the beautiful 1850 courthouse, is rapidly becoming one of the finest historical museums in the state. The Dayton Museum of Natural History is not only a museum but an important arm of education, strong in archaeology, geology and astronomy. Carillon Park, given to the city by Deeds and his family, stands in the shadow of one of America's eight carillons. Over the years, the park has grown to become a major attraction. It contains Newcom's Tavern; a canal lock; a Barney & Smith railway car; various pieces of memorabilia from NCR, Kettering and Deeds; reconstructions of the 1905 Wright Flyer and the Wright's bicycle shop, plus a grist mill and four different automobiles, all built in Dayton.

The fourth museum is one of Ohio's major tourist attractions, the Air Force Museum. People from all over America and the world come to see the largest—and probably the best —collection of the world's military aircraft.

Jack Nicklaus was among the pros appearing at the NCR Country Club in 1969 during the second PGA championship tourney hosted by Dayton.

The Dayton Art Institute (above), and a view of the city from the Art Institute (below).

Looking east across the Great Miami River from 1,000 feet up.

THE GEM CITY: Whether participating in the myriad activities at the Dayton River Festival (above) or the Oktoberfest (right) sponsored by the Dayton Art Institute, Dayton is the place to be.

Coda

Dayton's success is no more assured than is the success of any other community. But even the most cynical citizen cannot fail to be impressed by Dayton's entry into the '80s. Salesmen who visit the town once or twice a year rave about the downtown renaissance. Dayton's natives seem to have a long-standing inferiority complex about the city, despite national attention for Oregon Historic District, Courthouse Square or the new I.M. Pei and Partners' Gem Savings Building.

Problems continue as a heavily industrial town shifts over to service industries. (There were more than 3.5 service workers to each manufacturing worker in early 1981.) Frigidaire was sold in 1979, and the manufacturing operation moved to Cleveland. Firestone closed its Dayton Tire and Rubber plant, and Dayton Press (formerly McCall's) is struggling to survive. Yet two major GM plants have started up recently, and a strong, privately financed effort to make Dayton a "high technology center" shows great promise.

The area has given America some of her most important inventions, and there is no reason to assume Dayton will not continue to produce innovative creations for tomorrow. Its people have the right stuff, and the revitalization of the city's core has given Daytonians the confidence they need to make Dayton what the *Cincinnati Chronicle* called the city in August 1845, "the gem of interior towns."

PARTNERS IN DAYTON'S PROGRESS

The Dayton Overland Sales Company was one of many businesses to make its mark on the city.

The corporate community has made dynamic contributions to the growth, development and quality of life in Dayton. The city's leading businesses have lent their support and financial commitment to the publishing of DAYTON: THE GEM CITY. Their corporate histories follow.

The Montgomery County Historical Society

The Montgomery County Historical Society is a child of the Dayton Centennial Celebration of 1896. The original local historical organization was formed in that year to "save" Newcom Tavern, Dayton's oldest building. The tavern, hidden for years under clapboards and plaster, was nearly demolished for an apartment building. When the building's identity was discovered, the hastily formed "Log Cabin Committee" (with the help of John H. Patterson, president of the National Cash Register Company) moved the cabin to a river-bank location in Van Cleve Park. With the tavern safe and enthusiasm still high, the "Friends of the Old Log Cabin" decided to start a historical society.

When the Dayton Historical Society incorporated in 1897, it had few members, less money and a headquarters sorely in need of restoration. The journey of the society through its early years was a tortuous one; growth was slow and activity levels low. In 1932, after 35 years of existence, the society had only 135 members. Financial reports during this same era show receipts and expenditures of only a few hundred dollars per year. Lack of member involvement and the absence of broad community support hampered progress. The old tavern was perhaps the saddest case of all. It had deteriorated so badly by 1933 that one board member seriously suggested enclosing the entire building in a giant glass case before the city's 1946 sesquicentennial.

It was the Old Court House which provided the rallying point needed to transform the Society into a modern organization.

Society trustees had dreamed of converting the Old Court House into a museum as early as 1928, but the goal was not to be realized until 40 years later. Long-range planning and decisive action were difficult in those early days. Even a simple merger with the Montgomery County Historical and Archeological Society (approved by the executive committee in 1939) did not become a reality until 1947, despite the fact that the two societies had operated jointly under the same president since 1933!

However, with the threatened demolition of the Old Court House in the mid-1960s and the leadership of Glenn Thompson, editor of the Dayton *Journal Herald,* the society began to change. It was under Thompson, local architect John Sullivan Jr. and others, that the Board of Trustees decided to hire the Society's first professional director. From that point on, the history of the society is a dynamic one.

Newcom Tavern, the first home of the Montgomery County Historical Society, circa 1897.

Under the supervision of Gary D. Schuman, the first director, membership more than quadrupled and the Society signed a lease for the Old Court House. Under later directors, staffing increased and in 1973 the Society opened the Old Court House as a museum. In 1974, it established the state's second Regional Preservation Office, and a year later assumed responsibility for the administration of the Patterson Homestead, the historic house museum and meeting facility at 1815 Brown Street in Dayton. In the late 1970s and early 1980s, the Historical Society completed the restoration of the Old Court House and greatly expanded its exhibit and education programs.

Professional staffing and such projects as the Historic Markers Program, the Miami Valley Memoirs TV series, expanded publications, upgraded school programs and a series of ever-improving exhibits have brought the Society fully into the modern era. The days ahead look promising. With the continued support of the membership and the community, local history has a bright future in Montgomery County.

The 1850 Montgomery County Courthouse, the present museum and headquarters of the Montgomery County Historical Society.

In pursuit of perfection: the history of the Sheffield Corporation

Today, the Cordax® Coordinate Measuring Machine is the world's most widely known inspection machine of its type, manufactured by the Bendix Automation & Measurement Division at its 721 Springfield Street location. In 1981, the Dayton manufacturer provided the Cordax® Coordinate Measuring Machine for final inspection of tiles for the space shuttle *Columbia*.

This page in Dayton history is dedicated to Louis Polk, founder of the Sheffield Corporation, which has become the Bendix Automation & Measurement Division. "It was a wonderful experience to participate with many friends and associates, inside and outside the organization, in helping build the Sheffield Corporation. Both credit and my greatest thanks to all of them," wrote Polk in recalling Sheffield's history.

Sheffield evolved from a merger of two companies. The original company, City Machine & Tool Works, later known as Cimatool Corporation, was organized in 1906 by O.M. Polk and became a successful tool and die shop. In the late 1920s, City Machine & Tool first added machine tools and other products to its offering. These included gear chamfering machines, gear burnishing machines and gear chucks. Later it also added burnishing rolls, master crushers, taps and thread dies, drills, Microform grinders, crush-form grinders and ultrasonic machines.

"In late 1932," Polk continued, "I was approached by parties who inquired about my interest in purchasing a smaller company, Sheffield Machine & Tool. After negotiations, the acquisition was completed just prior to the banking holiday of 1933. . . . Since the Sheffield Machine & Tool Company was going to continue in the gage business, I changed the name to Sheffield Gage. It prospered, and in 1941 I merged it with Cimatool Corporation and changed the name to the Sheffield Corporation."

The Dayton native and graduate from Miami University, Oxford, Ohio, was to emerge as one of the nation's most distinguished industrial leaders while at the helm of the birthplace of metrology and measurement. He has been described as a "tireless promoter of industrial standards . . . a twentieth century crusader for the acceptance and application of precision measurement and inspection techniques."

Polk's contributions go far beyond those made specifically to automation and measurement, though with sense for the integration of technology and society. "The nation's technical progress is limited by the ability to split the inch into smaller and smaller parts," said Polk at one of hundreds of speaking engagements in the '50s. "It's time that all of us work together to raise our sights . . . industry, government, banking must set sights at a higher level for tomorrow than they are for today."

During the mid-'50s, Sheffield was approached by the Bendix Corporation. "Though we turned down many other offers, we decided to consider their proposal. After extensive negotiations, we became a subsidiary of the Bendix Corporation, December 18, 1956. At that time, I became a corporate officer and member of the Bendix board and its committees," recalled Polk.

"In the course of growth over the years, we had founded the Eli Whitney Laboratory, which was the most advanced metrology lab in the world and back-up to the National Bureau of Standards. Additional products were added to the instrument gaging area including multi-check machines that measure 50 or more dimensions at a time. Another product added was the visual optical comparator. All this brought us further into the electrical and electronic gaging business," said Polk.

Polk is now chairman of the U.S. Metric Board. Bendix Automation & Measurement Division is the largest manufacturer of coordinate measuring machines, a leader in the manufacture of metrology instruments and a major supplier of manual production gaging, back-up gages for automatic gages used throughout the automobile, aerospace, off-road equipment and appliance industries.

"The diverse mix of technologies, engineering and manufacturing experience have provided a dynamic foundation from which to continue our leadership," said Jack Hubbard, group vice president and general manager of the Bendix Automation & Measurement Division. "Mr. Polk's spirited and conscientious drive is ever present in our organization today. It is the pursuit of perfection which has become our theme."

City Machine & Tool Works, circa 1906.

Benham's

Specialists in fine foods for three generations

Good food, prepared attractively, is a Benham's tradition (left). A garden party catered by Benham's offers not only fine food but beautiful surroundings as well (right).

From chicken dinners served in their country home in the '30s, Verna Benham's family-owned company has grown to serve catered parties over a five-state area. From the first pies baked in her kitchen, top quality has been the family's trademark for 50 years.

The catering came into existence in the mid-'20s in George Benham's homestead in nearby Lebanon, Ohio. (Three generations of George's family had resided there; the Benhams themselves were fourth cousins. Their ancestry is traced to Captain Robert Benham, a veteran of the Revolution and major Indian battles, and his sister, Catherine Benham, the first white woman to set foot on the soil of Dayton, Ohio, in 1796.) To supplement the farm income for the extended family of ten, Verna's children carried full meals including her blue-ribbon cakes and pies to customers.

In 1934, Verna Benham and her family opened their home, Brookside Farm, on Sundays as a restaurant. Her sons Jim and Lyle waited table, while the rest of the family, including daughters Betty and Roberta, cooked dinner in a converted coal shed. Typical meals featured their own chickens (pan fried with mashed potatoes and gravy), corn fritters and homegrown vegetables. Pies and cakes were served with homemade vanilla ice cream. After the meal, customers relaxed on the front lawn and listened to the Cincinnati Reds on the radio.

In 1941, the farm was sold; Verna's sons had entered the service, her daughter Betty had married and her husband George was in failing health. Her second Brookside Farm was a boarding house for war materials employees, with about 30 for supper each evening. The Benhams then moved to Dayton in 1944 to start an entirely new food venture. Meadow-brook Country Club, which had been closed during the war, was re-opening. Verna be-

came club manager, and Roberta was the bookkeeper. Verna operated two other country clubs before opening the Far Hills Restaurant in 1947 with her son Jim as partner.

Verna's long-range goal had been to manage a full-time catering operation. Soon she and Jim closed the restaurant, outfitted its basement with war surplus kitchen equipment and bought used vans to transport food and dishes to the party sites. During the '50s, Jim's customers were industrial and commercial accounts (with executives of Frigidaire, E.F. MacDonald, Citizens' Federal, Gallaher Drugs, L.M. Berry, Egry Register, Third National Bank and NCR). Home weddings, luncheons and lawn parties remained Verna's forte. When she passed away in 1962, her daughter Betty returned to catering as her brother Jim's party consultant. Betty's daughter and son-in-law, Becky and Bill Howser, joined the company, and Bill purchased it from Jim Benham in 1970.

The basement operation on Far Hills Avenue was moved in 1973 to downtown Dayton. During the 1970s, the business expanded, not only in the quantity of functions, but in the distance traveled to reach customers. Adapting the equipment to portable use (refrigerators, freezers, propane ranges and generators) has created a demand in Cincinnati and in Lexington and Paris, Kentucky.

The size of the staff grew along with the enlarged physical operations. John Gummel became general manager in 1977. Since most parties are on weekends, the ten full-time and fifteen part-time employees are joined by 35-50 additional personnel, depending upon the season or size of the function. The family aspect of the staff remains, in that Verna Benham's daughter Betty and granddaughter Becky manage the kitchen, while Becky's husband Bill Howser is the owner. Another active granddaughter is Roberta's daughter

Whether a wedding or a wine and cheese tasting party, Benham's offers only the best.

Susan. Thirteen other third generation cousins have worked for the family company through the years.

While maintaining product quality, however, Benham's has had the opportunity to serve a variety of functions too, from formal dinners, wedding and debutante receptions and charitable balls to much more casual affairs — Western barbecues, a catfish fry and a potato chip gala. In the annual Dayton Art Institute's Oktoberfest, Benham's features county fair waffles, strawberry crepes and quiche Lorraine.

The Benham tradition of giving a host or hostess the very best in food and services is quite singular. Verna Benham's concern for her "very best customers" will continue.

International yellow pages advertising sales firm started from one desk

When Loren M. Berry was born in 1888, the event did not take place in the town about which this book was written; but the Miami Valley was part of his future. And selling was in his soul. He was ready when fate stepped in 22 years later, in Marion, Indiana.

In 1910, the young Berry was winding up his interurban timetable sales when a friend asked him to stay in town to sell advertising for the local telephone company's directory. That was the unheralded beginning of L.M. Berry and Company, then called Ohio Guide Company, and the ultimate selection of Dayton as the town in which it would become established and grow. Berry chose Dayton because he knew the town's business conditions were excellent. The cash register and the auto industries were flourishing, and the Wright brothers were working on improvements to their airplane.

The newcomer secured a room (for $12 a week) for himself and his bride. He then found desk space in the tallest building in town, the U.B. Building. From there he contacted his first directory advertising sales customer, Dayton Home Telephone Company. In the allotted two weeks, Berry sold $700 worth of advertising — at that time a sizable amount.

Contracts with other telephone companies followed in nearby cities and towns. By 1914, Berry had hired additional salespeople, and within the decade, moved his offices to the Keith building. The year 1931 brought a contract with Ohio Bell to handle the Dayton directory's advertising, precipitating Berry's occupancy of the third floor of the Ohio Bell building and prefacing the company's surpassing $1 million in revenue handled by 1939.

Berry's son John W. Berry joined the yellow pages sales company in 1946. He became general sales manager in 1948 and company president in 1963. At that point, Loren Berry became chief executive officer and chairman of the board.

Under John Berry's direction, the company maintained its strong people orientation, while new energies were invested in training programs for clerical and sales people, as well as in improving systems for billing procedures and reports.

His plan was to keep abreast of the telephone industry and to establish an organization that would meet the demands of big business and the expanding marketplace. Divisions and territories were formed and became the nucleus of the nationwide company today.

Technical developments have affected L.M. Berry and Company — the computerization and photocompilation of directories, centralized selling by telephone over WATS lines. Company offices were moved to the present Kettering Boulevard location in 1964. From

The U.B. Building, where the young Loren M. Berry worked from rented desk space (left) and L.M. Berry and Company's corporate headquarters building, now one of three buildings at Kettering Boulevard, as it appeared at its completion in 1965 (above).

there spreads the network which handles directory advertising sales for approximately 500 Bell and independent telephone company customers throughout the U.S. and Canada. An international joint venture was established in 1967 between ITT and the Berry Company, ITT World Directories, Inc., which currently handles telephone directory publication and advertising sales in eight foreign countries. In 1981, international revenues exceeded $300 million.

In 1971, a third generation member of the Berry family, John W. Berry Jr., arrived on the corporate scene and was named an assistant vice president eight years later. It was Loren Berry's pleasure to see his grandson advance to that post well before the older man's death in 1980. At that time, Loren Berry was vice chairman of the board, and John Berry was chairman of the board. Ray H. Eshelman had been elected president of the company, succeeding J. William Craig Jr., who had held the job for the seven previous years.

Loren Berry was fond of saying that his company grew because he had good people around him. The same is true today. The company's general office at Kettering Boulevard in Dayton employs approximately 600 people from the surrounding communities. Nationally, it employes over 2,200 people to handle its directory advertising sales. For 1981, the company's domestic sales hit $380 million.

Success continues as an outgrowth of continued media acceptance, increased market penetration and additional innovative products such as neighborhood directories, business directories and business-to-business advertising. There are coupons, red ink and innovations yet to come, which are now mere glimmerings of ideas in the minds of Berry's research and development people.

One thing does not change, however, and that is L.M. Berry and Company's continued commitment to sell for its telephone company customers ". . . the largest amount of advertising revenue consistent with maintaining the best public relations with subscribers."

Blue Bird Baking Company

Keeping the human touch in mass production

Louis D. Preonas was born in 1897 in Klivonos, Thessaly, where he became an apprentice and then a master baker. After arriving in the United States about 1914, Preonas worked as a baker in several midwestern cities, finally settling in Dayton and founding the Bluebird Baking Company in 1923.

The first plant was at 10 Horton Street. In 1928, the first new building was erected at 521 Kiser Street, and this building has been added on to in 1948, 1955 and 1961. In 1931 Blue Bird expanded sales in Columbus, Ohio, and later more cities were eating Blue Bird pies. In 1932, the next bakery was added in Cincinnati; eventually sales and plants spread out of state. Later, Blue Bird owned its own fruit orchards, and in 1945 the company built a quick freeze and storage plant in Mitchell, Indiana. The company built and bought out more bakeries, built garages for its delivery trucks, and increasingly mechanized its production.

During World War II there were shortages of workers and of material — flour, sugar, fruits and shortening were rationed. Blue Bird had to discontinue the manufacture of the "nickel pie" (5¢); 500,000 a week were being produced until that time.

Eisenhower's road building programs made timely deliveries from a central point of production more desirable, and this led to the closing of plants in Troy, Columbus, Cincinnati, Louisville and Indianapolis. So as business grew, production at first spread out with sales, but later production was centralized once more. Now from Dayton fresh pies and

An early fleet of Blue Bird delivery trucks (below) and Louis D. Preonas, president and founder of Blue Bird Baking Company (right).

cakes are distributed within a radius of 300 miles to major metropolitan areas including Chicago, Detroit, Cleveland, Pittsburgh, Cincinnati and Louisville.

Blue Bird's rapid growth is attributed to Preonas' philosophy of work and management. As an immigrant from the old country, he was in love with the idea of democracy and thought of his employees as co-workers, as family. The company began publishing a company magazine called "Bluebird Briefs" in 1941. The old issues of the magazine are quite revealing of the atmosphere Preonas worked to create in his business; the very existence of the magazine is significant.

There are lots of little articles about company personnel, with their photographs, written in a friendly, folksy style. For example, the

headline about one Harry Kelonis is "Always In the Dough! Once He Wrestled For It, Now Wrestles With It." Kelonis, production manager, had immigrated from Greece and was described as "A Greek by blood and brand, Constantinopolitan by birth, American citizen by choice, Wrestling Champion by courageous strength and skill, Play-boy by inclination, Hardworker by necessity, Pie Maker by profession, adored by his loving wife and two children." "A Budding Executive," Earl Helm was "a nice fellow and everybody likes him." There are also many photos of employees at work and at play, and photos of children of workers. There are philosophical and inspirational essays and poems, there are jokes, there are stories about company parties, there are speeches by Preonas in which he admonishes, encourages, advises and praises his workers in a most paternal fashion.

Today, the Blue Bird Baking Company wants people to think of Blue Bird as a steady, conservative provider of quality baked goods. Rather than numbering its employees, the company counts about "500 families who make a living and help in all communities our territory covers." The current president and general manager is the son of the founder, and most of the other officers of the firm are family members.

Louis Preonas made each person feel that he was working for himself. He said that the company did not pay the employee; the employee was paid by the work he did. Preonas bound able men and women to him and his enterprise by a personal loyalty and devotion which drew from them far more energetic, cheerful and concentrated effort than could be bought with money.

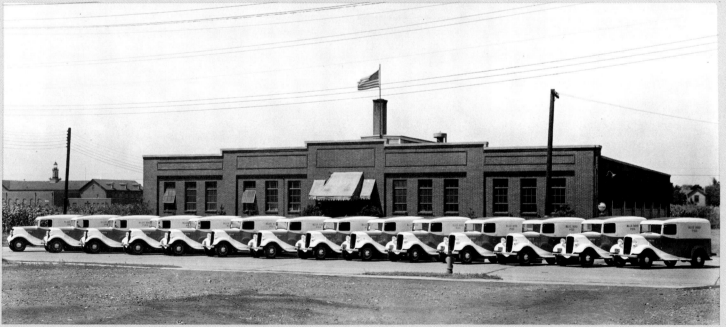

Where history lives — milestones in transportation

When Edward A. Deeds came to Dayton in 1899 fresh out of Denison University with an electrical engineering degree, he joined the National Cash Register Co. (now NCR Corporation) as an engineer. That was the start of a long association with Dayton, the Gem City, and a subsequent desire to provide the community with historical milestones in transportation.

During World War I, Deeds became chief of aircraft procurement for the United States Army and became a colonel. Deeds was associated with Charles F. Kettering in development of the first successful automobile self-starter, and they subsequently founded the Dayton Engineering Laboratories (Delco), now a division of General Motors Corp.

Because of his interest in Dayton, Colonel Deeds, who became chairman of NCR, decided just after World War II to establish a museum where future generations could look at transportation developments through the years.

The result was historic Carillon Park, a 65-acre wooded development with more than a score of buildings and over 50 exhibits on the southern edge of the city.

The park gets its name from the 40-bell Deeds Carillon bell tower built in 1942 as a gift of the late Mrs. Deeds. She was a life-long lover of music and an accomplished musician. Her desire to share that expression with others led to Deeds Carillon. Concerts are presented at the Dayton landmark bordered by Patterson and Carillon boulevards each Sunday evening, May through October.

Carillon Park, which is supported by a non-profit foundation established by Colonel and Mrs. Deeds and administered by a board of trustees, is under the direction of Joseph A. Usellis. The park rose from a swamp to become one of Gem City's finest tourist attractions.

Newcom Tavern once served as a temporary courthouse. The structure dates back to 1796.

The exhibits at Carillon Park, opened in 1950, cover a wide range of transportation developments and historical artifacts. Most noteworthy of the exhibits is the Wright Flyer III airplane in Wright Hall. Described by Orville Wright as the plane in which he and his brother, Wilbur, learned to fly, the craft is one of the priceless relics of aviation history. Orville Wright, a friend of Colonel Deeds, donated the plane to Carillon Park shortly before his death.

Charles Harvard Gibbs-Smith, British aviation historian, calls the Wright Flyer III "one of the most precious aeronautical treasures in the world. This machine was the world's first practical powered airplane and later the first airplane in the world to make successful flights with a pilot and passenger."

Orville and Wilbur made the world's first powered, sustained and controlled airplane flight on December 17, 1903, at Kill Devil Hills, Kitty Hawk, North Carolina. The Wrights built the Carillon Park machine in 1905, recalls Gibbs-Smith, and finally learned the secrets of powered flight and solved its basic problems.

The park also has an authentic replica of the Wright Cycle Shop, formerly located on the west side of Dayton, where the Wrights manufactured and sold bicycles.

Visitors see Newcom Tavern, Dayton's oldest building, dating back to 1796; an authentic one-room schoolhouse; a restored 1894 railroad station; an early blacksmith shop; an 1815 pioneer home; a grist mill; a steam fire engine; a 1903 open street car; a 1903 Barney & Smith wooden railroad coach built in Dayton; a 1912 New York Central steam locomotive, tender and wooden caboose.

Other interesting exhibits are the "grasshopper" Baltimore & Ohio locomotive #1, which helped open the Midwest to commerce; a covered bridge; a section of the Miami and Erie canal, fitted with one of the original locks; a Conestoga wagon; a Concord coach; and a 1912 Cadillac, first car equipped with Kettering's self-starter, an invention that made motoring more practical.

The newest exhibit, attracting the greatest number of visitors, is the antique automobile showroom housing four automobiles made in Dayton during the early part of the century.

The four cars include a 1908 Stoddard-Dayton; a 1910 Courier roadster; a 1910 Speedwell touring car, and a 1923 Maxwell sports touring car. Other exhibits in the building include a 1908 Dayton motor bicycle, a 1909 Custer electric three-wheel invalid car; plus two motorcycles, one made in Dayton and one in Cleveland.

The building includes a two-car showroom, parts department and service department.

More than 100,000 visitors worldwide tour Carillon Park annually without charge. The park is open Tuesday through Sunday from May through October. It is closed Monday, except when Monday is a holiday. Tour guides are provided and adequate parking is available. Several thousand school children visit Carillon Park each year during the school period.

The Wright Flyer III in which the Wright brothers learned to fly.

Central Printing Company

Growing with Dayton industry by innovation and service

Today's Central Printing Company is a far cry from the little job-shop started by Philip Burger and Albert Horstman after the disastrous flood of 1913.

From a storeroom on West Third Street between Broadway and Williams, the company moved to the 500 block on Wayne Avenue. In January 1920, Burger and Horstman bought from Upton German the Central Printing Company on East Fourth Street, just off Main Street. A year later, the two owners decided to go their separate ways, and Philip Burger retained Central Printing, which he incorporated in 1921.

The company grew during the 1920s and managed to survive the Great Depression. In 1939, Central was the third printing firm in the area to install an offset press.

In 1953, the company built a new building on Stanley Avenue only to have it taken the next year by condemnation proceedings clearing the way for Interstate 75.

The year 1956 saw great change. By then the company had to move to leased quarters at East Second and Sears streets. Philip Burger died that year, and his sons took over management of the company. George J. Burger became president and treasurer; Franklin, vice president; and Walter, secretary.

The period from 1952 through 1962 saw the company's greatest growth to date. Employment passed 50 and sales increased 500 percent, due in large part to the efforts of a salesman hired in 1952 named Peter J. Trohatos. In 1960, he became the company's first sales manager.

In 1972, Trohatos purchased control of the family company, taking on the responsibilities of chairman, president and treasurer. Central embarked on a decade of growth that saw sales increase from $1.2 to more than $13 million.

In October 1975, the company moved into its new 47,000-square-foot building at 2400 East River Road in Moraine. The facility was designed from the ground up as a model of printing efficiency.

During the next five years, Central installed the first commercial web press in the area, an investment of over $1.1 million, and added 12,000 square feet of leased warehouse space. It also added a plant in Fairfield, Ohio, a Cincinnati suburb, and opened sales offices in Columbus and Fairfield, Ohio, Fort Wayne, Indiana, and Lexington, Kentucky. By 1981, Central had over 175 employees and had completed a 33,000-square-foot addition to the plant.

Although printing-industry observers credit the company's exceptional growth to Trohato's leadership, he says the credit belongs to all the employees. "Everybody

Central Printing Company moved into their current facilities at 2400 East River Road in 1975.

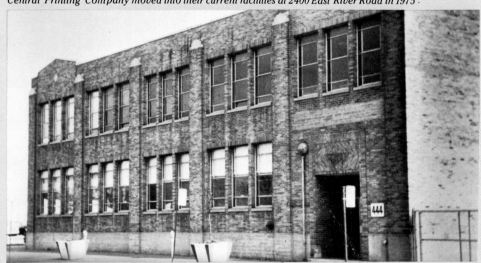
Central Printing Company in 1956 at Second and Sears streets.

puts the customer's needs first, regardless of what kind of effort it takes," he said. "Those millions of dollars of presses and equipment don't mean a thing without great people running them! Our success is attitude . . . of not just management, but everybody in our company."

Along the way, Trohatos and the company have been a major supporter of the community's business, cultural and civic efforts. Over 50 community projects enjoy this kind of continuing support.

Interestingly enough, most of the company's growth came during the 1970s when the Dayton area was in the throes of major

economic problems affecting many manufacturing-based cities. In 1975, the company ran advertising in regional editions of *Time, Newsweek, U. S. News* and *World Report* and *Sports Illustrated* directed at top management, not at printing buyers. And in 1981, it took a full page in the Dayton Sunday newspaper to tell both labor and management that "if you give a damn" you can make it big in Dayton.

"Good people and good equipment can knock the socks off the so-called Sun Belt companies." And that's not just Pete Trohatos talking: that's everybody at the Central Printing Company.

Dayton Malleable Inc.

A company shaping change

The roots of Dayton Malleable Inc. reach deeply into Dayton's history. Started in 1866, it is reported to be the second company west of the Alleghenies to make malleable iron. It is now the country's largest independent foundry organization. Charles Newbold and Peter Loeb formed The Dayton Malleable Iron Company, as it was named until 1973, as a partnership. It was incorporated in 1869 with Daytonian Colonel Edwin Parrott elected the first president in July. Originally located in east Dayton, the operation was moved to West Third Street in 1872. It produced both malleable iron and gray iron.

The young company produced saddlery parts such as bits and stirrups, soon followed by hardware for carriages, wagons and buggies. By 1882, product lines included farming equipment and bicycle parts, and sales had reached over $100,000 a year. In those days, variety was the spice of business, and parts for stoves, radiators, lawn mowers, and all types of machinery were produced as well. DMI's biggest impetus, however, came from the advent of the railroad late in the century and the automobile during the early 1900s. DMI "hitched a ride" and supplied castings for the budding transportation industry.

The first expansion outside Dayton was made in 1916 when the Ironton Division in Ironton, Ohio, was acquired. This proved to be a timely move as both the Dayton and Ironton plants were extremely busy during the war. The Ironton facility is now a leader in the production of nodular iron castings.

DMI's gray iron production from the Dayton plant was absorbed by the G.H.R. Division on Detrick Street in Dayton. Once known as the Gartland-Haswell-Rentchler Foundry Company, then the G.H.R. Foundry Company, the facility became a wholly-owned DMI subsidiary in 1935 and a division of the corporation in 1943. The plant is now one of the country's largest fully-mechanized

Edwin A. Parrott, elected the first president when DMI was incorporated in 1869, served for thirteen years.

DMI is the largest manufacturer of aluminum master brake cylinders in the United States.

gray iron foundries and has 500 employees. Production of malleable iron was continued at DMI's West Third Street plant until 1953 when it was moved to other manufacturing facilities.

Control of the Pratt & Letchworth Division, Buffalo, New York, was purchased in 1923, but it operated as a separate corporate entity until it became a DMI division in 1952. This foundry was formed in 1848 and was the first steel casting facility in the United States to operate commercially. Of the steel companies established before 1880, only the first company, Buffalo Malleable Iron Works (later Buffalo Steel, now Pratt & Letchworth Division of DMI), still manufactures steel castings.

In response to an emerging demand for light metal castings, DMI purchased the Meta-Mold Aluminum Company, Cedarburg, Wisconsin, in 1955.

To increase malleable and nodular iron capacity, the Meadville Division, Meadville, Pennsylvania (formerly Meadville Malleable Iron Company) was acquired in 1967. Then, in 1968, America's second oldest malleable iron foundry, Belcher Malleable Iron Company, Easton, Massachusetts, merged into DMI and is known today as Belcher Division.

A need for in-house machining capabilities led to the 1970 formation of the Peerless Division, Ironton, Ohio, a wise investment, as evidenced by several expansions.

In 1976, the Attalla Division in Attalla, Alabama — formerly Unexcelled Manufacturing Division of Twin Fair, Inc. — was purchased to enhance the company's gray iron manufacturing capabilities and to share in the growth of the Sunbelt.

The Columbia Division, Columbia, Louisiana, was added in 1977 to keep abreast of customers' needs for lighter castings. Aluminum parts can weigh up to half as much as similar iron castings; therefore, they play an important role in vehicle weight reduction.

DMI prides itself on the flexibility and quality it provides. Over 2,500 people are employed at the nine divisions and Dayton headquarters on South Dixie Avenue, which were built in 1958. A research center was added in 1965 and is one of the largest and most complete in the industry. The company has technical aid agreements with casting producers in Mexico, England, France and Belgium.

DMI's history began with bits and stirrups. Its future is being built on continued attention to the needs of American industry. The foundry industry itself is the fifth largest in the United States and DMI for 115 years has been an important contributor to its growth.

The Dayton Power and Light Company

Dependable service since 1911

On February 13, 1882, electricity was introduced to Dayton when the first electric light was illuminated in the office of the *Dayton Morning Journal*.

The city's initial electric light and power service came from a number of small companies. The Brush Electric Light and Motor Company of Montgomery County and The Dayton Gas Light and Coke Company were two small companies doing business in the early days of electricity.

In March 1883, these two companies merged to form The Dayton Electric Light Company. The city's first electric generating plant, built in 1883, was a combination water power and steam driven generating station. That same year, Dayton was one of the first cities in Ohio to light its streets with electricity.

In 1905, The Dayton Electric Light Company and a local competitor, The Dayton Lighting Company, merged under the latter name. The new utility enlarged the generating plant on Fourth Street and sold electricity to residents in the Dayton View and Riverdale areas, west on Third Street, south on Main and Brown streets and east on Third, Valley and Keowee streets to the corporation lines. Steam also was produced at the Fourth Street station as a by-product of the reciprocating engines and turbines used to generate electricity. The steam was distributed underground to a few downtown residential and industrial customers.

A rival utility — The Dayton Citizens Electric Company — built another coal-fired electric and steam plant in 1907. Competing utilities often installed power lines side by side. At that time, the charge for a kilowatt hour of electricity was about fifteen cents — almost three times more than electric rates today.

In 1911, the two utilities merged under the name The Hills and Dales Railway Company to generate, transmit and supply electricity and steam to Dayton. This company also constructed, maintained and operated the city's electric street railway.

The railway company was re-named The Dayton Power and Light Company (DP&L) on May 5, 1911. That October, Frank M. Tait, an associate of Thomas Edison, was elected DP&L's first president.

After the great flood of 1913, DP&L began expanding its lines to every corner of the city and adjacent territories. The company also purchased power plants and property in cities and villages surrounding Dayton. The addition of new territories to the system demanded greater power production stations. The company's first major coal-fired generating station began producing electricity in 1918. Miller's Ford Station, located on

the Miami River south of downtown Dayton, was re-named Frank M. Tait Station in 1946, in honor of the man who served as company president for 34 years.

In 1925, DP&L purchased The Dayton Gas Company. With this addition, DP&L became a combination gas, electric and steam utility. Natural gas was first introduced to the city in 1889. Presently, natural gas service is provided to 264,000 customers in sixteen counties.

Today, DP&L's service territory encompasses a 24-county, 6,000-square-mile area of West Central Ohio. The company provides steam service to nearly 400 customers in downtown Dayton for heating and industrial processing. DP&L also supplies over 400,000

customers with electricity generated at seven power plants. One of the nation's largest generating plants, J.M. Stuart Station was completed in 1974 and is jointly owned by DP&L, Cincinnati Gas & Electric and Columbus & Southern Ohio Electric companies. Located on the Ohio River, Stuart is operated by DP&L and represents nearly one-third of the company's total system generating capacity.

The Dayton Power and Light Company's corporate headquarters are located on Courthouse Plaza in the heart of downtown Dayton. The company is committed to providing dependable electric, natural gas and steam service to Dayton, the City Beautiful, and to the 268 other communities it serves in West Central Ohio.

An exterior view of Fourth Street Station in 1907.

Stuart Station, located on the Ohio River, was put into operation in 1970 with a generating capacity of 2,400,000 kilowatts.

Dayton-Walther Corporation

From cornfield foundry to multi-national manufacturer

President Theodore Roosevelt asked Colombia for permission to build the Panama Canal in 1903, the same year young George Walther embarked on a second voyage to the United States from Germany.

Walther had just completed a year's study in his homeland, augmenting ten years' experience gained in the foundry business in the United States.

Walther pursued metal working in Dayton upon his first arrival here in 1892. He resumed this work in 1903, then matriculated to other foundry towns, formulating ideas about the art of working with molten metal. His goal was to implement his knowledge of American foundry sciences, tempered by his own experience, into his own business.

He intended to put down roots in Dayton where other family members had settled, and he also recognized an opportunity in a city that was then the hub of a fledgling automobile industry.

Walther rented a cornfield just outside of town, built a small furnace and sheltered it with a tent, later replaced by a one-room foundry. Thus was born in 1905 the Dayton Steel Foundry Co. at a total expense of $4,000, thirteen years of backbreaking effort and a lifetime of planning.

Small steel castings for the automobile industry were among the company's first products and Walther's business quickly earned a reputation for quality.

Growth accompanies success and Dayton Steel Foundry prospered. Walther soon spent much time traveling, marketing Dayton castings for passenger cars.

As trucks entered the scene, Walther found he was well prepared for the opportunities they presented. Wooden wheels, such as used on cars, could not accept the punishment of heavy loads. Walther decided that initial steel wheel models he saw would not work either, so he set about perfecting his own.

In 1912, DSF produced the first acceptable cast steel cruciform wheel. The next year, Walther won a patent for the wheel. Soon, every major truck in the United States rolled on Dayton wheels.

It was during World War I that George Walther's energy and initiative resulted in a major breakthrough. The United States Army called foundrymen to Washington, stating the country's war effort demanded a strong steel wheel, and asking when such an effort could be completed. Walther's answer to unbelieving Army officers was six months.

Six months later, he boarded a train transporting the first Dayton Cast Steel Wheel designed for the Army.

Dayton Steel's growth now became a floodtide of success, the Dayton plant enlarging and expanding constantly.

An early photo of the original Dayton Steel Foundry Company, manufacturers of steel castings (above). The company which first occupied a tent in the middle of an Ohio cornfield now boasts this stylish and efficient corporate headquarters near Interstate 75 (left).

In post-World War II America, Dayton Steel was the company the industry looked to for wheel-end products. This industry-leading position led to new facilities in Portsmouth and Moraine, Ohio, and then to Canada in the 1950s.

George Walther Sr. was succeeded as president of Dayton Steel in 1961 by his eldest son, George Jr., who was to lead the company into its greatest period of growth. George Walther Jr. presided over a company that soon made wheels, hubs, brake drums, fifth wheels, landing gears, suspensions and other products for heavy-duty trucks and semi-trailers and was to make products for mobile homes and recreational vehicles, refrigerators for executive, recreational and home use.

While Dayton remained home base for the company, facilities were acquired in Cincin-nati, Ohio; Muncie, Indiana; and Fayette, Ohio. Other acquisitions were accomplished in Canada, Michigan, Kentucky and Tennessee.

Acquisitions and licensee arrangements led to manufacture of Dayton products in Mexico, France, Spain, Switzerland, England, Colombia, Brazil, Venezuela and Australia.

By 1972, Dayton Steel Foundry had outgrown the restrictive identity its name sometimes imposed. Now worldwide, it needed a new identity.

So was created, in 1973, the Dayton-Walther Corporation. And the progress continued, until today Dayton-Walther's manufactures are made in 39 facilities in ten states and ten foreign countries.

In 1978, President George Walther Jr. was elected chairman of the board and was succeeded as president by William D. Walther.

Celebrating its 75th anniversary in 1980, Dayton-Walther was the world's largest maker of spoke wheels for heavy-duty trucks and semi-trailers. Its divisions, affiliates, subsidiaries and licensees manufactured a growing line of products for the truck, semi-trailer, automobile, mobile home, recreational vehicle and construction industries and for the home.

Many factors insured Dayton-Walther's steady growth in the past, not the least of which was a reputation for quality, performance and dependability. It moves through the 1980s as a healthy, diversified corporation, guided by a management team that is both mature in judgment and youthful in outlook.

The future of Dayton-Walther is just as bright today as when George Walther lit the flame under the first furnace in 1905.

The Grand Lady of Ludlow

The Daytonian is a memorable hotel even beyond its services and special touches because it rekindles the spirit of a Grand Old Lady, The Algonquin Hotel, built in 1898 at this location. The Algonquin Hotel, originally built as an apartment house, was opened as a first-class hotel the following year, and during the early 1900s, it became the largest and most modern of the Dayton hotels. It was one of two downtown buildings using water from its own private wells.

Charles Insco Williams, a well known Dayton architect, designed the building for the original owner, J. Elliott Pierce. Small but elegant, The Algonquin expanded several years after its opening into a 300-room hotel. Complete with a roof top garden and the grandest ballroom in Dayton, The Algonquin charged $2.50 and $5.00 a night.

The Algonquin hosted one of National Cash Register's International Sales Conventions in 1910, housing businessmen from around the world. In 1913, the flood devastated downtown and caused serious problems for the hotel. The water reached its second floor and covered the public rooms and the lobby.

Pierce sold The Algonquin Hotel in 1918 to Michael J. Gibbons. The "face" had changed, but the building was still "lively to the eye." The Algonquin Hotel became The Gibbons Hotel.

The new hotel was managed by Gibbons until his death in 1925. Then his sons took it over until 1939, and after that the Gibbons Company was formed to take over operations.

In 1958, a bold experiment was tried at the hotel—about 350 University of Dayton freshmen turned part of the building into a dormitory to ease the acute housing problem. (Two years later, the university made a men's dormitory out of the vacated Brown hospital at the VA center.)

Days were numbered for the Gibbons Hotel, but almost immediately the new Dayton Inn was planned: a plush motor hotel with meeting rooms, swimming pool, parking deck and fully air-conditioned rooms. The twelve-story Dayton Inn was remodeled and opened in 1962.

In the early '70s, many of the hotels in downtown Dayton began having difficulties. There wasn't enough convention business to keep all of the downtown hotels full. It seemed economically unfeasible to continue operating the 235-room hotel, and the Dayton Inn closed its doors on December 31, 1977.

In 1978, William F. and Gretchen Gorog launched an extensive campaign to completely rebuild the only one of seven downtown hotels to survive from the turn of the century. After one and a half years of renovation, the property was restored to elegance as The Daytonian.

The Gorogs, who are Dayton natives, were

The Algonquin Hotel, ancestor of the new Daytonian, used water from its own private wells.

G.G.'s Restaurant is part of the new Daytonian Hotel.

well acquainted with the Dayton business community and expected an excellent response to The Daytonian from the business leadership of the city, which had long noted the absence of a luxury hotel in the area.

The ambience of The Daytonian is largely created by the structure of The Algonquin Hotel. The interior design has fourteen different room floor plans on the eight floors of The Algonquin section of the hotel. The public rooms reflect the dignity and elegance of turn of the century decor.

General Manager John G. Wilderman and his Daytonian staff take pride and pleasure in carrying on the tradition of quality and service.

As the city of Dayton grows larger, travelers will continue to find comfort and luxury in the Grand Lady of Ludlow.

The Elder-Beerman Stores Corp.

Dynamic partner in Dayton's growth

Employees of the Elder & Johnston Co., predecessor of Elder-Beerman, posed in 1908.

In 1920, young Arthur Beerman arrived in Dayton with his retail apprenticeship behind him and an innovative business career ahead of him.

After employment at several local department stores, Beerman became interested in real estate and eventually became a developer. With his sister, he opened several small shops catering to local apron and housedress customers. Because of the seasonal nature of the business, infants' and children's wear were added. The five shops were appropriately named "Beerman Youth Centers."

The decade of the 1950s was a period in which America's department stores began to expand their marketing perimeters to suburban areas. Taking advantage of this trend, Beerman, in 1950, opened McCook, a junior department store in a strip shopping center. With the success of this venture, a similar store, Eastown, followed four years later. A third store, Westown, opened for business in 1956. That same year saw the Beerman organization's acquisition of The Home Store, at the downtown location on Third and Main streets. Van Buren opened in 1958.

In 1961, the company merged with the Elder & Johnston Company, a major retailer in the community located at the corner of Fourth and Main streets. One important result of the acquisition was an increased ability of the Beerman retail operations to bring a greater selection of nationally recognized brand merchandise to its customers. Another outcome was the corporate name, The Elder-Beerman Stores Corp.

With this incentive to further expansion, Elder-Beerman continued with its customary vigor to remodel Northwest and to open Cen-terville and Hamilton in 1967. Since that time, other department stores have opened in Lima; Piqua; Fairborn; Middletown, Ohio and Richmond, Indiana.

Following the death of Beerman in 1970, Max Gutmann, a co-founder of the Bee-Gee Shoe Corporation with Beerman, was elected president. In 1973, Gutmann was elected chairman of the board. At his directive, announcement was made in 1974 of plans to construct a full-line department store on Dayton's developing Courthouse Square. As one of only two department stores in the nation to be built at a downtown location in several decades, this flagship store exemplified Elder-Beerman's continuing allegiance to a policy of community involvement. The grand opening of Courthouse Plaza, as it was named, was held in October 1976. In the spring of 1978, the four Mabley and Carew stores in Cincinnati were purchased from the Allied Stores Corporation. In April 1981, another store opened its doors in Chillicothe, Ohio.

Today, the Elder-Beerman department store group consists of twenty department stores and three furniture stores. The El-Bee Office Outfitters operate three stores in Dayton and Hamilton.

With the summer of 1981, Elder-Beerman accepted yet another challenge. Based on experience gained in the operation of 68 El-Bee Shoe Outlets in Ohio, Kentucky, Indiana, West Virginia and Texas, 69 women's specialty shops named Margo's were purchased from an established retailer, along with two shops devoted to childrenswear, Young Ages. This acquisition brought the corporation into the Sun Belt.

The Elder-Beerman Stores Corp. continues to consider Dayton its home and its corporate headquarters — an intimate partner and good neighbor in the business and civic life of Dayton. The major ownership of the corporation remains in local hands and is exemplified by Mrs. Barbara B. Weprin (the Beerman daughter) and Leonard B. Peal (the Beerman nephew), members of the corporation's board of directors, and by Mrs. Arthur Beerman.

The growth outside of the Dayton community has increased the strength of the corporate headquarters. Employment now numbers approximately 6,000 and increases seasonally.

Elder-Beerman Courthouse Plaza, August 1981.

Gem Savings

Building continuity at Dayton's crossroads

The Third and Main streets' crossroads in downtown Dayton has been a hub of human enterprise since the late eighteenth century. From the building of a log cabin Presbyterian meeting house on the northeast corner in 1799 to the 1981 opening of Gem Savings' modern corporate headquarters, Gem Plaza, Daytonians have conducted their commercial and personal business at this location opposite the busy courthouse.

On October 27, 1887, The Gem City Building and Loan Association was incorporated. A board of nine leading members of the community opened the new association in a small second-floor law office in the "Callahan block," as the Third and Main northeast block then was known. The rent was $10 per month.

Business was conducted in the friendly homespun style of that era. According to board minutes of September 1890, a "housewife" purchased a $1,700 property with a $100 down payment and a $1,600 mortgage from the association. She agreed to pay at least $30 a month on the loan as long as Dr. Weaver and Mr. Elder (directors) boarded their horses at her husband's livery stable. All parties agreed.

The standard for personal service and convenience established in those early days would have a reverberating impact on the training and performance required of future management and employees. To this day, with almost two dozen branch locations, with services that have multiplied and been automated and with almost 175,000 customers, individualized service is still the keystone of Gem Savings' operations.

As early as 1895, 1,000 pamphlets on the subject of savings were ordered at a cost of $20. Today, a specialized staff of nearly 450 uses marketing data and communications media to sell a growing number of banking services.

The original one-room office was open only a few hours each Saturday and Monday for the "reception of dues." Today, service is available every day with automated Gem Card Tellers. Offices and loan centers are established in seven counties of southwest Ohio. Services include checking accounts, home improvement and home equity loans, flexible rate-type mortgages, cash reserve loans, money market and other certificates, retirement plans and conveniences such as telephone transfer, automatic loan payments, direct deposit and payroll deduction savings.

Another early indicator of Gem Savings' future can be found in the association's story of the 1913 flood. Waters rose to ten feet in the ground-floor Wells Fargo office (Gem Savings' second location), sweeping typewriters, adding machines and ledgers off the highest counters. On that morning of March 25, O.J. Bard, general manager, and Daniel Dotson, a future officer, worked until the last moment before exiting out of the high back windows.

Gem Savings' first association-built headquarters in 1920.

Gem Savings' new I.M. Pei-designed headquarters opened in 1981 at Third and Main streets.

Later, electric irons dried notes and mortgages, and $5,000 was authorized by the board for the flood prevention fund.

This tradition of "holding the fort" and supporting the community was to persist through the Great Depression, two world wars and the continual fluctuations of local and national economies.

The doors of Gem Savings have always remained open through each difficult period to assure the security of savings during the Depression and to provide mortgage funds during the post-World War II housing boom to mention only two instances. Today sound assets of well over $1 billion and strong liquidity and reserve positions are maintained

under the leadership of Warren R. Ross, chairman of the board, and Ronald K. Dickerson, president.

Gem Savings has lent money for renovation projects which benefit the community, including Arcade Square, The Daytonian Hotel and the Old Post Office, among others.

Gem Plaza at the Third and Main crossroads is the latest addition to the continuing renaissance of the city. Gem Plaza, embracing the neighboring Courthouse Square, was designed by the internationally acclaimed firm of I.M. Pei and Partners. The modern headquarters represents a continuation of service pledged nearly a century ago to the city of Dayton and its people.

Medical excellence marks 50th year

Good Samaritan Hospital and Health Center was dedicated on May 12, 1932 (above). Good Samaritan Hospital and Health Center, 1980 (below).

The spirit of the founding of Good Samaritan Hospital and Health Center — meeting the challenge of change to provide vital medical care and concerned hospital service — has remained a distinguishing characteristic throughout its service to the Dayton area.

In 1927, the Dayton Research Association recognized the need for more hospital beds in Dayton, prompting the offer of support from the Sisters of Charity of Cincinnati, Ohio. Their commitment was to finance and staff a 250-bed hospital and provide education for registered nurses.

A Dayton physician, Dr. D.W. Beatty, donated land for a site while other citizens pledged more than $1 million.

It was a severely depressed economy that witnessed groundbreaking in 1930 and the dedication of Good Samaritan on May 12, 1932. The construction was the first of nine building projects begun during the next 50 years.

The School of Nursing, housing 105 residential student units, served the Dayton area for 40 years. In 1972, the program was transferred to Sinclair Community College.

Technological advances challenged the capabilities of health care institutions. A three-story west annex containing 108 beds was added in 1944 followed in 1952 by the Madonna Pavilion, a 110-bed structure housing maternity services and improved facilities for surgery, radiology, laboratory, maintenance and laundry. The $1 million raised by Dayton citizens for the Madonna expansion was matched by the Sisters of Charity.

Building expansion in 1956 added 96 units to the Good Samaritan School of Nursing. A

cafeteria, convent, administrative offices and what was then called the Emergency Room were built in 1965.

A 500-space parking facility was constructed in 1968 on the site of a farmhouse on Philadelphia Drive. It soon was overshadowed by the South Building, which cost more than $33 million and replaced many outmoded health care facilities. The South Building included the 2200 Building, a structure containing physicians' offices, outpatient care areas and space shared with the affiliated Wright State University School of Medicine.

Good Samaritan Hospital added "and Health Center" to its name for good reasons. Beyond the walls of Good Samaritan are the Vogel Health Center and West Dayton Health Center. The Good Samaritan Community Mental Health Center reaches out to people through satellite locations and works with local law enforcement agencies and the court system.

At the Maria-Joseph Living Care Center,

Good Samaritan provides a paramedic training program to thirteen counties. The program has graduated more paramedics than any other program in the United States. The Center also houses Samaritan Hall, a 25-bed alcohol and substance abuse facility.

In 1932, its first year of operation, Good Samaritan cared for 1,614 patients. By 1981, in-patient hospital services were rendered for more than 20,000 people with nearly 40,000 treated in modern Emergency Department facilities.

Sister Mary Daniel Twohig, the first administrator of Good Samaritan, was succeeded by seven Sisters of Charity with representation from business, industry and the medical community. As Good Samaritan's 50th anniversary is marked in 1982, James P. Fitzgerald serves as president. One-third of the trustees are Sisters of Charity. The hospital, in addition, is guided by the Sisters of Charity Health Care Systems, Inc., a corporation of seven hospitals subscribing to the policies and philosophy of the Sisters of Charity of Cincinnati.

Good Samaritan Hospital and Health Center in 1981 achieves medical excellence through the efforts of more than 500 physicians and cares for patients in its 547 beds with more than 2,600 full and part-time employees.

All health care needs whether as simple as small lacerations or as complex as open heart surgery are met by Good Samaritan Hospital and Health Center in a responsible and responsive manner. Hundreds of volunteers offer talents while Good Samaritan Foundation donors provide voluntary dollars.

Heidelberg Distributing Company

Innovative services complement quality products

Original Stewart Street warehouse and office circa 1945 (above) and Centre City Building, 40 South Main Street, Dayton, Ohio (left). Close photo of offices, garage area and main beer warehouse. Lower right building is the wine warehouse with a portion left off (below).

The most valuable thing that Albert Vontz had brought from Germany in 1907 was his knowledge of the brewing industry. With a background as brewery worker, barkeep and part owner of the Vienna Brewery in Cincinnati, it was a natural transition for Vontz to purchase a wholesale beverage distributorship in Dayton in 1937.

The distributorship began as a branch of the Heidelberg Brewing Company, and it took its name from that brewery. The small 5,000-square-foot warehouse was located at 133 East Stewart Street in the shadow of the National Cash Register complex.

In 1940, Albert Vontz Jr. joined his father at Heidelberg. That year also marked the addition of wine to the beer sales distribution. Heidelberg Brewery closed in 1946, but the distributorship steadily added new brands to its inventory. As consumer interest in light alcoholic beverages increased, the company prospered.

Heidelberg Distributing Company was incorporated in 1959 with the father and son as partners. There followed a period of expansion when other distributorships were consolidated. Palazzola Wine Companies in Cincinnati and Dayton were purchased in 1959 as was the Anheuser-Busch branch distributorship in Cincinnati. Service Distributing Company, the present site of Heidelberg's Dayton operation, was added in 1961. Next came Air City Distributing Company of Dayton (1963), Berman Wine Company of Toledo (1967) and

Fisher Brothers Distributorship of Cincinnati (1978).

In 1975 the historic Centre City Building at Fourth and Main streets was purchased to house Heidelberg Distributing Company's corporate headquarters. There are now over 100 in-town and over-the-road trucks and some 350 Heidelberg employees. The company is southwestern Ohio's largest beer and wine distributor — number one in wine distribution and number two in beer distribution for this state.

Heidelberg Distributing Company has made many contributions to the wholesale beverage industry, not the least of which is the graduation of numerous "alumni" of the company sales and management teams to responsible positions in wineries, breweries and distributorships across the nation.

Heidelberg pioneered the use of dual sales and delivery forces to handle beer and wine. In the late 1960s, the company was among the first in the industry to use data processing to handle inventory maintenance and incoming orders. In 1970, Heidelberg was the alcoholic beverage distributor to initiate use of industrial revenue bonds to finance new construction. In 1978, solar collection panels were built into the newest of the company's Leo Street warehouses to heat the buildings and aid in the nation's energy conservation efforts.

In the last two years, the company has also innovated the use of radio-dispatched trucks

to better service customers and save vehicle mileage.

Diversification has ranked with innovation as a Heidelberg hallmark. The company owns WNOP, Cincinnati's floating "Jazz Ark" radio station, and KSNO, a radio and cable TV station in Aspen, Colorado. The 740 Marina on the Ohio River; the Captain's Anchorage, a floating restaurant also on the river; and real estate holdings in Ohio, Colorado and Florida complete the list of company concerns.

The family tradition remains at Heidelberg. Albert Vontz III entered the business in 1975 and serves as executive vice president of the Cincinnati operation. Vail K. Miller, son-in-law of Al Vontz Jr., is president of Dayton Heidelberg Distributing Company. The dreams of the German immigrant have come true in the Gem City.

From sewing machines to the largest producer of bicycles in the United States

The machine shop at Huffman's Gilbert Avenue factory, October 1926 (above). During World War II, Huffman converted to war production, manufacturing automotive service equipment, bicycles and shell primers for the armed services (left).

The Huffy Corporation's origins go back to 1887 when George P. Huffman purchased all the assets of the Davis Sewing Machine Company and moved it to Dayton. In 1892, the company began to manufacture bicycles, making the Huffman family pioneers in the bicycle industry. The Davis Company entered the new field of electric washing machines in 1913. In 1925, after the sewing machine business was sold to Eastern interests, the name of the company was changed to The Huffman Manufacturing Company, headed by H.M. Huffman Sr.

The company saw opportunity for growth in the budding automotive industry and went into the manufacture of service station equipment, starting with a line of oil measures. The Huffman Manufacturing Company was the first to make a canned oil dispenser and invented several key service products for the automotive industry which are still in use today.

As the company continued to grow,

Huffman was quick to build a team of employees that could move the company ahead. It had begun to diversify and was on its way to becoming an important manufacturing and sales company.

In the depth of the Great Depression, Huffman, sensing a resurgent interest in bicycles throughout the country, expanded bicycle production. During the war years, under the leadership of H.M. Huffman Jr., Huffman joined many companies in producing products for the war effort.

Realizing post-war production would be limited by the availability of parts and raw materials, Huffman instituted a work simplification conference for all of its major suppliers with the objective of helping suppliers increase output to meet the challenges of the future. The post-war boom continued for two years with Huffman running at maximum production, and, when the expected post-war recession began, the company introduced the famous "Huffy Convertible" bicycle. An immediate success, it became the foundation upon which the Huffy brand was built.

The company needed seasonal products to manufacture during the winter months. In 1949, Huffman made the decision to go into the electric lawnmower business and was one of the first companies in the rotary mower business. In the 1950s, the company moved the Dayton bicycle manufacturing facilities to a large new plant in Celina, Ohio. It also acquired a manufacturing facility in Delphos,

Ohio, for the automotive service equipment product line. In addition, Huffman acquired its California bicycle plant in Azusa, California, thereby becoming the only major manufacturer of bicycles with a West Coast facility. Huffman continued on the move and by 1960 was the third largest bicycle manufacturer in the country.

In 1964, the acquisition of the Dille & McGuire Manufacturing Company in Richmond, Indiana, added important product manufacturing capabilities for the outdoor power equipment division. Total sales climbed rapidly to $42 million by 1969, and a success story was recognized across the country with Huffman stock's listing on the American Stock Exchange. In 1964, the company corporate offices were moved to a new building in Miamisburg, south of Dayton.

When Stuart J. Northrop joined as president in the early '70s, Huffman formed a new management team with Frederick C. Smith as chairman of the board and Horace Huffman Jr. as vice chairman.

During the bicycle boom in the early '70s, Huffman instituted aggressive advertising, thereby capturing the major share of the bicycle market in the latter part of the decade. Sale of the lawnmower business allowed Huffman to concentrate on its number one product lines — bicycles and automotive equipment. A new bicycle manufacturing facility was started in Ponca City, Oklahoma. In addition, during the '70s, the decision was made to change the name from The Huffman Manufacturing Company to the Huffy Corporation, and the Huffy Corporation was listed on the New York Stock Exchange.

As a logical extension of product lines, the Huffy Corporation purchased the Frabill Manufacturing Company in Milwaukee, Wisconsin, a primary manufacturer of sporting goods. To continue doing what Huffy knew best, the decision was made to go into the exercise bicycle business and related fitness equipment to be produced through the Milwaukee Division. In 1978, Harry A. Shaw was elected president and Stuart J. Northrop chairman of the board.

By the 1980s, more than 3,000 employees were contributing daily to the Huffy story. The little company that began in Dayton as a manufacturer of sewing machines in 1887 now owned over 2.5 million square feet of office and plant area in six locations.

Through 94 years of responsible leadership and employee dedication, the Huffy name has gained a reputation for quality and integrity, and Huffy Corporation has become the largest bicycle manufacturer in the United States. Innovation instituted by the industry leader has proven to be successful and stands as a promise for the future.

Ledex Inc.

Emphasizing ingenuity in engineering and performance in the product

In the early 1940s, just prior to Pearl Harbor, the U.S. Army Air Corps needed engineering talent and needed it fast. In the very shadow of Wright Field, the development center in Dayton, the Air Corps Armament Lab discovered that George H. Leland — engineer/entrepreneur/manufacturer — was available because he had recently given up his duties as chief operating executive of his company to become chairman. A restless and creative type already past middle age, Leland was more challenged by "unsolvable" engineering problems than by repetitive production. He took on numerous Air Corps assignments and with his newly organized

engineering company turned out one after another ingenious solution for some other company to manufacture for the war effort.

One of his development contracts was an electric bomb release which could withstand the severe vibration and shock of turbulent air and battle damage that the Flying Fortresses were experiencing over Germany. The key to a shock-resistant bomb release, reasoned Leland, would be a *rotary* solenoid rather than the conventional *linear* solenoid (a solenoid is an electro-magnetic actuator which can convert an electrical impulse into a short but powerful mechanical stroke). Within a few weeks, Leland had designed and produced prototypes of a solution to the bomb release problem. Simultaneously, and without realizing it, he had laid the groundwork for a business, based on solenoid technology, which would flourish and continue to grow for another 40 years and beyond.

At the close of hostilities, with a second generation of Lelands shedding uniforms for

A 1953 photo of the original building on Webster Street, vacated for new facilities in 1978 (below) and George H. Leland (1887-1969) discusses one of his most important inventions, the rotary solenoid (left).

civilian clothes, the whole family pooled their financial resources and launched a new manufacturing business. At first, the new corporation was called G. H. Leland Inc., but the name was later changed to Ledex Inc. Aggressive sales promotion, a receptive marketplace and an idea-fertile engineering department were the important contributors to the company's early success. The rotary solenoid found its way into new generations of labor-saving automation equipment. One new application in particular was the use of the rotary solenoid to drive a gang of rotary switches. Soon every basketball arena and football field had electric scoreboards using the company's stepping switches to control the lights on the "figuregrams," replacing the numbered shingles hanging on a nail.

As the world entered the space age, the young company was among the active participants. All the early satellites carried Ledex solenoids doing such critical jobs as advancing the tape in a magnetic recorder, tripping shutters for the first close-up pictures of Mars or operating latches on manned space capsules.

In the early '60s, Ledex acquired a small Detroit company, Bramco Inc., and moved it to Piqua, twenty miles north of Dayton. This acquisition gave Ledex its entree into electronic systems, and the company is now a leader in audio tone technology with a family of remote supervisory and status monitoring equipment for critical applications in the pipeline, petroleum and utilities industries.

A second major expansion move for the company was the starting of a new operation making rotary band-type switches. Located 35 miles southeast of Dayton in Wilmington, this move was necessary to solve a critical supply problem and broaden the product line.

Ledex met the challenges of the Vietnam War by contributing solenoids, switches and precision intervalometers while building its reputation in non-defense markets. The explosive growth of computers in the '70s set off an equally explosive demand for high speed printers, word processors, copiers and related paper handling office machinery. To meet this challenge, Ledex developed a whole line of precision *linear* solenoids to satisfy the demand for high speed, reliability and long life in the computer world.

As the company entered the '80s, it utilized over 150,000 square feet of office and factory floor space and employed more than 500 people. It continued to grow with a domestic and global network of sales representatives and licensed foreign affiliates. Ledex has managed its growth as a corporation closely held by the members of the family, employees and associates.

The E. F. MacDonald Company

A company . . . an industry

The story of The E. F. MacDonald Company and that of the incentive industry go hand-in-hand. One rarely hears the word incentive mentioned without reference to the industry's first incentive company and its founder, Elton F. MacDonald.

In 1922, Elton F. MacDonald was hired as a clerk by William F. Cappel, head of A. Cappel and Sons, a Dayton company primarily involved in the manufacture and sale of luggage and umbrellas.

MacDonald advanced quickly at Cappel and within eight months was making outside calls selling briefcases, portfolios and a variety of leather goods. He soon recognized an interest among companies such as NCR and Delco to provide merchandise awards to top salesmen.

Reasoning that other businesses might buy prizes to award salesmen who achieved certain goals, MacDonald plunged full-force into selling incentive campaigns.

Company sales volume grew steadily, reaching $100,000 in 1926. One year later, the company's first major automotive sales campaign proved to be an important breakthrough, boosting annual sales to $600,000!

With the success of the incentive business came the need for a wider choice of prizes. This need was filled through the publication of the first incentive award catalog, which included two of the basic principles of the incentive business — choice and family influence.

Originally, incentive campaigns were directed to the "stars" of the salesforce. Prizes were awarded only to those persons who achieved their quotas. This practice left the "average" performer with little incentive to work harder.

Consequently, the Cappel, MacDonald partnership, formed in 1937, introduced the "point system," thus permitting every salesman to compete against his own past performance. All salesmen were motivated rather than just a few. This technique remains the keystone of 99 percent of all modern incentive activities.

This change in the motivation philosophy brought a turning point in the growth and development of both Cappel, MacDonald and the sales incentive industry. Sales volume rose steadily, reaching $1 million in 1947, $10 million in 1952 and $25 million in 1955.

In 1947, Cappel, MacDonald & Co., an Ohio corporation, was formed, replacing the original partnership. Early in the '50s, it had become clear that additional types of awards were needed. Travel proved an excellent answer, and, by 1954, Cappel, MacDonald & Co. had expanded to include a travel service.

The year 1958 witnessed the birth of The E. F. MacDonald Company. In 1961, a Delaware corporation bearing the same name was formed, absorbing by merger the business and properties of the Ohio corporation. The

Front cover of the 1927 merchandise catalogue for Willard Storage Battery Co.

Merchandising selections from the 1928 Goodyear catalogue included ladies' golf clubs and early airplane wardrolette (top) and the 1929 Goodyear catalogue added the latest selections of furniture for the home (above).

year 1961 also marked the first offering of company shares to the public and a new sales record of $50 million.

During the '60s, E. F. MacDonald established The E. F. MacDonald Stamp Co. Plaid Stamps were distributed through the A & P grocery chain and other merchants.

At present, The E. F. MacDonald Company is an international corporation with 28 U.S. incentive offices and nine offices in Europe and Australia. Other E.F. MacDonald Companies include: Mail-A-Way, Inc., one of the country's largest mailing facilities; E.F. MacDonald Creative Marketing, offering complete marketing and advertising services; MacDonald Motivational Research Center, Inc., specializing in psychological research and training; and E.F. MacDonald Showroom Sales

Centers, Inc., displaying retail catalog merchandise.

The company employs 1,500 people worldwide, and 800 of those employees are in Dayton. These employees have supported their community in a variety of ways, most notably through annual donations to United Way and the Community Blood Center.

The 1980s will be an exciting period for MacDonald. There are plans for a merger between Carlson Companies, Inc. of Minneapolis and The E. F. MacDonald Company. The merger plans assure MacDonald's continued growth in Dayton.

The company is also planning a move to the corner of Second and Main streets in downtown Dayton. As Board Chairman George C. Gilfillen Jr. has stated, "E. F. MacDonald is going to stay in Dayton. We will reaffirm our Dayton roots by moving just four blocks from our current downtown headquarters. In fact, we look forward to being even *more* downtown."

The E. F. MacDonald Company will continue as a vital part of the Dayton community. Dayton, the home of aviation and innovation, is truly "The Wright Place to be."

The Martin Electric Company

From light bulbs to robots

John P. Martin, along with other stockholders, founded the Martin Electric Company on August 13, 1940. The company started operations at 310 East Second Street, wholesaling electrical supplies to Dayton and the surrounding areas.

During World War II, business prospered as Ohio's Wright-Patterson Air Force Base needed more supplies. Industry had to retool to produce war materials, and so required new electrical fittings. After the war, the company continued to grow, and in the summer of 1960, the Martin Electric Company opened a branch in Hamilton, Ohio.

The company has grown because it has always carried a great variety of electrical supplies; this diversity and flexibility is the basis of its continuing success — "one stop shopping" might be its motto.

The current product lines include full industrial and commercial electrical supplies for motor control, lighting systems, light bulbs, fans, baseboard heating, wire, conduit, switches, recepticles, connectors and minicomputers. As the technology of electronics is evolving dramatically, the Martin Electric Company sees itself becoming a supplier for systems of the future such as programmable controls and industrial robots.

In 1976, the Martin Electric Company moved to a renovated car dealership building at 701 South Patterson Boulevard. In March of that year, the building was stripped down to its concrete shell. Nine months later a new home for the Dayton operation was born. The lower floor is used solely as a warehouse, while the upper floor is not only used as a warehouse but also contains shipping and receiving, counter, reception and office spaces. The 40,000-square-foot structure is newly faced with brick, and paved parking and landscaping completed its exterior improvements. The renovation was so successful that the city of Dayton presented the company with the City Beautiful Award.

Since the death of the founder, John P. Martin, the company has had three presidents, Howard E. Hull (one of the original founders), Robert E. Martin and current President and Secretary John R. Martin, all natives of Dayton. John R. Martin is the son of the founder, and two directors, Robert Kronauge and J.E. Follick, are family members by marriage. Otto Huber is the other director, and Robert Musselman is vice president of Hamilton operations. This family-owned business participates in community affairs and fully supports its employees in their activities in charitable organizations.

Today the Martin Electric Company employs 54 people in Dayton and seventeen in Hamilton. By stocking over 12,000 different electrical items, the company can offer the customer complete inventory as well as technical support and prompt service to back it up.

The new Martin Electric Company building, renovated from a car dealership, won Dayton's City Beautiful Award in 1976.

An interior view of the new Martin Electric Company Building.

Mead Corporation

Major U.S. forest products company born in Dayton in 1846

An engraved plaque in the lobby of Mead's new 27-story World Headquarters building reads, "It is only by dealing honestly and fairly in all things that real success is attainable." The quotation by George H. Mead, grandson of the founder of the company, reflects the philosophy that continues to guide company actions. This philosophy and a commitment to its human resource have served to make Mead a major asset to the many communities it serves.

Even though Mead is highly decentralized with more than 150 mills, plants and distribution centers spread over all parts of the country, the company headquarters remain in Dayton, the site of its original paper mill. Basically a forest products company which makes pulp, paper, paperboard products and lumber, Mead is also a major distributor of paper, school supplies and industrial materials including pipe, valves and electrical items. Other businesses include a coal mine and the manufacture of molded rubber products and ductile iron castings. Mead's Advanced Systems group develops businesses for the future, involving the storing, retrieving and reproducing of data through the innovative application of digital technology.

Mead had its start in 1846 when Daniel Mead, an enterprising young bookkeeper, used his accumulated capital to join a Dayton firm named Ellis, Chaflin & Co. to go into the papermaking business. The company changed names and partners several times until 1881, when Mead became the sole owner and adopted the name The Mead Paper Company. With the purchase of a pulp and paper mill in Chillicothe, Ohio, the company became a two-division operation.

After the elder Mead's death in 1891, the company declined. On the verge of bankruptcy, it was reorganized in 1905 by a group of Chillicothe bankers and George H. Mead, grandson of the founder. Within several years, the company consolidated manufacturing operations in Chillicothe, leaving only a small office in the Reibold building in Dayton.

Under George H.'s management, the paper company grew steadily as new assets were acquired and existing ones strengthened. In 1930, Mead was incorporated under its present name, the Mead Corporation, with Mead as president. At that time, the company had plants in four states and about 1,000 employees. The Mead family remained in Dayton, but the principal offices were moved to Chillicothe in 1933, only to be returned to Dayton in 1944.

From 1955 on, Mead diversified into its present broadly-based organization. During the 1970s, more than $1.5 billion was spent to make existing facilities more cost effective and to increase capacity in targeted areas. Capital investments from 1980 to 1984 should exceed $1.5 billion, the most agggressive capital spending in its history. Net sales grew to a record $2.7 billion in 1980 and net earnings of $128.6 million, second best in Mead's history.

In 1977, Mead dedicated its new World Headquarters building overlooking Courthouse Square in downtown Dayton. Of the 25,000 people employed by Mead worldwide, about 1,000 are based in the headquarters building and more than 500 work in the new computer center located south of Dayton and other area locations.

"Consumption of paper is the measure of a people's culture," said the sign on Mead's float in an 1890s parade in Dayton.

In March 1977, employees moved into Mead's new World Headquarters building on the northeast corner of Courthouse Square Plaza.

Miami Valley Hospital

Preparing today for the future

In 1890, Dayton's community of 61,000 was in short supply of medical care for its populace plagued by malaria, diptheria, typhoid, pneumonia and the "fevers." Convinced the city needed a new hospital, the Reverend Carl Mueller, a German Lutheran minister, gathered 803 Daytonians who subscribed $1 each to form the Protestant Deaconess Society, predecessor of today's Miami Valley Hospital Society.

On October 18, 1891, in a converted house, Miami Valley Hospital officially opened its doors beginning what would become one of the nation's 100 largest health care institutions.

MVH started with seven physicians and 37 beds. The nurses, recruited from a deaconess mother home in Germany, worked twelve- to fourteen-hour days, scrubbing floors on their hands and knees, boiling laundry, preparing meals and even sleeping at night beside the beds of critically ill patients.

Contributions from Daytonians kept the larders full of food. Volunteers, active then as now, raised money for a new laundry, sewed nightgowns, sheets and tablecloths and decorated the hospital for Christmas.

Herbs, roots, barks and vegetables filled the pharmacy shelves. The first pharmacist, Otto Moosbrugger, ground dandelions, then boiled them in alcohol and tincture to treat bronchitis, lung diseases and pneumonia. Pills were made by hand, until 1892 when coal tar products came on the market, and with them the age of aspirin.

Soon a larger hospital was needed, and gifts of land paved the way for one atop Charity Hill overlooking Dayton. Dedicated in 1894, the hospital's location proved advantageous in 1913, when the worst flood in Dayton history spared the hospital for service to flood victims.

In 1899, the Miami Valley Hospital School of Nursing, now one of the state's largest nursing programs, opened its doors. By 1916, Miami Valley had grown to five buildings and after World War I had more refined lab tests and x-rays, a dental clinic, a new surgical building and a center to treat crippled children.

Critical overcrowding created pressure in the 1920s for additional facilities, but by 1931 the Depression had hit Miami Valley Hospital. Many areas needed repairs, and patients were unable to pay their bills.

Despite these difficulties, the hospital continued to expand, setting up clinics for heart disease, diabetes control and tuberculosis diagnosis. In the 1930s, technicians from across the country traveled to MVH to inspect Charles F. Kettering's famous Hypotherm, a device then used to treat arthritis and vascular diseases by inducing fever. With the economy improving, the trustees hoped to proceed with building expansion, but World

The Miami Valley Hospital as it appeared in 1910.

An artist's conception of Miami Valley Hospital as it will appear in 1983.

War II stalled construction of the present main hospital until the early 1950s.

In the meantime, as polio epidemics swept the nation, Miami Valley Hospital became the regional center for polio treatment in the 1940s and 1950s. Polio vaccines eventually eliminated that center, which was converted to a physical medicine and rehabilitation center. The 1950s also saw the first cardiac catheterization, the city's first artificial kidney machine and the development of an intensive care unit. Today, open heart surgery and kidney and cornea transplants are commonplace.

The hospital now serves as a regional center for treatment of high risk pregnancy, cancer therapy, kidney dialysis, physical medicine and rehabilitation, chronic pain management, alcoholism recovery, adult burn and cardiac care. In 1981 the hospital's Emergency Center was designated a regional trauma center by the United States Department of Health and Human Services and the

American College of Surgeons.

Miami Valley will serve approximately 27,000 inpatients and 220,000 outpatients in 1981. With 3,100 employees, it is the area's fifth largest employer and boasts nearly 700 physicians.

In 1980, under the leadership of Frederick C. Smith, chairman of the board of trustees, L.R. Jordan, president and chief executive officer, and Allistair Dunn, chairman of the planning committee, construction began on a $65 million modernization and development program. This project promises new jobs for the community and responds to the new "wellness" concept in medicine. Scheduled for completion in the near future, the addition will consolidate ambulatory services, provide facilities for additional education, expand surgery, cardiology and critical care, add physicians' offices and a parking garage.

As a vital part of Dayton for over 90 years, Miami Valley Hospital is ever growing to serve the patients of southwest Ohio.

NCR Corporation

Poised for a new century of growth

NCR one of the first multinational corporations. By 1980, more than half the company's customer revenues were being generated outside the United States. Its Dayton headquarters is the center for activities in over 100 countries, including marketing and supporting products through 1200 offices and operating 90 facilities worldwide for the development and manufacture of NCR products. The NCR logo has become a familiar sight wherever business is conducted around the globe.

One word sums up Patterson's multifaceted character — *innovative.* Generally recognized as a pioneer in American industry, he first put into practice many marketing, employee training and manufacturing principles that still guide successful businesses everywhere. His innovative style was also transmitted to the company he founded. From its beginnings, NCR has followed his admonition, "We progress through change."

In the 1920s, progress meant the addition of general accounting machines to the company's product line. In the 1930s, it meant developing machines to help financial institutions cope with ever increasing volumes of paper-based transactions. In the decades following World War II, progress required entry into the electronic age, including introduction of the first fully transistorized business computer.

In the early 1960s, microelectronics, the technology that integrates large numbers of electronic components into tiny complex circuits, emerged as a revolutionary force in data processing. By 1963, NCR had established a small microcircuits laboratory in Dayton to explore the potential of the technology and, in 1966, expanded the laboratory into a limited production facility.

Five years later, the company constructed a separate microelectronics facility just south of Dayton, in Miamisburg, Ohio. Here NCR develops and fabricates proprietary circuits and non-volatile memories used throughout its product line. In the decade since the Miamisburg facility was completed, it has been expanded several times. Additional facilities have also been constructed in Colorado, and NCR has begun marketing non-volatile memories and semi-custom logic circuits to other manufacturers.

Advances in microelectronics have resulted in increased product reliability, improved energy efficiency and lower product cost. They have also permitted NCR to develop increasingly more "intelligent" products which users can configure to their exact information processing needs.

Microelectronics is only one of many technologies NCR and its subsidiaries are employing to develop systems for tomorrow, systems that will ensure the company's continued growth through its second century as a corporate citizen of Dayton and the world.

Daytonian John Henry Patterson was a man of considerable vision. However, not even he could have foreseen that the company he founded in 1884 with thirteen employees and 3200 square feet of factory space would grow in less than a century into a multibillion dollar, multinational enterprise.

Patterson started his company to manufacture and market a "new-fangled" product for merchants, the cash register, invented in 1879 by two Dayton brothers, James and John Ritty. By the time he purchased controlling interest in the invention for $6,500, it had passed through several hands without having any significant impact on the mercantile scene. Patterson, however, was determined to make a success of his new business.

In the years since, NCR has become a leader in the development of new ways to collect, process, store and communicate information for businesses of every size. Today, it is one of the world's largest producers of general business systems.

NCR products now include electronic data processing systems; special-purpose terminals for retail, financial and manufacturing organizations; general-purpose data entry and retrieval terminals; communications processors and networking software; micrographic systems, business forms and related media. The company also operates a worldwide network of data processing centers to service businesses whose requirements do not justify installation of in-house computer systems.

Approximately one-third of company revenues are currently generated by sales of

NCR Corporation world headquarters, Dayton, Ohio (above) and John Henry Patterson (1844-1922), founder, NCR Corporation (below).

point-of-service systems to the retail sector, where NCR remains one of the world's largest suppliers. Another third comes from supplying computer systems, terminals and proof equipment to financial institutions. (Most of the company's financial terminals are manufactured in Dayton.) The remaining third is derived from sales of systems and software to manufacturers, distributors, construction and transportation companies, hospitals, schools and government offices.

About a year after he founded his company, John H. Patterson authorized an overseas distributorship in Liverpool, England, making

Philips Industries Inc.

Manufacturing quality components for better building

Although Philips Industries began in Dayton more by accident than design, it has remained there because of Dayton's central marketing location and the easy lifestyle the city affords its employees. Philips owns two manufacturing plants and a new headquarters building in Dayton, employing 500 people in the area.

In 1981, Philips Industries, with headquarters in Dayton and listed on the New York Stock Exchange, operated 30 plants in the United States and Canada and employed more than 3,400 people. Marketing its products internationally, the company's sales exceeded $250 million. Philips is a broadly diversified manufacturer of components for manufactured housing and recreational vehicles, products for residential, industrial and commercial construction and industrial products.

The growth of this international structure of people, plants and products began 24 years ago in October 1957, when Jesse Philips purchased a small Dayton company. Philips, a graduate of Oberlin College and the Harvard Business School, left a successful career in retail merchandising to undertake this new enterprise which had one plant employing twenty people manufacturing one product — aluminum windows. Basing his plans on a strong sense for the potential of the manufactured housing industry, he soon had the company on the road to profitable growth.

During the 1960s, the manufactured housing industry and the comparable recreational vehicle industry grew rapidly. Philips kept up with this growth, adding production facilities and broadening its product line. It soon became a dominant factor as the largest supplier exclusively serving these industries.

During the early 1970s, Philips entered the second phase of its growth by diversifying to serve all segments of the total building industry. Entering the conventional housing market for the first time, the company acquired Malta Manufacturing, a producer of quality wood windows and patio doors. This acquisition was followed shortly by the merger of Philips with the Dayton-based Lau Blower Company. Lau manufactures fans and blowers for domestic, industrial and commercial heating and air-conditioning applications and a quality line of humidifiers.

Philips also acquired Lasco Industries, with headquarters in Anaheim, California. Lasco increased Philips penetration of the residential construction market with its fiberglass bath fixtures and opened up new industrial, commercial and agricultural markets with its established and expanding lines of fiberglass building panels and plastic pipe and fittings. Subsequently, Philips added the manufacture of insulating glass panels for all types of construction by acquiring Twin Pane of Livonia, Michigan.

Philips Industries has held to a steady

When Jesse Philips founded Philips Industries in 1957, it produced one product — aluminum windows for mobile homes (above), and today Philips Industries' 30 plants produce components for all segments of the building industry (right).

course of growth, adjusting to changing economic conditions by maintaining sound management principles to build both its operating capacity and its financial strength. Today the company is structured with eight operating divisions and an international marketing division.

Each operating division is responsible for developing its own products, producing them with maximum efficiency and delivering them on time. Overall management of Philips Industries is maintained in the Dayton headquarters where financial controls and corporate planning are centered. The headquarters staff also provides specialized assistance to operating managers. The principal officers are Jesse Philips, chairman and chief executive officer, and Robert H. Brethen, president and chief operating officer.

Entering its 25th year, Philips Industries is poised for new growth. It has seasoned management at all levels. Its primary asset is a loyal, dedicated work force. More than 1,000 employees have served for ten years or more. Over 300 of these are members of the Dayton community.

The company is well into the third phase of its development. It has continued to maintain its leadership as a supplier to the manufac-

tured housing and recreational vehicle industries. It has diversified and matured into a manufacturer of products for all segments of the construction market. Most recently, it is becoming established as a supplier of components for a widening range of industrial and agricultural applications.

Philips Industries and its employees have been leaders, financially and with personal commitment, in most of the important civic, cultural and social concerns of the Greater Dayton area. As it has been throughout its history, Philips Industries remains committed to deepening its roots in Dayton and to contributing to the growing vitality of this city's life and economy.

Ponderosa System, Inc.

A system for success brought success to the system

A Ponderosa Steakhouse, circa 1969.

Founded in 1965, Ponderosa now operates the largest family-priced steakhouse chain in the United States. Approximately two-thirds of these facilities are company-owned. Total annual sales will soon exceed one-half billion dollars, and the corporation is now studying opportunities presented by overseas markets.

Of course, Ponderosa hardly began "at the top." There were only 25 restaurants in the fledgling chain when the firm moved its headquarters from Kokomo, Indiana, to Dayton in 1968. Ponderosa went public that year and has weathered three major recessions, growing stronger each year — and increasingly convinced as time passes in the soundness of its "system" approach.

A respected food service trade magazine attributes much of Ponderosa's growth and stature to "superior executive talent (and) a structured approach . . . to expansion."

A system for success, then — a strategic management system — has been pivotal in bringing solid success to the Ponderosa system.

Gerald S. Office Jr., chairman of the board and president since 1969, concurs with that assessment. "Restaurant chains that have employed professional management concepts along with sophisticated marketing and distribution techniques — and who have committed themselves to developing human resources — are the ones who will prosper," he states.

Today, Ponderosa is structured into three distinct strategy centers to pave the way for future growth. The largest of these centers is North American Steakhouse operations housed in separate headquarters off Interstate 75. ESI Meats, Inc., a wholly-owned subsidiary of Ponderosa System, Inc., operates the world's largest portion control and freezer facility under one roof, located at Bristol, Indiana. This plant, and a second located in Tampa, Florida, serve both the needs of Ponderosa Steakhouses and other commercial customers. The third strategy center, International Development, is responsible for overseas expansion with primary emphasis on Europe and the Far East.

Ponderosa has defined a set of corporate values and beliefs — an organization philosophy — which management believes to be the foundation for the company's future.

The goals for Ponderosa and its divisions are threefold.

1. For customers. The corporation wishes to be perceived as "the best eating-out value of any restaurant chain." Thus, management is pledged to strive continually for improved quality, productivity and cost controls.
2. For shareholders. The corporation's goal is to protect and increase the value of shareholder investment through sound management, prudent expansion and the achievement of a dominant market position.
3. For Ponderosa employees. The company recognizes that its success is dependent on the creativity and commitment of its people — and strives for a stimulating and challenging climate which emphasizes the full participation of all employees.

There are two other points which are driven home time and again by Office and other executives at Ponderosa's corporate headquarters.

First, Ponderosa considers its relationship with Greater Dayton — as well as other communities in which the company does business — to be of major importance. Therefore, the company encourages and supports employees' personal and corporate community activities. Office himself has devoted time by serving on the board of trustees of the Dayton Development Council, the Area Progress Council, the board of directors of United Way, the board of trustees at the University of Dayton and as honorary chairman for the Special Olympics of Dayton in Montgomery County, Inc.

Second, Ponderosa feels an obligation to protect and foster principles of democracy and private enterprise.

"In our philosophy," says Office, "we state that, 'With a strong belief in political and economic freedom, it is appropriate that we devote resources to support the private enterprise system. We recognize a special obligation to those young people whose employment by Ponderosa may be their first "real job" by providing a work experience and leadership that fosters a belief in and support of private enterprise.'"

That, of course, is a restatement of Ponderosa's own belief in "the system."

One of many Dayton area Ponderosa Steakhouses today (below) and PSI headquarters near the Dayton International Airport (left).

Price Brothers Company, Inc.

Attracted by city's need to rebuild, firm became part of growth

Precast revetment blocks from Price Brothers Company were installed on both banks of the Great Miami River. Threaded together on cables, these blocks formed rugged concrete mats that continue — even today — to resist erosion and protect flood control levees of the Miami Conservancy District (above). Harry S. Price stands inside a section of 84-inch-diameter precast concrete pressure pipe (below) used to build the main water supply line for the city of Dayton's water treatment plant. This pipe is still in service today.

Harry Steele Price, a Michigan-based builder of bridges, hydroelectric dams and electric power plants, saw an opportunity in the Miami Valley after Dayton's disastrous flood of 1913.

In 1916, just prior to the start of World War I, Price was awarded a contract for rebuilding the dam in the Great Miami River at Island Park. No sooner had work begun than the war took the attention of the entire community. Wages for construction workers jumped from 17.5 cents per hour to 60 cents per hour within a few months. Consequently, finishing the dam was a long struggle. By 1919, at the age of 43, Price had lost most of his firm's working capital, but his professional reputation survived.

His friend Arthur Morgan, who was gaining prominence as grand designer of the Miami Conservancy District, persuaded Price to move his company and family to Dayton in 1920 because his talents were needed in the major construction effort Morgan envisioned.

Over the six decades that followed, Price Brothers Company not only has helped Dayton build many of its dams, levees, bridges, water and sewer lines and important buildings but it also has grown into one of the city's leading locally owned corporations. From its 1899 origin as a small construction

company, it has evolved into a manufacturing company with production facilities serving the eastern half of the United States.

The firm's success during the 1930s, '40s, and '50s in pioneering the use of precast concrete for pipelines and buildings made it a leader in both the waterworks and construction industries. A large share of the water and sewer lines in the Dayton area have been built with precast concrete.

In 1926, Price Brothers supplied the city's water supply facility with newly designed,

reinforced concrete pressure pipe — 84 inches in diameter, over 25,000 feet long — and connected water wells opposite Wright Field to a pumping station on Ottawa Street near the Keowee Street bridge.

In 1942, Dayton witnessed one of the first major installations of Flexicore — a hollow-core concrete floor and roof slab developed by Price Brothers — in the construction of the large Frigidaire production plant in Moraine. The rugged slabs still serve in the building, presently used by General Motors.

Price Brothers' pressure pipe and Flexicore were soon followed by other precast concrete pipe and building products as the company's operations expanded to other states. Production facilities in the Dayton area also increased to include a new pressure-pipe plant on Webster Avenue in 1949, two Flexicore and sewer pipe plants in New Carlisle during the 1950s and expansion of the original plant facilities on East Monument Avenue.

In 1969, a new four-story corporate headquarters became one of the first structures in Dayton's urban renewal program. This building typifies the strength, lifetime economy and architectural beauty that can be achieved with the firm's precast concrete building components. Other Dayton area structures built with Price Brothers' precast concrete building systems include the international headquarters of NCR Corporation and the Midwest headquarters of Metropolitan Life Insurance Company, as well as many hospitals and apartment projects.

In 1933, two of the original Price brothers withdrew from the corporation, and a second generation of Price brothers took over — Harry's two sons, Gayle and Harry Jr. Now a third generation member, Gayle Jr., heads the company which operates five corporate divisions and manufactures products in over twenty plants. A leader in the manufacturing of precast concrete construction material, Price Brothers has diversified into the design and production of fiberglass reinforced plastics.

With its headquarters and long history in Dayton, Price Brothers Company has evidenced a strong sense of community involvement. Both Harry Jr. and Gayle Jr. have served many community causes and have encouraged active civic participation by all of the company's employees. In 1980, the firm announced an employee stock ownership plan to extend its ownership base and more fully recognize the contributions made by its employees.

When Harry Price arrived to build a dam and help Dayton recover from its tragic 1913 flood, it is doubtful whether he suspected how much he would ultimately contribute to the city's growth.

Innovation keyed growth from print shop to major systems company

When Lucius D. Reynolds came to Dayton to found Reynolds + Reynolds in 1866, it was not uncommon to see livestock meandering about the town's broad, dusty dirt streets. The Miami Canal snaked sluggishly through the city and was the community's freight connection with the rest of the world. The town of 25,000 enterprising souls was still in the aftermath of the Civil War.

This was the Dayton in which the dark-bearded Reynolds teamed with his brother-in-law James R. Gardner to form the Gardner & Reynolds print shop near First and Main streets where the Victory Theater now stands.

A former Bellefontaine, Ohio, newspaper editor, Reynolds had returned to Ohio after a stint in Washington where he worked for the Lincoln government.

Within a year, Gardner sold out to Reynolds' father, Ira Reynolds, and the fledgling firm took on the name it bears today — Reynolds + Reynolds.

The firm had a distinctive concept. It was to produce large quantities of standard business forms in long press runs, and then sell the forms in small quantities to many customers at a cheaper price than competitors could offer on their short runs of forms designed for each customer. That concept of standardization is still a cornerstone in the company's philosophy.

Father Ira quickly contributed by developing a popular duplicate sales book much like that still used in many stores. The sales book was a major item for many years as the company prospered and outgrew several succeeding locations.

Then in 1898, it built a plant at 800 Germantown Street which today is the firm's corporate headquarters and the heart of its complex of six structures.

The firm incorporated in 1889, and in 1927, sold its unprofitable tablet division. It also made a historic marketing move in 1927 by beginning production of standard accounting systems for auto dealers. Today, auto dealers account for more than half of the firm's total sales.

After financial problems during the 1930s Depression, the firm was acquired from the Reynolds family in 1939 by the late R.H. Grant Sr., a Daytonian who had achieved national fame as a top General Motors marketing executive.

R.H. Grant Jr. became president in 1941 and held that post until 1957 when he succeeded Grant Sr. as board chairman when the latter died. Grant Jr. remains chairman today and his family retains controlling interest of the firm.

Under Grant family ownership, the firm returned to prosperous ways and entered major new forms markets in the 1950s. In 1956, it began printing "pegboard" or "one-write" manual systems and in 1960 started producing forms and manual systems for the medical field.

By this time a variety of other printed products had faded from the product line leaving its presses to churn out almost every type of form used by business today.

But 1960 produced a more momentous decision for the company when, under the presidency of the late Frank F. Pfeiffer, it took its first steps toward providing electronic data processing for auto dealers. From this beginning emerged the firm's computer-related business, which in 1980 accounted for $122.5 million of the company's total sales of $210.2 million. Today the company is the nation's largest supplier of computer systems and services to auto dealers and is expanding into other major markets for its computer systems and services.

From the 1960 beginning, all of the computer hardware it used for services or sold to its customers was made by other firms. In 1979, it formed a manufacturing unit in Cincinnati to produce terminals and computers for the new medical and contractor markets.

The firm has regional computer centers at Grand Prairie, Texas; Elmwood Park, New Jersey; Chicago; Atlanta; Walnut Creek, California; and Brampton, Ontario, Canada. It also has 140 sales offices and operates time-sharing computers in principal cities.

Reynolds + Reynolds also operates six printing plants — Dayton and Celina, Ohio; North Hollywood and Tulare, California; Grand Prairie, Texas; and Brampton.

In 1980, the firm completed its 22nd consecutive year of record sales. Under chief executive officer E.F. Strasser and president Robert G. Timberlake, Reynolds + Reynolds is recognized as a leader in business forms and computer systems and services.

Reynolds & Reynolds delivery truck (above), circa 1915. The Germantown Street plant (below) in the mid-1930s when the company also produced advertising literature.

St. Elizabeth Medical Center

The spirit of St. Elizabeth

The story of St. Elizabeth Hospital begins with one man's dream. By 1875, Father John F. Hahne, pastor of Dayton's Emmanuel Catholic Church, had built a church, a school and an orphanage. He had one goal left — a hospital for Dayton, a city of 40,000 with no public health-care facility. In the 1870s, "hospitals" were thought of as "pest-houses," fit only for the containment of contagious fatal illness. But Father Hahne knew what good medical care could achieve.

In the spring of 1878, he signed a lease for an old saloon, Zweisler's Inn, which stood where Chaminade-Julienne High School is now. Next, he wrote to Sister Vincentia of the Franciscan Sisters of the Poor in Cincinnati, who had as their cause the care of the sick and destitute. Sister Vincentia sent two nuns to run the new hospital; they arrived July 2, 1878, after a two-day canal boat trip up the Miami River. Sister Emilie and Sister Columba set to work with $700 from the women of Emmanuel's St. Elizabeth Society. It was from this society, named for the charitable queen, St. Elizabeth of Hungary, that the hospital got its name.

A week before the official opening, St. Elizabeth received its first patient — the victim of a railroad accident. Nineteen-year-old John Slattery's arm had been crushed and had to be amputated. But he recovered without complications — proof that this hospital was different.

Dedication took place August 15, 1878. It was not an elaborate event, for the sisters had to run their business on a shoestring. Each day, they made rounds of bakeries, grocers and butcher shops, asking for food. The hospital rapidly became a popular cause, and the nuns were able to acquire food with little cash.

The hospital's staff of seven physicians was headed by Dr. John C. Reeve, who during the early years served at the hospital free of charge. In its first three years of existence,

The first hospital was in Zweisler's Inn, an old saloon.

nearly 1,000 patients were cared for. Dayton's expanding population and the increase in accidents due to new railroads, machine shops and factories increased demand for services.

The sisters later purchased a fifteen-room house and four acres of land on the west bank of the Miami River, then began to plan a five-story brick hospital, but they needed more than $100,000. Now, however, people of Dayton were wholeheartedly in favor of the idea. With $30,000 collected, construction began on the new hospital.

On dedication day, November 19, 1882, 20,000 people paraded from the old hospital to the new with a marching band plus the banners and uniforms of a dozen church societies. Now there were 260 beds, new operating rooms, a large laboratory, a huge kitchen. In 1903, the hospital's first extensive addition brought the number of beds to 425.

Hundreds of patients could not pay during difficult times such as the Depression, but generous support from Daytonians kept the hospital going and growing.

The hospital's reputation for excellent education began with the opening of a school of nursing in 1915. In 1946, the schools of medical and X-ray technology were opened, the first such facilities in the Dayton area.

In the 1950s, the sisters decided to move the hospital, in stages, across Hopeland Street to face Miami Boulevard, and in 1954, the first new building was completed. During the next 20 years, all the hospital's facilities were transferred to the new location.

The late 1960s saw the naming of the first lay administrator, E.C. Kuhbander, and the changing of the hospital's name to St. Elizabeth Medical Center to reflect the wide range of services offered, particularly in family medicine, physical therapy, outpatient surgery and cardiac care. In 1971, a new wing was built to house patient records and a medical library. St. Elizabeth's nationally recognized Family Practice Residency Program began in 1972. The southwest wing was finished in 1973, and the Family Medicine Center in 1976. Also in 1976, St. Elizabeth began its affiliation with Wright State University School of Medicine.

Today more than 2,000 employees and a medical staff composed of more than 600 physicians work in a modern facility with 608 beds. Together, they carry on the compassionate care and the special spirit that distinguish St. Elizabeth.

The new St. Elizabeth Medical Center.

Shopsmith Inc.

A tradition of building close customer relations

In 1972, John R. Folkerth, a Dayton stockbroker, went looking for a part for a secondhand woodworking machine. The search took him to Raymond, Mississippi, where he discovered that the machine was no longer being produced. But not only were parts available, so was an inventory of the machines, plus machining and dies for their manufacture.

Folkerth got his part and quite a bit more — an entire company. It took foresight to see the potential of a fine line of woodworking equipment. But before the year was over, Folkerth obtained a limited stock offering and a loan to form Shopsmith Inc.

The line of tools acquired had its beginning in 1946 when inventor Hans Goldschmidt formed Magna Engineering Corporation to manufacture and market a revolutionary multi-purpose woodworking tool. The original model was improved and refined until, in 1953, the MARK V was introduced. Later, the company changed ownership and, in 1967, a decision was made to discontinue production. The production line was at this point when Folkerth appeared on the scene.

A year was spent in moving equipment, organizing and setting up production. The first Shopsmith MARK V came off the production line in Tipp City on March 31, 1973. The challenge then became one of marketing the machines.

After an unsuccessful attempt to revive the previous dealer distribution network, Shopsmith established the concept of dealing directly with the consumer, initially through woodworking demonstrations in shopping malls. The first of these promotions was held in Dayton's Salem Mall. The idea was a success from the start, and today Shopsmith woodworking demonstrations are held in shopping centers across the country.

The next step was to market Shopsmith tools and accessories through direct mailing. As a result, Shopsmith has become a major leader in the direct response market.

In 1976, the company moved to Vandalia and, in 1979-1980, expanded to several different locations in Dayton. Over 1,100 employees work in these facilities and in the Shopsmith-Missouri subsidiary, located in Jefferson City.

Shopsmith sales have grown at a dramatic rate. In the four year period from 1978 to 1981, sales increased from under $8 million in 1978 to $16 million in 1979, $30 million in 1980, and over $62 million in 1981 — just about doubling every year.

President Folkerth's goal for Shopsmith is for it to become a major corporation with $150 million or more (expressed in 1980 dollars) in annual sales by 1985.

The top of the Shopsmith line is the five-in-one multi-purpose woodworking tool which is a table saw, drill press, boring machine, lathe and disc sander—in one compact and economical unit. In addition, Shopsmith produces special purpose tools—bandsaw, jointer, belt sander and jigsaw—and a complete line of woodworking accessories. The Jefferson City, Missouri, subsidiary manufactures and distributes the BenchMark line of benchtop and portable power tools.

Shopsmith has built a wide base of loyal and satisfied customers who look to the company for quality tools, the education to use them and a lifetime of dedicated service. In turn, Shopsmith has a commitment to develop and maintain this unique customer/company relationship.

Catalog operations sell Shopsmith accessories and allied home workshop products manufactured by other companies. Sales are also generated through Shopsmith's woodworking magazine, *Hands On!,* published bi-monthly and distributed through retail outlets called Shopsmith Showrooms. This program is being expanded to include stores in key market areas across the country.

In 1981, Ohio Governor James A. Rhodes honored Shopsmith with an award for being one of the fastest growing businesses in the country. This recognition was the result of a survey done by *Inc.* magazine, a business publication, which listed Shopsmith as 29th among the 100 fastest-growing, independent, publicly-held corporations in the United States — and first in Ohio for 1980.

Shopsmith is dedicated to striving for a close relationship with the do-it-yourselfers and home craftsmen in order to supply their needs for complete home workshop capabilities.

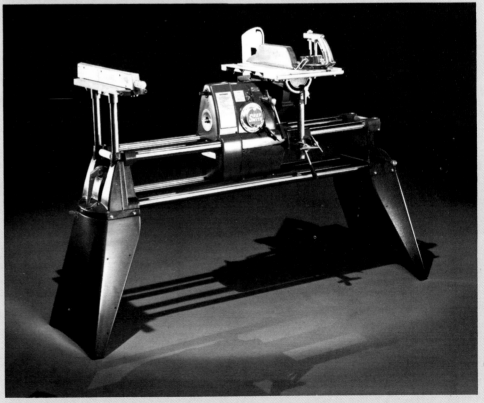

John R. Folkerth, president of Shopsmith Inc. (left). Shopsmith Mark V multi-purpose woodworking tool is the top of the Shopsmith line (below).

The Specialty Papers Company

Packaging for yesterday, today and tomorrow

The original building on Miami Chapel Road appeared this way in 1934 (above). Today's Specialty Papers offices include a new building connected to the old via a skywalk (below).

Waxed paper was impetus to the birth of a company. Life-styles had become more complicated. People were in transition from self-sufficiency to convenience. Nowhere was change more evident than in the way people provided for their food requirements and personal needs. All of this was apparent in 1919. Bread available from bakeries and commercial soap were packaged in waxed paper. Family kitchens were incomplete without a supply of waxed paper to store leftovers.

Van Hamm Wilshire recognized this need and began producing waxed paper when he started the Specialty Papers Company on August 5, 1919, in small rented quarters at 841 E. Monument Avenue.

As the new business grew, Specialty moved in 1925 to its present location, and after several expansions, Miami Chapel Road continues to be the company's principal office and largest manufacturing location. During World War II, Specialty produced protective paper for guns, for weapon parts and for military food packaging. After the death of Wilshire in 1946, James A. Strong, the company's sales manager from the early days, took over as president until his retirement in 1951.

As supermarkets replaced Ma and Pa groceries, low prices became more important than personal service. Refrigeration became economical. Foods could be frozen and stored for freshness. New materials, such as aluminum foil and cellophane, became available. William P. Patterson, president from 1951 until his retirement in 1968, guided the

shift in the company's product line to meet these new opportunities. During this period, Specialty initiated printing by both the rotogravure and flexographic processes and became a pioneer in the field of polyethylene extrusion laminating and coating. These new printing and laminating processes became the backbone of the business as waxed paper products gave way to laminates of paper and foil, as well as other more sophisticated products.

The decade of the '70s brought new packaging requirements and, as a result, more opportunities for Specialty Papers. Fast food restaurants needed foil sandwich wrap to retain heat and freshness. Unit packaging of powdered drink mixes, tea and soups required pouches. Since 1968, the company's

current president, John L. Schaefer, has anticipated the requirements of flexible packaging.

Innovation, versatility, aggressiveness and acquisitions have become synonymous with growth. Acquisition of the Master Packaging Company provided a plant in Shreveport, Louisiana — now operated as the Film Division — and allowed expansion of the product line to include laminations and printed films not possible in Dayton. A small company in Chicago, 3 Sigma, Inc., was purchased in 1980 and moved to Covington, Ohio. A producer of pressure sensitive materials, 3 Sigma specializes in tapes for disposable diapers. With advanced equipment, the Dayton operation moved into new products, including packaging for both the confections and medical industries. In 1981, a new Dayton office building was erected to prepare for future growth. Specialty, originally one of several waxed paper producers, is the only one that has remained an independent company.

Specialty Papers, in many ways, is a slice of America. Its products are sold from shore to shore, from border to border. Many of the early day customers are still customers today and are among the largest corporations in the country. Packaging materials produced in Dayton are used to wrap hamburgers and cookies, soup mixes and cake mixes, medicines and medical supplies. Specialty's history can be traced from just after the first World War to the space age. Its future will continue to be based on a vision of tomorrow's packaging needs.

Vulcan Tool Company

Building the tools of manufacturing for the world

Early Vulcan employees posed in front of the East First Street Shop around 1920.

A small group of toolmakers founded Vulcan Tool Company in 1916 by establishing a shop at 418 East First Street. In 1917, the late Lee Amos Jones purchased control of the company from this group. The company grew through World War I and struggled through the depression of the early '20s and the Great Depression of the '30s when employment levels fluctuated from as few as two men up to 35.

In 1927, L.A. Jones moved the company from East First Street to 213 North Beckel Street where both the tool room and the design room were enlarged. In 1933, Lee Warren Jones, son of the founder and present chairman of the board, joined the company, and in 1939 founded Tube Products Company which is located north of Dayton in Troy. Although the economy was stagnant during the early '30s, the past performance and quality workmanship of Vulcan's skilled craftsmen kept the company afloat. Throughout those lean years, Vulcan never missed a single pay day.

During World War II, Vulcan designed and made the tools and dies needed to change U.S. manufacturing facilities into producers of war weapons. At the end of World War II, Vulcan bought the Dayton Tool and Engineering Company and moved to the expanded plant and offices at 730 Lorain Avenue in East Dayton.

Since its founding, Vulcan has trained employees in toolmaking and designing. Many tool companies in the Dayton area were founded by men who learned and developed their craft while at Vulcan.

Diversification became a necessity with the changing times. The creative minds of Vulcan invented the Vulcanaire grinder which be-

came Vulcan's first proprietary product in 1949. The diversification continued in 1956 when Vulcan entered into an agreement with Steel Products Corporation for the right to manufacture "Brehm Shimmy®" dies and also acquired the rights to the "Brehm®" Tube Cutter shortly thereafter. In 1959, Howard H.H. Jones, Vulcan's current president, and grandson of the founder, established Production Tube Cutting, Inc., with branches in France and England. In the late '50s and early '60s, Vulcan displayed its new products at machine shows throughout the world, and by the mid-'60s both the Vulcanaire and "Brehm®" Tube Cutter were being sold worldwide.

In the late '60s and on through the '70s, Vulcan continued to improve its proprietary items. In 1964, Vulcan purchased the assets of Arbor Tool of Iowa and established Vulcan Tool of Iowa. This acquisition included Dubuque Industrial Supply, a tool supply distributor. In 1973, Tube Products merged with Vulcan Tool Company to form Vulcan Tool Corporation. Tube Products operates plants in Troy, Ohio and Louisville, Kentucky which produce auto and truck tail and exhaust pipes for the auto and truck industries and also for the replacement parts industry.

In 1976, Vulcan was approached by the Jackes-Evans Company to develop a machine, the "Ringmaster," which today is one of Vulcan's own products. This makes Vulcan one of the largest manufacturers of tube-cutting equipment in the country. The company has added many numerical control machines to its production facility that enable it to meet the ever-increasing accuracy required by today's manufacturing technology.

Over the years, Vulcan has been active in the Dayton community. Its employees and staff have performed volunteer work for the Red Cross, United Way, Boys Club, the YMCA and high school boosters, among others. It is the desire of the company, its management and its employees to keep Dayton the Gem City through their actions, their volunteer work and their contributions.

From its humble beginnings in 1916, Vulcan now operates plants in three states and employs more than 400 people. One of the largest tool and die manufacturers in the country, Vulcan will be servicing the manufacturing industry of the country for years to come from its birthplace — Dayton, Ohio, a gem of a city.

In 1927, the company moved to 213 North Beckel Street and enlarged tool and design rooms.

An impressive past — a new beginning

TV2 can boast that it is not only Dayton's oldest but also its newest television station. The switch from old to new occurred in 1981, when Hearst Broadcasting bought WDTN. In June 1976 the station was purchased from Avco Corporation by Grinnell Communications Corporation. After 27 years of broadcasting, WLWD became WDTN. Grinnell Communications Corporation had only one broadcasting property: TV2. WDTN was one of the few commercial stations ever to be purchased by an educational institution. This purchase enabled TV2 to embark on an ambitious program of capital improvements.

TV2 was Dayton's first licensed television station. Licensed by the FCC in 1947, the station made its first broadcast in 1949. The premiere performance was *Texaco Star Theatre* with Mr. Television himself, Milton Berle.

For most of its existence, TV2 was a part of Avco Broadcasting (Aviation Corporation of America), founded by Victor Emanuel, a native of Dayton. Avco built its broadcasting business on the work of Powell Crosley Jr. In 1921, Crosley, who merely wanted "to sell more radios," produced a "broadcast" from his living room with an oatmeal container, some copper wire and 20 watts of power. A year later, Crosley's experiment became WLW, the first commercially licensed radio station in Ohio. Crosley Corporation was sold to Avco in 1945.

From 1954 to 1968, TV2 provided Daytonians with programming from both NBC and ABC. But Avco believed that a television station should have a strong local identity and should produce its own programs, of local interest, with local talent.

TV2's local production was of such high quality that its programs were often sought for wider broadcast. ABC's *Midwestern Hayride* originated in Dayton. And *Wide, Wide World* often called upon TV2 to help with its production. The McGuire Sisters made their television debut at TV2, and Steve Allen chose TV2 as the spot for the first out-of-town broadcast for his *Tonight Show.* Gordon Jump of TV2 had a leading role in the series *WKRP.* Phil Donahue's talk show had its beginning on TV2 in 1967, with Madalyn Murray O'Hair as the first guest. *Donahue* now originates from WGN in Chicago, its home since 1974.

WDTN is especially proud of its long association with the Cincinnati Reds. Since 1956, Reds games have been a TV2 exclusive. TV2 has been a pioneer in sportscasting in many fields. Only two months after the station went on the air, it broadcast a Dayton Indians game and became the first station in the country to air a Class A baseball team in action. Only a year later, TV2 became the first station in the world to carry a sports event produced exclusively for television viewers and staged in a television studio before a studio audience. The event was live studio wrestling, and it marked the beginning of a lively tradition in American broadcasting. TV2 was the first in the area to carry live bowling from an area bowling alley, the first to broadcast University of Dayton basketball, the first to broadcast night-time baseball and the first in the country to televise live automobile racing.

WDTN understands that it exists not only to make money but to serve its community. TV2 was the first station in Dayton to produce a show on issues of interest to the black community — *Livin' Black.* In addition to its regular public service programming, TV2 produces special shows as the community need arises. During the notorious blizzard of '78, for example, the station stayed on the air for 44 consecutive hours. For days, WDTN was the only contact many area residents had with the rest of the world. Also in 1978, TV2 and the Dayton League of Women Voters successfully completed the largest, most ambitious public service project ever ventured in Ohio. *Rally '78* allowed 50 statewide and local candidates to state their case before the voters. WDTN assumed 100 percent of the cost. The accomplishment was enough to earn a front-page review in *Variety.*

If WDTN sees a community need, and an organization does not exist to serve that need, then the station will act to fill the vacuum. It was after perceiving such a need, for instance, that a TV2 staffer founded and chaired the Dayton Organization of Black Women for Professional Development.

On January 1, 1980, the station switched from NBC to ABC.

By any standard TV2 is a most unusual station — and a station of firsts.

The original logo of Channel 2 in Dayton.

Phil Donahue's talk show originated in Dayton on TV2 in 1967.

White-Allen Chevrolet/Honda

Here to stay: a downtown Dayton tradition since 1935

Ever since White-Allen Chevrolet first opened its doors in January 1935, the automobile business has been a family tradition for the Whites — a tradition providing quality products and complete service.

Hugh White had already been an automobile dealer for fourteen years when he co-founded White-Allen. His experience with his dealership in Zanesville taught him that there was a lot more to the business than selling cars. White believed that investing in people was just as important to the development of his business and the growth of the community. White and his partner, Don Allen, opened the dealership at 442 North Main Street to be part of the developing downtown community.

A few years later, Allen left the business and White continued on alone, building White-Allen into one of the largest car and truck dealerships in the tri-state area.

More than 500,000 new and used cars and trucks bearing the White-Allen imprint have rolled out of North Main Street over the past 46 years. While many of them were made by Chevrolet, there were also other makes sold by White-Allen. Imports sold by White-Allen at one time or another include Jaguars, Citroens, and even a Czechoslovakian import, the Skoda. (Since 1972, White-Allen has been a leading seller of a Japanese import, soon to be made in Ohio, the Honda.

Hugh White eventually sold White-Allen to his son Jim, who passed it on to his son Tim in 1980. (Other family members operate Chevrolet dealerships in Toledo and Columbus.)

Tim White now carries on the tradition, having learned the automotive business from every angle. A White-Allen employee since 1969, Tim has worked in parts, service, sales and the body shop. This wide range of experience gives him the background he needs to direct the entire operation today as White-Allen's president.

White-Allen continues to play an important role in downtown Dayton activities. Because of his commitment to the community, White was appointed general chairman for the '81 Dayton Holiday Festival. Each year the company sponsors a float and lends several cars for the annual Children's Parade which is the start of the Dayton Holiday Festival and Christmas season.

Young people in the community benefit from White-Allen's contributions to the Dayton Boy's Club and Junior Achievement. The dealership has also sponsored Little League baseball and basketball for many years.

Since 1948, White-Allen has been a major supporter of intercollegiate athletics at the University of Dayton. The dealership sponsors the annual Most Valuable Player awards in men's football and basketball as well as women's basketball and volleyball. White-

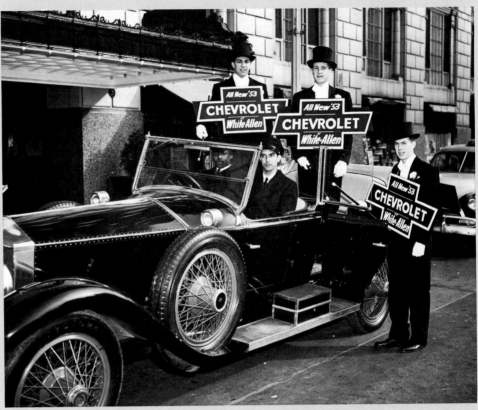

This advertising photograph was taken in front of the Biltmore Hotel (above); and White-Allen Chevrolet is seen in 1948 at the corner of North Main and McPherson (left).

Allen also contributes to the Dayton Ballet Company, the Dayton Performing Arts Fund and the Dayton chapter of the American Red Cross, of which Tim is a board director.

For three generations, White-Allen has played an active role in the growth and development of the community. This investment in the people of the Dayton area has paid special dividends in goodwill and public relations. It's a major reason for the company's continued success.

Today, White-Allen has over eight acres of space on both sides of North Main Street, with more than five acres roofed over. The large complex houses the dealership's new and used car and truck sales departments as well as one of the largest and best-equipped service and parts departments in the area.

In an era in which car dealers have been moving to the suburbs, White-Allen has remained a part of the downtown area, increasing the size of its operation as well as its

James F. White (left) receives a commemorative plaque from Chevrolet Motor Division congratulating Hugh E. White (picture) on 50 years as a Chevrolet Dealer on October 2, 1974.

contributions to the community.

White-Allen's 130 employees carry on the tradition established by Hugh White in 1935. It's a philosophy that might best be summed up as, "Sell a good product and make sure you put something back into the community." That philosophy tells how White-Allen has remained a major part of the downtown Dayton scene for over 46 years, and has inspired White-Allen's radio jingle:

"Downtown Dayton, We're Here to Stay!"

Winters National Corporation
Stability and customer service are keys to 166 years of growth

In a frontier setting of instability, the Winters National Bank and Trust Co. had its beginnings in 1813 when sixteen Dayton businessmen met to form a bank.

Located near the present day site of Winters, the bank began operations in August 1814, under the name of the Dayton Manufacturing Company, with assets of $123,505.

Withstanding unstable pressures, particularly the severe depression of 1821, Dayton's first bank proved to be one of the strongest institutions of its kind in the United States.

Business boomed for most of the 1830s but when depression struck in 1843, The Dayton Bank, as it was now called, closed its doors for the first — and last — time. Twenty-nine years was a remarkable record for a bank at that time.

In 1845, the new Dayton Bank opened, linked to the former institution through $45,000 in silver paid to businessman Jonathan Harshman in lieu of his stocks and deposits in the old bank. The money was then paid into the new Dayton Bank as part of the capital stock. Valentine Winters I became the bank's first cashier.

As Dayton grew, the bank grew and changed its name to the New Exchange Bank. Five years later, Winters brought his son Jonathan into the bank and, in 1857, with father and son as major stockholders, the bank was renamed V. Winters and Son.

In 1882, Winters joined the national banking system, and the name became The Winters National Bank. Jonathan Winters I, whom the Dayton *Journal* described as "among the most capable bankers in the West," was the first president.

Ten years later the bank moved to new quarters at Third and Main streets. In 1918, the move was made to 40 North Main Street. Shortly afterward, it was remodeled and became one of the most impressive looking banking establishments in the United States.

A request to operate a Trust Department was granted to Winters by the state of Ohio in 1924. The bank's name was changed to The Winters National Bank and Trust Company.

The sharp recession in 1924, following World War I, resulted in the directors appointing a committee of the board to explore sale, merger or acquisition possibilities. The committee called upon one of Dayton's leading citizens, Charles F. Kettering. When Kettering acquired the stock holdings offered by Winters, he provided the recognition and leadership needed to prevent a crisis. "The Boss," as Kettering was called, was an inventor of world renown, and his ideas have shaped the Winters' philosophy ever since. To bank employees and others in the community, he stressed his viewpoint that service was the greatest commodity that a bank had to sell.

Measured in monetary terms alone, Kettering's contribution to Winters was outstanding. In 1924, when he became chairman of the board, Winters' total assets measured $10 million. When he was made honorary chairman in 1958, assets totaled $250 million.

The next two decades marked a period of accelerated growth for the bank that has continued into the 1980s. In 1971, Winters moved into its present location, the Winters Bank Tower at Second and Main Street. The largest building in Dayton, it was one of the first facilities constructed in a major downtown development effort that has resulted in a host of new and renovated buildings. That same year, Winters formed the first bank holding company in the Miami Valley. In this capacity, the corporation could extend its service through new banking and financially related subsidiaries.

Currently, Winters National Bank operates 41 offices with assets of $1.14 billion, making it the largest financial institution in the Miami Valley. Nationally, the bank ranks 172nd among the nation's 15,000-plus banks. Assets of Winters National Corporation and its subsidiaries totaled $1.46 billion at year-end 1980.

Winters calls itself "the bank with the answers." This theme summarizes the ingredients for success that have contributed to the bank's continued growth through its 167 years as a financial institution. Winters' leadership in the banking industry reflects the bank's emphasis on convenient, quality service and financial products that can be tailored to individual customer needs. This commitment will continue to guide Winters in the future.

Downtown main office crowds were common in the '30s and '40s prior to widespread branch banking.

The Dayton Manufacturing Company, Dayton's first bank, was located near the present day site of the Winters Bank Tower.

Dayton Area Chamber of Commerce
Charged with the spirit

Dayton began as a small settlement in Indian Territory in 1796. Its growth and progress is a tribute to the spirit, initiative, dedication and far-sighted thinking of its past and present leaders in business and government. Today, Dayton is known throughout the world as the Birthplace of Aviation, as well as the birthplace of a number of technological, mechanical, industrial and civic innovations.

The first factory in the Dayton area was a grist mill, believed to have been located about three miles up the Mad River from the junction of Miami River. (The original mill burned to the ground in 1820.)

By 1798, there was another grist mill, a sawmill and acorn cracker south of town, powered by waters from Rubicon Creek. The industrial life of the young community had developed to such an extent by 1810 that Dayton, with a population of 383, had a printing office, two cut nail factories, a tannery, a brewery, three tailor shops, three cabinet-making shops, a watch maker, a jeweler, a sickle maker and a wagon maker.

The population and industry of Dayton grew rapidly throughout the first half of the nineteenth century. An 1842 record shows 188 manufacturing plants in operation. With that growth came the need for an organization to represent the business interests of the growing community.

Dayton has had a succession of such organizations. The first, the Dayton Exchange, was established December 1, 1873, with the objective of securing a railroad to the Jackson County coal mine. This was accomplished in 1881 with the building of the Southeastern Railroad, and the Exchange was dissolved.

The Board of Trade was established and incorporated in the spring of 1887 and enrolled 336 members. Its activities were aimed at securing a new union railway station.

The Chamber of Commerce emerged February 15, 1907, a combination of the Booster's Club, the Commercial Club and the Board of Trade. The Receivers and Shippers Association became a department of the Chamber in 1908. Its first president was a local coal operator, Theodore Fluhart. The objective of the newly formed Chamber was "to foster the business interests of the City, promote its growth and prosperity and in all available ways to advance its general welfare."

Through the years, a dedicated business leadership has espoused that philosophy and, at the same time, expanded its scope to include responsible concern for the quality of life in the total community.

The first Chamber of Commerce began the promotion of Dayton through various Chamber publications. An 1890 publication, *City of a Thousand Factories,* reflected the area's assets, as did the monthly magazine, *Greater Dayton.*

Concerned with improving the community as well as with industrial growth, the Chamber was asked by the City Council to assist in planning improvements such as straightening the channel of the Miami River, proving that there was cooperation between public and private sectors. From the beginning, the Chamber has kept its finger on the pulse of the community.

In 1913, the year of the Great Flood, the name was changed to the Greater Dayton Association. Until 1918, it

was headquartered in the Raub Building under the leadership of Frederick H. Rike and Fred J. Ach. In 1918, under Lee Warren Jones, the organization was renamed the Dayton Chamber of Commerce.

In the score of years before 1938, the Chamber moved several times, always retaining its primary goal. From 1938 to 1947, however, its focus shifted to the issues of those years — civil defense, World War II, community stability— and it tried to maintain a secure business environment in the face of international upheaval.

Through the 1950s the Chamber worked to promote business and industry, to provide information and assistance for orderly growth and expansion of the area and for specific firms. In 1956, the name was again changed to the Dayton Area Chamber of Commerce because it had grown to service the entire metropolitan area.

In the '60s, the epidemic of social unrest and urban decay that was sweeping the nation hit Dayton, compounded by national escalating inflation. The business

Seated to the far left at this 1903 meeting of the Dayton Board of Trade is John H. Patterson, world famous Dayton industrialist. Diagonally across from him is Morris Woodhull, another prominent man in Dayton's history.

community scrutinized the Chamber and began to alter it dramatically, with concentrated programs aimed at strengthening human relations, economic development, downtown redevelopment and education. With an eye toward the future, extensive development began along the River Corridor.

The '70s brought major shifts in employment. Throughout the decade, the cities of the Northeast and Midwest faced a changing business climate with the loss of manufacturing industries and jobs. The Chamber, now a full partner in the community decision-making hierarchy, pooled the time, talent and resources of its membership to build programs and strengthened its working relationship with government. The Chamber added the Miami Valley Alliance of Business as an affiliate to provide training and retaining of individuals to meet the needs of business. The efforts of the Dayton/Montgomery Convention and Visitors Bureau that had become an affiliate in the '60s began to generate revenue for the community. Downtown redevelopment gener-

ated more than 30 new buildings, representing an investment of more than $250 million. During these years, energy and environment became priorities, and Chamber task forces addressed these issues. Renewed economic development efforts resulted in a capital investment of $143 million and 5,600 new jobs from 1971 to 1981, and in 1980 the Dayton Development Council became a Chamber affiliate.

Today, long-range planning remains a key issue and research is a major activity of the Chamber, with the collecting, analyzing and distributing of information to business leadership in the community. No one can predict the future, but the Dayton business community does have goals and will continue working for the best interests of the Dayton area, charged with that pioneer spirit.

Department of second chances

In late August, the editors informed Judith Wehn, Karen Copher and the Ronalds that — because of book design requirements — there was one page remaining to be filled. We jumped at the chance to include some material which had been squeezed out of the book for one reason or another.

A chance meeting with the Reverend William P. Dugger produced an interesting reminiscence from the 1913 flood. On Tuesday morning Dugger started for work from his westside home. Soon he realized he could not reach his employer's business and returned home, crossing the Fifth Street bridge. He heard a wagon crossing the bridge behind him, then a crash. The horse was caught up in the collapsing bridge and did not escape (see photo on page 103). Dugger never saw what happened to the driver or wagon.

Reverend Dugger also believes there was a black baseball team playing in Dayton before the flood. Perhaps W.G. Sloan (page 98) was a member of this team, which preceded the Negro League.

The famous story about John Van Cleve can't be left out. John, extremely portly, was asked by a small boy, "Mr. Van Cleve, when you was a little boy, was you ever a *little* boy?"

Many old-time Daytonians would be disappointed if we didn't mention the Green & Green Cracker Company, whose "Wolf's cracker" was known throughout southern Ohio. Another Dayton tradition, still thriving, is Esther Price's Candy.

The Maxwell car question became the final mystery of the book. On page 115 we quote from the *Dayton Daily News* that Maxwell car production is occurring in Dayton. We do not list Maxwell on page 116 as an auto manufacturer. A 1970 *Gem City Saver* states that Maxwell parts were made in Dayton, but not cars. The Dayton Motor Car Company was part of a huge combine formed around 1910-12. Probably about 1913 the firm was producing the Maxwell. About 1923, Walter Chrysler joined the Dayton Motor Car Company, now the Dayton-Stoddard, and in 1924 the firm produced an automobile bearing the Chrysler name. In 1924 the Maxwell was phased out. The Dayton Motor Car/ Stoddard plant eventually became Chrysler Airtemp, and Dayton became a Chrysler town as well. (And we still don't know if Maxwell cars were made in Dayton!)

We know there's more — everyone who reads the manuscript has something to offer. That's what made *Dayton: The Gem City* so much fun for the four of us.

Karen Copher's favorite photo is this shot of the welcome-home party held in the Arcade for Daytonian Steve Lauterbach, one of the U.S. hostages in Iran. It was, ironically, the first photo we all knew we wanted, as it would anchor the book in 1981. Karen recalls nearly being shoved over the Arcade railing by a burly news photographer who coveted her ideal location for the photo.

Judith Wehn's favorite historical picture comes from the Kern collection of 40,000 glass plate negatives. The entire collection would have been destroyed had not the Historical Society intervened. This particular photo from 1892 shows Third Street looking east from Ludlow toward Main. The side view of the Courthouse is unusual.

Bibliography

General histories

Brown, Ashley, ed. *The History of Montgomery County, Ohio Containing a History of the County; Its Townships, Cities, Towns, Schools, Churches, Etc.; General and Local Statistics; Portraits of Early Settlers and Prominent Men; History of the Northwest Territory; History of Ohio; Map of Montgomery County; Constitution of the United States, Miscellaneous Matters, Etc., Etc.* Chicago: W. H. Beers & Co., 1882.

Crew, Harvey W. *History of Dayton, Ohio With Portraits and Biographical Sketches.* Dayton: United Brethren Publishing House, 1889. (Very complete.)

Conover, Charlotte Reeve, ed. *Dayton and Montgomery County.* New York: Lewis Historical Publishing Co., Inc., 1932.

——————. *Dayton Ohio: An Intimate History.* reprint ed., Dayton, Ohio: Landfall Press, 1970. (A shorter version of the above.)

Curwen, Maskell E. *A Sketch of the History of Dayton.* Dayton: James Odell, Jr., 1850. (The earliest history and the one most free of errors.)

Drury, Rev. A. W. *History of the City of Dayton and Montgomery County, Ohio.* Chicago-Dayton: The S. J. Clarke Publishing Co., 1909. (Very complete.)

Edgar, John F. *Pioneer Life In Dayton and Vicinity, 1796–1840.* Dayton: U.B. Publishing House, 1896; reprint ed., Evansville, Indiana; Unigraphic, Inc., 1976. (The 1976 version has an excellent annotation.)

Hover, John C. et al., *Memoirs of the Miami Valley.* Chicago: Robert O. Law Company, 1919. (Covers entire valley, not just city or county.)

Howe, Henry, LL.D. *Historical Collections of Ohio in Two Volumes.* Cincinnati: C. J. Krehbiel and Co., 1907.

Steele, Robert W. and Steele, Mary Davies. *Early Dayton: With Important Facts and Incidents From the Founding of the City of Dayton, Ohio to the Hundredth Anniversary, 1796–1896.* Dayton, Ohio: U.B. Publishing House, 1896.

Books

Aughinbaugh, B. A. *Know Ohio.* Columbus: Department of Education, State of Ohio, 1939.

Bailey, Anthony. *America, Lost and Found.* New York: Random House, 1980.

Battery "D" History Committee. *Cease Firing: A History of Battery "D," 134th Field Artillery.* Dayton: The Walker Lithographing and Printing Co., 1921.

Boyd, T. A. *Professional Amateur: The Biography of Charles Franklin Kettering.* New York: E. P. Dutton & Co., Inc., 1975.

Bussey, C. Chester. *Origin and Development of Sinclair Community College, Dayton, Ohio 1887–1970.* Dayton: Montgomery Community College District, 1970.

Cellarius, Frederick Julius. *Atlas of the City of Dayton.* Dayton: F. J. Cellarius, 1907.

The Centerville Historical Society. *A Sense of Place.* Centerville: The Centerville Historical Society, 1977.

Conover, Frank. *Centennial Portrait and Biographical Record of the City of Dayton, Montgomery County, Ohio.* Logansport, Indiana: A. W. Bowen and Co., 1897.

Cox, James M. *Journey Through My Years.* New York: Simon & Schuster, 1946.

Crouch, Tom D. *The Giant Leap: A Chronology of Ohio Aerospace Events and Personalities, 1815–1969.* Columbus: The Ohio Historical Society, 1971.

Dayton. n.p.: International Publishing Co., 1889.

Dayton, a History in Photographs. Dayton: The Junior League of Dayton, Ohio, Inc., 1976.

Dayton Art Institute. *Fifty Treasures of the Dayton Art Institute.* Dayton: Dayton Art Institute, 1969.

Downer, Edward T. *Ohio Troops in the Field.* Columbus: Ohio State University Press for the Ohio Historical Society, n.d.

Dunbar, Paul Lawrence [sic]. *Majors and Minors.* Toledo, Ohio: Hadley and Hadley, 1895.

Eckert, Allen W. *A Time of Terror: The Great Dayton Flood.* Boston: Little, Brown and Company, 1965.

Erwin, Paul F. *Andrew S. Iddings, Explorer.* Cincinnati: Creative Writers & Publishers, Inc., 1967.

Faber, Charles W. *New Dayton Illustrated.* Dayton: The National Coupon Publishing Co., 1894.

Funk, Nellis R. *A Pictorial History of the Great Dayton Flood.* Dayton: The Otterbein Press, 1913.

Gerber, David A. *Black Ohio and the Color Line, 1860–1915.* Urbana, Illinois: University of Illinois Press, 1976.

Gist, Christopher. *Christopher Gist's Journals (With Historical, Geographical and Ethnological Notes and Biographies of His Contemporaries by William M. Darlington).* Ann Arbor, Michigan: University Microfilms, by Argonaut Press, Ltd., New York, 1966.

Great Dayton Flood. Dayton: K. M. Kammerer, 1913.

Harper, Robert S. *Ohio Handbook of the Civil War.* Columbus: Ohio Historical Society, 1961.

Heckewelder, Rev. John. *History, Manners, and Customs of the Indian Nations Who Once Inhabited Pennsylvania and the Neighboring States.* Philadelphia: Publication Fund of the Historical Society of Pennsylvania, 1876.

Henry, Alfred J. *The Floods of 1913 in the Rivers of the Ohio and Lower Mississippi Valleys.* Washington: U.S. Weather Bureau No. 520, 1913.

Historical Records Survey. *Ohio Inventory of the County Archives of Ohio, no. 57, Montgomery County.* Columbus: The Ohio Historical Records Survey Project, 1941.

Jackson, Kenneth T. *The Ku Klux Klan in the City, 1915–1930.* New York: Oxford University Press, 1967.

Kern, Albert. *First Regiment: Ohio Volunteer Infantry, 1861–1865.* Dayton: Albert Kern, 1918.

Klement, Frank L. *The Limits of Dissent: Clement L. Vallandigham and the Civil War.* Lexington: University Press of Kentucky, 1970.

Klopfenstein, Carl G. "The Removal of the Indians From Ohio." in Buchman, Randall L., *The Historic Indian in Ohio.* Columbus: The Ohio Historical Society, 1976.

Knopf, Richard C. *Anthony Wayne: A Name in Arms.* Pittsburgh: University of Pittsburgh Press, 1960.

Lafferty, Michael B., ed. *Ohio's Natural Heritage.* Columbus: The Ohio Academy of Science, 1979.

Life of Major General Robert C. Schenck, U.S.A. of Volunteers. n.p., n.d.

Lingeman, Richard R. *Don't You Know There's a War On? The American Home Front, 1941–1945.* New York: G. P. Putnam's Sons, 1970.

MacLean, J. P. *A Bibliography of Shaker Literature With An Introductory Study of the Writings and Publications Pertaining to Ohio Believers.* Columbus: Fred J. Heer, 1905.

Mahon, John K. *The War of 1812.* Gainesville: University of Florida Press, 1972.

Mangione, Jerre. *The Dream and the Deal: The Federal Writers' Project, 1935–1943.* Boston: Little, Brown and Company, 1972.

Marcosson, Isaac F. *Colonel Deeds, Industrial Builder.* New York: Dodd, Mead & Company, 1947.

——————. *Wherever Men Trade: The Romance of the Cash Register.* New York: Dodd, Mead & Company, 1945.

Marshall, Logan. *The True Story of the Great American Calamity by Flood, Fire and Tornado.* n.p.: L. T. Meyers, 1913.

Martin, Herbert Woodward. *Paul Laurence Dunbar, A Singer of Songs.* Columbus: State Library of Ohio, 1979.

MacDonald, Susanne Rike. *The Backward Look.* New York: Exposition Press, 1957.

McKee, Philip. *Big Town.* New York: The John Day Company, 1931.

McMurtrie, Douglas C. *Early Printing in Dayton, Ohio.* Dayton: Printing House Craftsmen's Club of Dayton and Vicinity, 1935.

M'Nemar, Richard. *The Kentucky Revival, or a Short History of the Late Extraordinary Out-pouring of the Spirit of God, in the Western States of America, Agreeably to Scripture-Promises, and Prophecies Concerning the Latter Day: With a Brief Account of the Entrance and Progress of What the World Calls Shakerism, Among the Subjects of the Late Revival in Ohio and Kentucky.* 1808. Cincinnati: Art Guild Reprints, Inc., 1968.

Mead, George H. *In Quiet Ways.* Dayton: The Mead Corporation, 1970.

Medal of Honor Recipients, 1863–1979. Washington: U.S. Government Printing Office, 1979.

Merrill, Francis E. *Social Problems on the Home Front: A Study of War-time Influences.* New York: Harper & Brothers, 1948.

Mills, William C. *Archaeological Atlas of Ohio.* Columbus: Ohio State Archaeological and Historical Society, 1914.

Morgan, Arthur E. *The Miami Conservancy District.* New York: McGraw-Hill Book Company, Inc., 1951.

Myers, Phineas Barton. *Ninety-Five Years After Lincoln: A History of the Urban League of Dayton, Ohio.* New York: Exposition Press, 1959.

Potter, Martha A. *Ohio's Prehistoric Peoples.* Columbus: The Ohio Historical Society, 1968.

Prufer, Olaf H. and Baby, Raymond S. *Paleo-Indians of Ohio.* Columbus: The Ohio Historical Society, 1963.

Prufer, Olaf H., and McKenzie, Douglas H. *Studies in Ohio Archaeology.* Kent, Ohio: Kent State University Press, 1967.

Reid, Whitelaw. *Ohio in the War: Her Statesmen, Her Generals, and Soldiers.* Cincinnati: The Robert Clarke Co., 1895.

Report of the Select Committee on Expenditures in the War Department. Washington: Government Printing Office, 1920.

Rice, Arnold S. *The Ku Klux Klan in American Politics.* Washington, D.C.: Public Affairs Press, 1962.

Rightor, Chester E. *City Manager in Dayton.* New York: The MacMillan Company, 1919.

Roberts, Carl. *200 Years of Progress: A History of Dayton and the Miami Valley.* Dubuque, Iowa: Feature Services, Inc., Kendall/Hunt Publishing Company, 1978.

Rodgers, William. *Think: A Biography of the Watsons and IBM.* New York: Stein and Day, 1969.

Ostendorf, Lloyd. *Mr. Lincoln Came to Dayton.* Dayton: The Otterbein Press, 1959.

Salley, J. P. *Journal,* in Gist, Christopher. *Christopher Gist's Journals.* Ann Arbor, Michigan: University Microfilms, by Argonaut Press, Ltd., New York, 1966.

Sharts, Joseph W. *Biography of Dayton; An Economic Interpretation of Local History.* Dayton: Miami Valley Socialist, 1922.

Katherine Houk Talbott, 1864–1935. Written by her sons and daughters for her grandchildren. Privately printed: Eliza T. Thayer, 1949.

Talbott, Nelson S., compiler. *Harry Elstner Talbot, 1860–1921.* n.p., n.d.

Thompson, Merle Raymond. *Trust Dissolution.* Boston: Richard G. Badger, The Gorham Press, 1919.

Vallandigham, Rev. James L. *A Life of Clement L. Vallandigham.* Baltimore: Turnbull Brothers, 1872.

Views of Dayton and Soldiers' Home. Dayton: John J. Keyes, n.d.

Vincent, Jerry Fox. *A Cabin Grows: The History of a Church.* Dayton: Westminster Presbyterian Church, n.d.

Werthner, Prof. W. B. *Backgrounds of Early Dayton.* Dayton: Dayton Torch Club, 1928.

West, J. Martin, ed. *Clark's Shawnee Campaign of 1780.* Springfield, Ohio: Clark County Historical Society, 1975.

Wiggins, Lida Keck. *The Life and Works of Paul Laurence Dunbar.* Naperville, Illinois: J. L. Nichols & Company, 1907.

Winters, Jonathan. *A Sketch of the Winters Family.* Dayton: United Brethren Publishing House, 1889.

Writers' Program of the Work Projects Administration. *The Ohio Guide.* New York: Oxford University Press, 1940.

Young, Rosamund McPherson. *Boss Kett: A Life of Charles F. Kettering.* New York: Longmans, Green and Co., 1961.

——————. *Twelve Seconds to the Moon: A Story of the Wright Brothers.* Dayton: The Journal Herald, 1978.

Pamphlets

Blades for Victory: The Story of the Aeroproducts Propeller and the Men and Women Who Build It. Dayton: Aeroproducts Division, General Motors Corporation, 1944 (?).

Carillon Park. Dayton: National Cash Register Co., 1950.

Conklin, William Judkins. *Montgomery County Medical Society: Its Founders and Early Members.* Dayton: Printed by order of the Society, 1901.

——————. *The Pioneer Doctor: A Medical Sketch of Early Dayton, 1796–1825.* Dayton: Montgomery County Medical Society, 1900.

The Dayton Chamber of Commerce. *Facts About Dayton.* Dayton: n.p., 1929.

Dayton Country Club. *History of the Dayton Country Club: Eightieth Anniversary Edition.* Dayton: n.p., 1976.

The Dayton Research Association. "The Controlling Principles of A Plan to Improve Local Government."

A polyglot of businesses on the Miami-Erie Canal in 1889, looking north from the Fifth Street Bridge.

Dayton: The Dayton Research Association, February, 1939.

──────── "The Gross Debt of the City of Dayton." Dayton: The Dayton Research Association, March, 1937.

Delco and Its People: A Brief History of Delco—The Plant—Personnel—Equipment—Production and Activities. Dayton: The Dayton Engineering Laboratories Company, 1919.

Edwards, Pat. "Our Common Heritage as Mountain People." Dayton: Our Common Heritage, July 14, 1975.

Hill, Leonard U. *A Reproduction of a Scrapbook from Newspaper Articles on Local and Regional History.* Piqua, Ohio: Leonard U. Hill, 1970.

History of the National Home for Disabled Volunteer Soldiers: With a Complete Guide Book to the Central Home, at Dayton, Ohio, by a Veteran of the Home. Dayton: United Brethren Publishing Establishment: 1875.

The Horizons of Mead. Dayton: The Mead Corporation, 1960.

Houk, Geo. W. *A Sketch of the Dayton Bar.* Dayton: United Brethren Publishing House, 1889.

Inland Division of General Motors, 1923–1973; 50th Anniversary: It Started With the Wheel. n.p.:n.p., 1973.

Johnson, Charlest R. H., ed. *A History of the Wesleyan Methodist Church of America: The Story of One Hundred Years, 1842–1942, of the first Wesleyan Methodist Church at Dayton, Ohio.* Dayton: n.p., n.d.

Kettering Digest: A Collection of Articles. n.p.:n.p., 1956.

Key Statistics About Minorities in the Dayton Area. Dayton: City of Dayton Human Relations Council, January, 1974.

Landis, Emerson. "Social Problems in Dayton, Ohio." Dayton: Board of Education, September 18, 1939.

McKee, Philip. "Great Days in Dayton." Dayton: Dayton Power and Light Company, 1940.

Metropolitan Community Studies. *Metropolitan Change.* Dayton: Metropolitan Community Studies, Inc., November 1959.

Reynolds and Reynolds. "110 Years of Historical Highlights of the Reynolds & Reynolds Company." Dayton: Reynolds & Reynolds, 1976.

Riordan, Robert V. and McIntyre, Jamie. "An Archaeological Survey and Assessment of the Chautauqua Road Bridge Replacement." Public Archaeology Report No. 11. Dayton: Wright State University Laboratory of Anthropology, 1980.

Schwartz, Robert. "The Campaign for Commission Manager Government in Dayton, Ohio, 1913." Dayton: University of Dayton, 1975.

Spayd, M. A. "A Business Built on Holes! 'The Standard Register Company'." New York: The Newcomen Society in North America, 1957.

U.S. Air Force. "The Materiel Center and You." Dayton: Wright Field Publications Unit, January, 1943.

Van Cleve, John. "A Trip From Dayton to Chicago by Water in the Year 1847 Described in Verse." Dayton: privately printed by Houston Lowe, Christmas, 1911.

Verity, Vic; Droege, John; and Ralph Ramey. *The Miami Canal from Cincinnati to Dayton.* Oberlin, Ohio: The Canal Society of Ohio, August 22, 1977.

"A Visit to Dayton Press." Dayton: Dayton Press, Inc., 1977.

Woodland Cemetery Association. *Woodland Cemetery.* Dayton: United Brethren Publishing Co., 1903.

Theses, Dissertations and Manuscripts

Alexander, Lynn Griggs. "Dayton's Living Room: The Dayton Art Institute in the 1930's." Master's Thesis, Wright State University, 1976.

American Association of University Women. "A.A.U.W. Arts Survey Project; Series II." Dayton, 1941.

Becker, Carl M. "Mill, Shop and Factory: The Industrial Life of Dayton, Ohio, 1930–1900." Ph.D. dissertation, University of Cincinnati, 1971.

Cichanowicz, Stanley R. "The Kossuth Colony and Jacob D. Moskowitz—An Experiment in the Settlement of Hungarian Immigrants in Dayton, Ohio." University of Dayton, 1963.

Condron, Jim. "The Institutional History of the University of Dayton Basketball Program: 1947–Present." University of Dayton, 1976.

Corley, Lisa. "The Rise of the Dayton Reds, The Gem City's First Professional Baseball Team." Wright State University, 1974.

Deem, Warren H. "The Employers' Association of Dayton, Ohio." Harvard University, 1953.

"Delco Light and Frigidaire." Montgomery County Historical Society, n.d. (typewritten.)

Doren, Alice M. "Foreigners in Dayton." YWCA Immigration and Foreign Community Department, Dayton, 1917.

Drake, Jack. "Cholera in Dayton." Dayton and Montgomery County Public Library, n.d. (typewritten.)

Gordon, Mary. "The Life of John Whitten Van Cleve." Master's thesis, University of Dayton, 1965.

Gravelle, Adrian J. "The Wayne and Fifth Street Railroad: The History of an Early Transportation System in Dayton." University of Dayton, 1963.

Hall, Agnes Anderson. "Letters From John." Dayton and Montgomery County Public Library, 1935.

Heilman, James M. and Hoefer, Roger R. "Astronomical Alignments in a Fort Ancient Settlement at the Incinerator Site in Dayton, Ohio." Dayton Museum of Natural History, 1980.

──────── and Schwab, Anne. "Fort Ancient in Southwestern Ohio." Dayton Museum of Natural History, 1980.

Howell, James C. "Community Transit Relations in Dayton, Ohio, 1869–1961." Master's thesis, Ohio State University, 1962.

Howson, Embrey Bernard. "The Ku Klux Klan in Ohio After World War I." Master's thesis, Ohio State University, 1951.

Hussong, Nicholas A. "Home Amusement Circa 1880." University of Dayton, 1964.

Ingram, Jefferson. "Did Colonel Robert Patterson Hold Slaves in Ohio After 1803?" Dayton and Montgomery County Public Library, April 10, 1975.

Kelly, Martin J. "That Part of the City Known as Oregon." Montgomery County Historical Society, 1966.

Knust, Edward H. S.M. "Hallowed Memories." University of Dayton, 1950. (Mimeographed.)

──────── . "Miscellanea." University of Dayton, 1950. (Mimeographed.)

Kokkinou, Epiphanie Clara. "The Political Career of Robert Cumming Schenck." Master's thesis, Miami University, 1955.

Lemmon, George J. "Interruption of Education of World War II Veterans." Master's thesis, University of Dayton, 1949.

Leyda, Martha S. "Robert Wilbur Steele, Daytonian Scholar, 1819–1891." Master's thesis, Miami University, 1963.

Lindenfeld, Charles Lloyd. "The Great Dayton Flood of 1913." Master's thesis, Ohio State University, 1962.

Lyle, Russell S. "Traction Lines in Dayton." Montgomery County Historical Society, n.d.

Marshall, Laurie. "Yours For Industrial Freedom: The Socialist Party and the Labor Movement of Dayton, Ohio, 1900–1921." Wright State University, 1971.

Martin, Russell A. "Historical Sketch of the City of Dayton." Dayton and Montgomery County Public Library, April 5, 1941.

Orear, Linn. "Language and Loyalty: German Americans in Dayton, 1918." Antioch College, June 4, 1962.

Perkins, James H. "Dayton During World War I, 1914 to 1918." Master's thesis, Miami University, August, 1959.

Rice, Robert Burton. "A History of Black Citizens in Dayton." Dayton, Robert Rice, Jr., June 1976.

Ronald, Bruce W. "George Rogers Clark Expedition of 1782." Dayton and Montgomery County Public Library, 1976.

Schwartz, Irving Lloyd. "Dayton, Ohio During the Civil War." Master's thesis, Miami University, June 1949.

Seewer, Michael L. "An Interpretive History of the National Cash Register Company Strike of 1901." University of Dayton, 1969.

Smith, Barbara. "The Threat to Move the National Cash Register From Dayton, 1907." University of Dayton, 1972.

"Smith School History." E.D. Smith School, Dayton, 1976.

Sollengerger, D.L. "The Development and Growth of the Public Secondary Schools of Dayton, Ohio from 1850–1935." Master's thesis, Ohio State University, 1935.

Van Cleve, Benjamin. "Memoirs of Benjamin Van Cleve." Dayton and Montgomery County Public Library, n.d. (handwritten)

Walker, Lois E. "Dayton's Growth and Decentralization: The Annexation of 1868." Wright State University, 1980.

"The Wayne and Fifth Street Railroad: Its Early History Gleaned From the Columns of the *Dayton Daily Journal.*" Dayton and Montgomery County Public Library, n.d.

Weaver, Norman F. "Knights of the KKK in Wisconsin, Indiana and Ohio." Ph.D. dissertation, University of Wisconsin, 1955.

Wehrle, Wm. O., S.M. "A History of the University of Dayton." University of Dayton, January, 1937.

Articles

The American Pioneer, A Monthly Periodical Devoted to the Objects of the Logan Historical Society; or, to Collecting and Publishing Sketches Relative to the Early Settlement of the Country I and II (1842, 1843).

Baby, Raymond S. "Prehistoric Architecture: A Study of House Types in the Ohio Valley." *The Ohio Journal of Science* 71, no. 4 (July, 1971).

Becker, Carl M. "A Most Complete Factory: The Barney Car Works, 1850–1926." *Cincinnati Historical Society Bulletin* 24 (1973): 49–70.

Bonnecamps, Father. "Account of the Voyage on the Beautiful River Made in 1749 Under the Direction of Monsieur De Celeron." *Ohio Archaeological and Historical Publications* 29 (1920): 397–424.

Burba, Howard L. "Miami Valley Local History and Various Other Subjects." Dayton: *Dayton Daily News*, 1932–1934.

Carson, Gerald. "The Machine That Kept Them Honest." *American Heritage*, August, 1966, pp. 51–59.

"Dayton's 'Homestead Unit No. 1'." *Architectural Forum* 59 (July, 1933): 78–79.

Dorn, Jacob H. "Subsistence Homesteading in Dayton, Ohio, 1933–1935." *Ohio History* 78, no. 2 (Spring, 1969): 77–94.

Dunbar, Paul Laurence. "Christmas Carol." *Dayton Tattler* 1, no. 2 (December 20, 1890).

Galbreath, C.B. "The Expedition of Celoron." *Ohio Archaeological and Historical Publications* 29 (1920): 331.

Gem City Saver, 1969 to 1979.

Hollingsworth, Virginia. "A Dedicated Life." *Wilson Library Bulletin* 28 (May, 1953): 782–787.

Joyner, Fred B. "Robert Cumming Schenck, First Citizen and Statesman of the Ohio Valley." *Ohio Archaeological and Historical Publications* 58, no. 4 (October 1949): 289.

"J.W." "Hugh Chalmers: A Man of Action." *Detroit Saturday Night,* January 1, 1910.

Lambing, A.A. "Celeron's Journal." *Ohio Archaeological and Historical Publications* 29 (1920): 335–397.

MacLean, J.P. "Origin of the Watervliet Ohio Shaker Community." *Dayton Daily News,* January 19, 1904.

Marshall, O.H. "De Celeron's Expedition to the Ohio in 1749." *Ohio Archaeological and Historical Publications* 29 (1920): 424.

Meek, Basil. "Gen. Harmer's Expedition." *Ohio Archaeological and Historical Publications* 20 (1911): 83.

Pioneer Association of Montgomery County, Ohio. "Old Settlers. A Collection of Biographical Sketches of the Surviving Members of the Pioneer Association of Montgomery County, Prepared by the Association and Published as a Series in The *Dayton Daily Journal,* July 14–Oct. 19, 1882." *Dayton Daily Journal,* 1882.

Smith, Samuel B. "Memoirs: 93rd OVI." Dayton and Montgomery County Public Library.

Swart, Stanley L. "A Memo on Cross Burning." *Northwest Ohio Quarterly* 43 (1971): 70–74.

Talbert, Charles G. "Kentucky Invades Ohio—1786." *The Register of the Kentucky Historical Society* 54, no. 188 (June, 1956).

Tucker, David A., Jr., M.D. "Notes on Cholera in Southwestern Ohio." *Ohio Archaeological and Historical Quarterly* 49 (1940): 378–385.

Van Cleve, John W. "A Brief History of the Settlement of the Town of Dayton." *Journal of the Historical and Philosophical Society of Ohio* 1, part 1 (1838): 73–81.

Wittke, Carl. "Ohio's German Language Press and the War." *Ohio Archaeological and Historical Society Publications* 28 (1919): 82–95.

Young, Roz. "Mrs. Hedges' House." *Montgomery County Historical Society Bulletin,* Summer, 1967.

Other sources

"Calendar of the Bickham Collection." Dayton: Dayton and Montgomery County Public Library, 1956.

Patterson, Robert. Petition for pension. *The Draper Manuscripts, MM.* Madison, Wisconsin: State Historical Society of Wisconsin.

Patterson, John. "What Dayton, Ohio, Should Do to Become a Model City." Speech at Dayton Centennial banquet, March 19, 1896.

Interviews:
Georgiana Harshman
H. Eugene Kneiss
Lloyd Ostendorf
The Reverend William P. Dugger
G.K. Biel
Melba Hunt

Newspapers

Daily Democrat
Dayton Daily Journal
Dayton Daily News
Dayton Evening Herald
Dayton Herald
The Dayton Journal and Advertiser
The Dayton Repertory
Dayton This Week
The Journal
The Journal Herald
Log Cabin
The Tattler
The Western Empire

Chapter One

[1] John Peter Salley, *Journal,* quoted in Christopher Gist, *Christopher Gist's Journals* (published for University Microfilms Inc., Ann Arbor, by Argonaut Press Ltd., New York, 1966), p. 258.

[2] James M. Heilman and Roger R. Hoefer, "Astronomical Alignments in a Fort Ancient Settlement at the Incinerator Site in Dayton, Ohio" (Dayton: Dayton Museum of Natural History, 1980).

[3] J. M. Heilman and Anne Schwab, "Fort Ancient in Southwestern Ohio" (Dayton: Dayton Museum of Natural History, August 28, 1980).

[4] Robert V. Riordan and Jamie McIntyre, *An Archaeological Survey and Assessment of the Chatauqua Road Bridge Replacement* (Dayton: Public Archaeology Report No. 11, Laboratory of Anthropology, Wright State University, 1980).

[5] Christopher Gist, *Christopher Gist's Journals* (published for University Microfilms Inc., Ann Arbor, Michigan, by Argonaut Press, Ltd., New York 1966), p. 47.

[6] Father Bonnecamps, "Account of the Voyage on the Beautiful River made in 1749 Under the Direction of Monsieur De Celeron," *Ohio Archaeological and Historical Publications,* 29 (1920), p. 410.

[7] Celoron de Blainville, "Journal," quoted in the Rev. A. A. Lambing, "Celoron's Journal," *Ohio Archaeological and Historical Publications,* 29 (1920), p. 374.

[8] Celoron, p. 375.

[9] Leonard U. Hill, *A Reproduction of a Scrapbook from Newspaper Articles on Local and Regional History* (Piqua, Ohio: Leonard U. Hill, 1970), p. 20.

[10] Charles G. Talbert, "Kentucky Invades Ohio—1786," *Register of the Kentucky Historical Society,* 54 (July 1956), p. 203.

[11] John F. Edgar, *Pioneer Life in Dayton and Vicinity, 1796–1840* (Dayton: U.B. Publishing House, 1896), p. 96.

[12] Talbert, p. 207.

[13] Robert Patterson, Petition for pension, *The Draper Manuscripts,* MM (Madison, Wisconsin: State Historical Society of Wisconsin).

[14] Talbert, p. 209.

[15] John Armstrong, "Journal," quoted in Basil Meek, "General Harmar's Expedition," *Ohio Archaeological and Historical Society Publications,* 20 (1911), p. 83.

[16] Benjamin Van Cleve, "Memoirs of Benjamin Van Cleve," Dayton and Montgomery County Public Library.

[17] Anthony Wayne to Henry Knox, quoted in Richard C. Knopf, ed., *Anthony Wayne: A Name in Arms* (Pittsburgh: University of Pittsburgh Press, 1960), p. 350.

[18] Knopf, p. 351.

Chapter Two

[1] A. W. Drury, *History of the City of Dayton and Montgomery County, Ohio* (Chicago-Dayton: The S. J. Clarke Publishing Co., 1909), p. 39.

[2] Benjamin Van Cleve, "Memoirs of Benjamin Van Cleve," Dayton and Montgomery County Public Library.

[3] Van Cleve, "Memoirs."

[4] John F. Edgar, *Pioneer Life in Dayton and Vicinity, 1796–1840* (Dayton: U.B. Publishing House, 1896), p. 50.

[5] Edgar, p. 78.

[6] Harvey W. Crew, ed., *History of Dayton, Ohio, with Portraits and Biographical Sketches* (Dayton: United Brethren Publishing House, 1889), p. 85.

[7] Douglas McMurtrie, *Early Printing in Dayton Ohio* (Dayton: Printing House Craftsman's Club of Dayton and Vicinity, 1935) n. pag.

[8] Henry Howe, LL.D., *Historical Collections of Ohio* (Cincinnati: C.J. Krehbiel & Co., 1907), p. 277.

[9] John K. Mahon, *The War of 1812* (Gainesville: University of Florida Press, 1972), p. 45.

[10] *Gem City Saver,* Summer 1975

[11] Robert W. Steele and Mary Davies Steele, *Early Dayton: With Important Facts and Incidents From the Founding of the City of Dayton, to the Hundredth Anniversary, 1796–1896* (Dayton: U.B. Publishing House, 1896), p. 127.

[12] Crew, p. 129.

[13] Crew, p. 343.

[14] Crew, p. 150.

[15] Drury, p. 145.

[16] Richard McNemar, *The Kentucky Revival* (Cincinnati: Art Guild Reprints, 1968), p. 61.

Chapter Three

[1] Jefferson Ingram, "Did Colonel Robert Patterson Hold Slaves in Ohio after 1803?" (Dayton & Montgomery County Public Library, April 10, 1975), n. pag.

[2] Harvey W. Crew, *History of Dayton, Ohio, With Portraits and Biographical Sketches* (Dayton: United Brethren Publishing House, 1889), p. 175.

[3] John F. Edgar, *Pioneer Life in Dayton and Vicinity, 1796–1840* (Dayton: U.B. Publishing House, 1896), p. 235.

[4] Robert W. Steele and Mary Davies Steele, *Early Dayton: With Important Facts and Incidents from the Founding of the City of Dayton, Ohio to the Hundredth Anniversary, 1796–1896* (Dayton: U.B. Publishing House, 1896), p. 174.

[5] Henry Howe, LL.D., *Historical Collections of Ohio* (Cincinnati: C.J. Krehbiel & Co., 1907), p. 278.

[6] Steele, p. 198.

[7] Ashley Brown, ed., *The History of Montgomery County, Ohio* (Chicago: W. H. Beers & Co., 1882), p. 691.

[8] Howard L. Burba, "Miami Valley Local History and Various Other Subjects," *Dayton Daily News,* 1932–1934, n. pag.

[9] Howe, p. 277.

[10] Carl M. Becker, "Mill, Shop, and Factory: The Industrial Life of Dayton, Ohio, 1830–1900," (Cincinnati: University of Cincinnati, 1971), p. 63.

[11] Woodland Cemetery Association, *Woodland Cemetery* (Dayton: United Brethren Publishing Company, 1903), n. pag.

[12] Edgar, p. 232.

[13] Brown, ed., p. 586.

[14] Jack Drake, "Cholera in Dayton," n.d., n. pag.

[15] Burba, March 8, 1931, n. pag.

[16] Maskell E. Curwen, *A Sketch of the History of Dayton* (Dayton: James Odell, Jr., 1850), p. 55.

[17] Burba, March 8, 1931, n. pag.

[18] Crew, p. 545.

[19] Curwen, p. 55.

[20] Burba, December 13, 1936, n. pag.

[21] Daniel Drake, M.D., Notice, quoted in David A. Tucker, Jr., M.D., "Notes on Cholera in Southwestern Ohio," *Ohio Archaeological and Historical Quarterly,* 49 (1940), p. 385.

Chapter Four

[1] Lloyd Ostendorf, *Mr. Lincoln Came to Dayton* (Dayton: The Otterbein Press, 1959), p. 14.

[2] Samuel B. Smith, "Memoirs: 93rd OVI," (Dayton: Dayton and Montgomery County Library), p. 11–12.

[3] Irving Lloyd Schwartz, "Dayton, Ohio, During the Civil War" (Oxford: Miami University, 1949), p. 98.

[4] Schwartz, p. 108.

[5] *Gem City Saver,* Spring 1973.

[6] Carl M. Becker, "Mill, Shop and Factory: The Industrial Life of Dayton, Ohio, 1830–1900" (Cincinnati: University of Cincinnati, 1971), p. 98.

[7] A. W. Drury, *History of the City of Dayton and Montgomery County, Ohio* (Chicago-Dayton: The S. J. Clarke Publishing Co., 1909), p. 172.

[8] Louis E. Walker, "Dayton's Growth and De-Centralization: The Annexation of 1868" (Dayton: Wright State University, 1980).

[9] Drury, *History of Dayton,* p. 761.

[10] Drury, p. 769.

[11] Whitelaw Reid, *Ohio in the War: Her Statesmen, Her Generals, and Soldiers,* 2 vols. (Cincinnati: The Robert Clarke Co., 1895), 1:518.

[12] Epiphanie Clara Kokkinou, "The Political Career of Robert Cumming Schenck" (Oxford: Miami University, 1955), p. 58.

[13] "Life of Maj. Gen. Robert C. Schenck, U.S.A. of Vols." (pamphlet in Dayton and Montgomery County Library, n.p:n.d.), p. 3.

[14] Reid, p. 521.

[15] Kokkinou, p. 227.

[16] Mary Hassett, quoted in John C. Hover, *Memoirs of the Miami Valley,* 3 vols. (Chicago: Robert O. Law Company, 1919), 2:348.

[5]Lindenfield, p. 98–99.
[6]Alfred J. Henry, *The Floods of 1913 in the Rivers of the Ohio and Lower Mississippi Valleys,* (U.S. Weather Bureau No. 520, Washington, 1913), p. 53.
[7]Isaac F. Marcosson, *Colonel Deeds, Industrial Builder* (New York: Dodd, Mead & Co., 1947), p. 177.
[8]Morgan, p. 344.

Chapter Eight

[1]Robert Schwartz, "The Campaign for Commission Manager Government in Dayton, Ohio, 1913" (Dayton: University of Dayton, 1975), p. 5.
[2]Schwartz, p. 8.
[3]Schwartz, p. 25.
[4]James H. Perkins, "Dayton During World War I, 1914–1918" (Oxford: Miami University, August, 1959), p. 44.
[5]Perkins, p. 71.
[6]Perkins, p. 72.
[7]Linn Orear, "Language and Loyalty: German Americans in Dayton, 1918" (Yellow Springs: Antioch College, 1962), n. pag.
[8]Charles E. Hughes, "Hughes Report," as quoted in *Report of the Select Committee on Expenditures in the War Department* (Washington, D.C.: Government Printing Office, 1920), p. 18.
[9]*Gem City Saver,* Summer, 1976.
[10]A. E. Roach, "Ket, America's Best Loved Inventor" (Dayton: Montgomery County Historical Society, n.d.), n. pag.
[11]Embrey Bernard Howson, "KKK in Ohio" (Columbus: Ohio State University, 1951), p. 22.
[12]Howson, p. 48.
[13]*Dayton Daily News,* September 24, 1926.
[14]Paul F. Erwin, *Andrew S. Iddings, Explorer* (Cincinnati: Creative Writers & Publishers, Inc., 1967), p. 196.

Chapter Nine

[1]*Dayton This Week,* Vol. 8 (1929), n. pag.
[2]The Dayton Research Association, "The Controlling Principles of a Plan to Improve Local Government" (Dayton: The Dayton Research Association, Feb., 1939), p. 34.
[3]Mary Ellen Fischer, "In Retrospect" *Ionic Columns,* 9, no. 6 (Aug./Sept., 1977), p. 4.
[4]Mary Ellen Lynch, "Recall to Work Made Him Happiest Man in America" *Dayton Daily News,* 26 June, 1962.
[5]The Dayton Research Association, "The Gross Debt of the City of Dayton" (Dayton: The Dayton Research Association, March 1937), p. 34.
[6]"Smith School History" (Dayton: Smith Elementary School, 1976), n. pag.
[7]Jacob H. Dorn, "Subsistence Homesteading in Dayton, Ohio, 1933–1935" *Ohio History,* 78, no. 2 (Spring 1969).
[8]The *Journal,* April 5, 1935.
[9]Al Foose, "Memoirs," unpublished manuscript.
[10]Lynn Griggs Alexander, "Dayton's Living Room: The Dayton Art Institute in the 1930's" (Dayton: Wright State University, 1976), p. 73.
[11]American Association of University Women, A.A.U.W. Arts Survey Project, Series II (Dayton, Ohio: A.A.U.W., 1939–1941), II:41.
[12]A.A.U.W., p. 41.
[13]"History of the Dayton Country Club: Eightieth Anniversary Edition" (Dayton: Dayton Country Club, 1976), p. 93.
[14]Personal communication, Georgiana Harshman, April 18, 1981.

Chapter Ten

[1]Bickham Collection (Dayton: Montgomery County Public Library).
[2]Edward H. Knust, S.M., "Miscellanea" (Dayton: University of Dayton, 1950), n. pag.
[3]"Annual Report, 1944" (City of Dayton).
[4]"A Visit to Dayton Press" (Dayton: Dayton Press, Inc., 1979).
[5]*Gem City Saver,* Winter 1969.
[6]Committee on Veterans' Affairs, United States Senate, *Medal of Honor Recipients, 1863–1978* (Washington: United States Government Printing Office, 1979), p. 687.

[17]Robert Steele, quoted in A. W. Drury, *History of the City of Dayton and Montgomery County, Ohio* (Chicago-Dayton: The S. J. Clarke Publishing Co., 1909), p. 607.
[18]Nicholas A. Hussong, "Home Amusement Circa 1880" (Dayton: University of Dayton, 1964), p. 33.
[19]Drury, p. 608.
[20]Hussong, p. 34.

Chapter Five

[1]Isaac F. Marcosson, *Wherever Men Trade* (New York: Dodd, Mead & Company, 1945), p. 27.
[2]Personal communication from H. Eugene Kneiss, NCR Historian, February, 1981.
[3]Marcosson, p. 134.
[4]Kneiss.
[5]Carl M. Becker, "Mill, Shop and Factory: The Industrial Life of Dayton, Ohio, 1830–1900" (Cincinnati: University of Cincinnati, 1971), p. 257.
[6]Isaac F. Marcosson, *Colonel Deeds, Industrial Builder* (New York: Dodd, Mead and Company, 1947), p. 71.
[7]Lisa Corley, *The Rise of the Dayton Reds, the Gem City's First Professional Baseball Team* (Dayton: Wright State University, 1974), n. pag.
[8]Charlotte Reeve Conover, *Dayton, Ohio: An Intimate History* (1931; reprint ed., Dayton: Landfall Press, 1970), p. 159.
[9]Susanne Rike MacDonald, *The Backward Look* (New York: Exposition Press, 1957), p. 11.
[10]Becker, p. 274.
[11]Conover, p. 137.
[12]Paul Laurence Dunbar, in Lida Keck Wiggins, *The Life and Works of Paul Laurence Dunbar* (Naperville, Illinois: J. L. Nichols & Company, 1907).
[13]Personal communication Cincinnati Reds publicity office, March 24, 1981.

[14]Personal communication with A. S. Bickham, March 24, 1981.
[15]Committee on Veterans' Affairs, United States Senate, *Medal of Honor Recipients, 1863–1978* (Washington: U.S. Government Printing Office, 1979), p. 369.
[16]Roz Young, "Mrs. Hedge's House," *Montgomery Historical Society Bulletin,* Summer, 1967.

Chapter Six

[1]Rosamond Young, *Twelve Seconds to the Moon: A Story of the Wright Brothers* (Dayton: Journal Herald, 1978), p. 16.
[2]Young, p. 35.
[3]Young, p. 43.
[4]*Gem City Saver,* Fall 1973.
[5]*Saver.*
[6]*Saver.*
[7]*Saver.*
[8]Merle Raymond Thompson, *Trust Dissolution* (Boston: Richard G. Badger, The Gorham Press, 1919), p. 196.
[9]John H. Patterson, March 19, 1896, speech given at Beckel Hotel, Dayton: reprinted by N.C.R.
[10]*The Federal Antitrust Laws* (Washington, D.C., Government Printing Office, 1916), p. 73–74.

Chapter Seven

[1]The *Journal,* April, 1913
[2]Charles Lloyd Lindenfield, "The Great Dayton Flood of 1913," (Columbus: The Ohio State University, 1962), p. 32.
[3]Arthur E. Morgan, *The Miami Conservancy District* (New York: McGraw-Hill Book Company, Inc., 1951), p. 78.
[4]Morgan, p. 81.

Index

Index

Publisher's Acknowledgments

The editors and publishers of *Dayton: The Gem City* wish to thank the special people who, by their interest and commitment, felt as we did that a premium history book of Dayton and Montgomery County was needed.

Some of those included, of course, authors Bruce and Virginia Ronald, current photographer Karen Keith Copher and photo editor Judith Wehn, whose sense of history and appreciation for the Dayton area are tremendous.

To the leadership and staff of the Montgomery County Historical Society, Trace B. Swisher, president, a hearty thank you.

Historical Society Executive Director Patrick Foltz provided fine professional advice and direction and it was appreciated. Others on the staff who lent support and personal involvement include Kim Wilson, Steve Germann, Teresa Prosser, Ruth Scott, Shirley Patterson and Dan Daniel.

A very special salute to Jack Sullivan and William Ford who believed in the project and lent considerable support and advice — we are indebted to you both.

The Daytonian general manager John Wilderman and his staff — Chuck Wade, Arthur Dukes, Jerry Brown, Ann Marie Welch, Connie Kozak, Debra Thomas, Craig Robinson and Lafayette Silar — provided fine hospitality and it was appreciated.

Anita Warden and Janet Dashiell were so helpful and a delight to work with throughout the Ohio projects.

Others who contributed to the success of *Dayton: The Gem City* and deserve considerable credit include Mickey Thompson, Tim Colwell, Barbara Jameson, Ruth Keipp, Marie Flagg, Sherry Suffens, Sharon Mason, Romaney Lee, Mary Schiermann, Craig Parks, Debra Donica, Gena Frye, Tami Clair and a special thanks to Tom, Dee, Jim, Ken, Chris, Alex and, of course, to Candace.

Credits

THE BUG: A testimonial to the technical inventiveness of Daytonians, this assembly line at "South Field, Moraine" was geared up to launch — about 20 years before its time — Charles Kettering's crude predecessor to the "buzz bomb" of WWII.

Authors' Acknowledgments

■ In late January, we were offered the opportunity to write this book. For four months, both of us worked at full-time jobs and wrote the first major new history of Dayton in 50 years. It seemed impossible then; it still seems so today. It could not have happened without the help of a great many people.

First, our respective employers who put up with our glassy stares on Monday mornings—Kircher, Helton and Collett, Inc., and Smith School in the Oakwood City School system. A special thanks to Gem Savings who allowed us to quote from the Gem City Saver and to use notes that were gathered but not used, in their publication. More special thanks to photo editor Judith Wehn and photographer Karen Copher. The four of us worked together from the start.

Most research starts in the public library and we were fortunate that the Dayton and Montgomery County Public Library is one of America's finest library systems. Although many others helped, the following people were especially helpful: Nancy Horlacher, Karen McDaniel, Marsha Cousino, Robert Thoman and Leon Bey.

The Dayton newspapers were quick to offer us full use of any and all material they had published. Without the year-end and decade reviews of the Dayton Daily News, the material from 1940 on could not have been included without months of laborious drudgery. Our thanks go to Arnold Rosenfeld, executive editor of both papers, the Journal Herald and the Dayton Daily News.

Thanks to all the publishers (listed in the footnotes) who gave us permission to quote from other volumes. Thanks to the people who granted us the rights to quote from memoirs, scholarly papers and interviews. They are listed in the bibliography.

A special thank you to Steven Germann and Patrick A. Foltz of the Montgomery County Historical Society, and Dr. Carl Becker, a respected American historian, head of the history department at Wright State University, who read the complete manuscript in an heroic effort to keep us as free from error as possible. Jamie McIntyre of Wright State and J. Heilman and Bill Mooney of the Museum of Natural History read the first chapter for anthropological accuracy. Fred Bartenstein of the city manager's office read the modern history chapter to help us with city history, where few written overviews exist.

And finally, our deepest personal thanks to Linda Larimore, Susan Fisher, Marilyn Kinsworthy and our daughter Kate who typed—and typed—and typed.

The Dayton News Boy's Picnic participants against the 1918 backdrop of Fourth and Ludlow streets.

Columbus Day Parade in 1892.

Concept and design by Continental Heritage Press, Inc., Tulsa.
Printed and bound by Walsworth Publishing Company.
Type is Cheltenham Book and Garamond Condensed Book.
Text Sheets are Mead Offset Enamel Gloss.
Endleaves are Eagle A.
Cover is Holliston Kingston Linen.

To a captious critic

Dear critic, who my lightness so deplores,
Would I might study to be prince of bores,
Right wisely would I rule that dull estate—
But, sir, I may not, till you abdicate.

—Paul Laurence Dunbar